Scandinavian Cities

Fodor's 90
Scandinavian Cities

Reprinted from *Fodor's Scandinavia '90*

FODOR'S TRAVEL PUBLICATIONS, INC.
New York & London

Copyright © 1990 by Fodor's Travel Publications, Inc.

Fodor's is a trademark of Fodor's Travel Publications Inc.

All rights reserved under International and Pan-American Copyright Conventions. Published in the United States by Fodor's Travel Publications, Inc., a subsidiary of Random House, Inc., New York, and simultaneously in Canada by Random House of Canada Limited, Toronto. Distributed by Random House, Inc., New York.

No maps, illustrations, or other portions of this book may be reproduced in any form without written permission from the publisher.

ISBN 0-679-01759-3

Fodor's Scandinavian Cities

Editor: Richard Moore
Associate Editor: Sean Connolly
Assistant Editor: Caz Philcox
Area Editors: Asgeir Fridgeirrson, Sylvie Nickels, Anita Peltonen, Philip Ray
Contributor: Andrew Brown
Drawings: Elizabeth Haines
Maps: Swanston Graphics, Bryan Woodfield
Cover Photograph: Robert Maass

Cover Design: Vignelli Associates

Special Sales

Fodor's Travel Publications are available at special discounts for bulk purchases (100 copies or more) for sales promotions or premiums. Special editions, including personalized covers, excerpts of existing guides, and corporate imprints, can be created in large quantities for special needs. For more information, write to Special Marketing, Fodor's Travel Publications, 201 East 50th Street, New York, NY 10022. Inquiries from the United Kingdom should be sent to Fodor's Travel Publications, 30–32 Bedford Square, London WC1B 3SG.

MANUFACTURED IN THE UNITED STATES OF AMERICA
10 9 8 7 6 5 4 3 2 1

CONTENTS

Foreword	vii
Hotel and Restaurant Rates	ix
Stockholm	1
Exploring Stockholm	4
Map of Stockholm 6–7	
Practical Information for Stockholm	12
Hotels	13
Restaurants	21
Copenhagen	25
Exploring Copenhagen	26
Map of Copenhagen 28–29	
Practical Information for Copenhagen	36
Hotels	37
Restaurants	46
Oslo	49
Exploring Oslo	51
Map of Oslo 52–53	
Practical Information for Oslo	60
Hotels	60
Restaurants	70
The Oslo Fjord District	73
Exploring the Oslo Fjord District	73
Practical Information for Oslo Fjord District	76
Hotels and Restaurants	76
Helsinki	80
Exploring Helsinki	81
Map of Helsinki 82–83	
Practical Information for Helsinki	88
Hotels	88
Restaurants	93
Prelude to Iceland	96
Exploring Iceland	101
Iceland's Capital Reykjavik	101
Map of Reykjavik 102	
Practical Information for Reykjavik	107
Hotels	108
Restaurants	112
Practical Information for the Rest of Iceland	113

Scandinavian History 117
    Map of the Vikings 120
    Map of the Swedish Empire 124
    Map of the Rise of the Modern States 129

Food and Drink 130

Index 137

FOREWORD

The Scandinavian capitals offer their guests a very special kind of experience. This is a group of cities—none of them large when set against Tokyo or New York, indeed, all having to some extent the feeling of a slightly over-grown country town—each with a very distinct character of its own. They are all orderly, indeed among Europe's best-run and safest towns; elegant, urbane and charming; all with a strong sense of the past.

The quality of their hotels is high and their restaurants offer not only the rich cooking native to each country, but a fair sprinkling of foreign cuisines, testimony to the far-flung wanderings of their people. They all can offer special travel bargains to their visitors—museum passes, inexpensive hotel packages, travel facilities—balanced out by some of the glossiest restaurants and highest-priced shops to be found anywhere.

Shopping, in fact, at all cost levels, is one of the chief joys of visiting the Scandinavian capitals. The craftwork which each produces is a sure lodestone to any visitor who likes beautiful, imaginative and skillfully-made things.

* * * *

We are indebted once again to the Directors of the Scandinavian National Tourist Offices in London for their generous cooperation; specifically to Boris Taimitarha of the Finnish Tourist Board and to Phyllis Chapman; to Barbro Hunter of the Swedish National Tourist Office; to Poul Christensen of the Danish Tourist Board; to Ivar Hauff of the Norwegian Tourist Board; and to Johann Sigurdsson of the Icelandic Tourist Information Bureau.

We would especially like to acknowledge the hard work and helpful interest of our team of Area Editors, Asgeir Fridgeirrson, Sylvie Nickels, Philip Ray, and Doreen Taylor, without whom this edition would not have been possible.

* * * *

While every care has been taken to assure the accuracy of the information in this guide, the passage of time will always bring change, and consequently the publisher cannot accept responsibility for errors that may occur.

All prices and opening times quoted in this guide are based on information available to us at press time. Hours and admission fees may change, however, and the prudent traveler will avoid inconvenience by calling ahead.

Fodor's wants to hear about your travel experiences, both pleasant and unpleasant. When a hotel or restaurant fails to live up to its billing, let us know and we will investigate the complaint and revise our entries where the facts warrant it.

Send your letters to the editors of Fodor's Travel Publications, 201 E. 50th Street, New York, NY 10022.

HOTEL AND RESTAURANT RATES

There are no official hotel price classifications in any of the Scandinavian countries. In general, rates in the towns and rural areas are somewhat lower than in the major cities. The following price categories are for the price of a double room.

	Stockholm (SEK)	Copenhagen (Dkr)	Oslo (NOK)	Helsinki (Fmk)	Reykjavik (US$)
Deluxe	1,000 and up	1,100 and up	950 and up	750 and up	
Expensive	800–1,000	800–1,100	650–950	550–750	120–150
Moderate	600–800	670–800	500–650	350–550	100–120
Inexpensive	under 600	under 670	350–500	under 350	50–100

Restaurants throughout the country chapters are generally rated expensive (E), moderate (M), and inexpensive (I). All restaurant prices are per person and exclude drinks. The categories break down approximately as follows:

	Stockholm (SEK)	Copenhagen (Dkr)	Oslo (NOK)	Helsinki (Fmk)	Reykjavik (US$)
Expensive	200 and up	185 and up	200 and up	170–220	45 and up
Moderate	100–200	100–185	100–200	110–170	25–45
Inexpensive	100 or less	under 100	60–100	75–110	under 25

STOCKHOLM

Open Nature and City Planning

Stockholm, Sweden's capital, has been called the most beautiful city in the world. This is open to debate, but few will deny that it is a handsome and civilized capital with a natural setting that would be hard to beat anywhere. When it was founded as a fortress on a little stone island where Lake Mälaren reaches the Baltic, nobody cared much about natural beauty. It was protection the founders were after, military defense. But around the year 1250, the fortress became a town, and the town, spreading to nearby islands and finally to the mainland, became a city. And, though Nature remained the same, men's opinion of it changed, and Stockholm delights the tourist today with its openness, its space, its vistas over a great expanse of water. Of course it's been called the "Venice of the North," but that happens sooner or later to any northern city with more water than can be supplied by a fire hydrant.

Stockholm's beauty has been jealously guarded by the city fathers. The town is full of parks, tree-lined squares and boulevards, playgrounds, wading pools and other amenities of urban life, and the building codes are extremely strict. Nature and city planning have thus combined to create a pleasing metropolis, and it is hard to realize as you gaze out over the water from a table on the Strömparterren terrace that you are in the heart of a bustling metropolis, a town that has grown from less than 100,000 inhabitants to over a million in the space of a century.

Nowhere is the striking modernity of much of Stockholm more obvious than in the brand new streets and squares around Sergels Torg, a startling glass and steel tower in the heart of the new city, and the rail station, where multi-lane highways, skyscrapers and underground shopping malls have all sprung up in the space of a few years. Yet no more than five minutes' walk will bring you to the medieval heart of the city on the islands of Gamla Stan (Old Town), where narrow twisting streets huddle around the bulk of the imposing Royal Palace, the Cathedral and the Riksdag, the Parliament.

June, July and August are the best months to visit this capital. Then you have the best weather and the greatest variety of sight-seeing facilities. Bring a reasonably warm coat along. What most people would call a mild summer day is apt to be announced in the Stockholm papers as a heat wave. In May or October the weather is brisker, but so is the normal life of Stockholm.

History and Growth

The earliest origins of Stockholm are largely unknown. Perhaps the first somewhat reliable report is a Viking saga, which, as all Viking sagas should, ends in violence. It seems that Agne, a warrior king of the Ynglinga dynasty, had been off on a visit to Finland. There, among other treasures, he had acquired a chieftain's daughter named Skjalf, by the effective if crude device of cutting down her father. Coming home, he stopped on the shore of an island which is now a part of Stockholm, to drink the health of his new bride and a proper toast to his late father-in-law. The mead flowed freely, Agne slept, Skjalf freed her fellow Finnish prisoners, and they hanged Agne. Then the Finns safely sailed home. The place was subsequently called Agnefit, or Agne Strand.

The first written mention of Stockholm in preserved chronicles gives the date 1252. Tradition—and some historical evidence—has it that a powerful regent named Birger Jarl here founded a fortified castle and city, locking off the entrance to Lake Mälaren and the region around it. At all events, it is known that a castle of substance was built in the 13th century, and during the same period the Great Church was begun (dedicated to St. Nicholas, patron saint of shipping) and the first monasteries.

From these dim beginnings the history of the city can be divided into four fairly distinct epochs: the erratic, confused first centuries; the arrival of King Gustav Vasa, who made Stockholm a capital beginning in 1523; King Gustavus Adolphus, who made it the heart of an empire a century later; and the modern era.

After the time of Birger Jarl the Swedish nation, still unorganized, groped its way forward. Up to this time Stockholm had not been the capital; the latest city to enjoy the favor had been Sigtuna. The real physical heart of Sweden remained uncertain. Nevertheless, Magnus Eriksson, a king of some importance, was crowned here in 1336. Toward the end of the century Sweden, Norway, and Denmark were united under one ruler. A period of confusion and revolt followed. Stockholm continued to be a commercial center, with monopoly trading rights for much of the territory around.

On Midsummer's Eve, 1523, when King Gustav Vasa returned from his victorious uprising for Swedish independence from the union (and from a Danish king), the real history of Stockholm began. Vasa was a powerful figure, sometimes called the George Washington of Sweden, and, although he moved from castle to castle throughout the country, his treasure chamber was in the old Stockholm Royal Palace. Succeeding kings tended in the same direction, making Stockholm more and more important.

Under Gustavus Adolphus, a great organizer as well as a military leader, who reigned from 1611 to 1632, the city became a capital in fact as well as name. Sweden had already begun to engage in political machinations and wars on the Continent and in Russia. It was partly his need to keep his military forces at top efficiency, his need for tax money, for supplies and for men that led Gustavus to concentrate the administration of the country in Stockholm. When he died on the battlefield of Lützen in 1632, Protestantism had been saved, Sweden had become an empire and Stockholm was its capital.

Prosperity and population grew accordingly. Gustavus himself, in a farewell address of 1630, had told the citizens of Sweden's cities that he hoped "your small cottages may become large stone houses". Many of them did. From a population of perhaps 3,000 when Gustav Vasa came home victorious, the number of inhabitants had grown to some 9,000 by the time Gustavus Adolphus fell, and rose to perhaps 35,000 by 1660. Meanwhile, the wars continued. Fortunately for Stockholm, they were fought on foreign soil. This did not, however, diminish the importance of the city, for it functioned as the capital even during the long absence of hero King Charles XII, who spent almost his entire reign in the field—losing much of what Gustavus Adolphus had won.

Rulers came and went, political battles were fought, won, and lost. But the building of Stockholm went on, sometimes in the hands of eminent architects like Nicodemus Tessin and his son, who are responsible for both the Royal Palace and Drottningholm Palace, as well as many other buildings which still stand. In the 18th century, Stockholm began to attract scientists and scholars, to share the spotlight with Lund and Uppsala as a center of learning. Gustav III (assassinated in 1792), a dilettante who could put on steel gauntlets when required, did much to make Stockholm a cultural, musical, and dramatic capital.

In 1850 Stockholm was still a quiet town. It had many of the stately buildings which even now give it its characteristic profile, but it numbered less than 100,000 people—a peaceful administrative center, perhaps dreaming of past glories. The first municipal cleaning department was established in 1859, the first waterworks in 1861, and gaslights had arrived but a few years earlier. As late as 1860, Drottninggatan, the most prominent commercial street, had no sidewalks. But the same year the first train arrived from Södertälje, 25 miles away. Modern communications had been born. The new era had begun.

Modern Development

The last 100 years of Stockholm's history are the story of a peaceful revolution, of industrialization, and of the remaking of a government from a monarchy with four estates in the parliament—nobles, clergy, farmers, as well as burghers—into a full parliamentary democracy with a king at its head. As the country has progressed and grown, Stockholm has progressed and grown with it. You will see the physical evidence wherever you go—the squat Parliament House on the site of one-time royal stables; the City Hall, a splendidly quirky and lavish brick creation overlooking the waters of Lake Mälaren; the extensive and striking developments in the center of the city; and two huge satellite suburbs to the west and east of the city.

Exploring Stockholm

If Stockholm's island geography poses communication problems, it has the advantage of dividing the city neatly into sections and of making it possible to know easily where you are.

Gamla Stan. The Old Town, site of the Royal Palace and center of the city and nation, and the adjoining islands, Riddarholmen (The Isle of Knights), and Helgeandsholmen (Island of the Holy Spirit).

Södermalm. As the name implies, this is the southern section, across the bridge leading from the Old Town.

Norrmalm. North of the Old Town, the financial and business heart of the city. The new building construction from Hötorget to Klarabergsgatan, which forms the new commercial center of Stockholm, constitutes the most important part of the redevelopment of Nedre Norrmalm (Lower Norrmalm).

Kungsholmen. A large island west of Norrmalm, site of the Town Hall, and most of the offices of the city government.

Östermalm. East of Norrmalm, largely residential, many embassies and consulates.

Djurgården. The huge island which is mostly park, projecting east toward the Baltic Sea in the channels between Östermalm and Södermalm. Here are concentrated museums, including Skansen, the open-air museum, amusement parks, and restaurants.

Regardless of how long you intend to stay and how thoroughly you expect to see the city, begin by one or more boat excursions. Nothing else can give you a quick idea of the unique nature of Stockholm.

Let's take as a starting point the south of the large downtown park known as the Royal Gardens (Kungsträdgården), just across the rushing channel from the Royal Palace. It's an ummistakable point, easy to find. Immediately beside you is the striking profile of the statue of King Charles XII, arm raised and pointing east; behind him stretches the long park; to his right the unmistakable solid stone of the Royal Opera House, a block or so to his left the familiar façade of the Grand Hotel; and across the water the dominating walls of the palace. Furthermore, just at the water's edge at both sides of the bridge there are kiosks that serve as starting points for some of the boat and bus excursions which show you the city.

The best way to see the city is by boat—there is practically no major place of interest in and around Stockholm that isn't within easy reach of the many little boats that ply around the busy harbor. But you'll find it equally easy to explore the city on foot. Most of the principal sights are concentrated in the center of Stockholm and are relatively close to one another. If you feel like venturing further afield, use the excellent subway system, the T-banan; many of the stations are carved from solid rock, creating an eerie, grotto-like atmosphere.

Gamla Stan

The best place to begin your exploration of the city is the Old Town, Gamla Stan, situated on three little islands. From the statue of Charles XII at the foot of the Kungsträdgården, there are two bridges leading to the Old Town, both no more than a couple of minutes' walk away. The more interesting, however, is the second, the Norrbro, leading directly to

STOCKHOLM

the imposing bulk of the Royal Palace. As you cross the bridge, you'll also see the Parliament building, a ponderous stone structure dating from the turn of the century, on your right. And just behind and to one side of the Parliament building is the one-time building of the Bank of Sweden, the oldest existing bank in the world, founded in 1656.

The Royal Palace is not old, as palaces go, but the site is. It was here that Stockholm was born. The original palace, the Three Crowns, burned down one night in 1697, with the exception of the northern wing of today's palace. A new palace on the old site was ordered immediately. Three generations of Sweden's most famous architectural dynasty had an important part in its creation—Nicodemus Tessin the Elder planned the exterior and began the interior decoration, which was continued by his son, Tessin the Younger, and grandson, Carl Gustav Tessin. The whole project took more than 60 years, and was not completed until 1760. The building consists basically of a perfect square—enclosing a large court—with two wings sticking out on the east side and another on the west.

A number of interiors are open to the public. You may be interested in the Hall of State, which contains the king's silver throne. The Chapel Royal in the same wing has, among other impressive historical and artistic treasures, pews saved from the old palace. If you have time, look in on the Apartments of State, the Apartments of King Oscar II and Queen Sophie, and the Guest Apartments, notable for the furnishings and extremely fine Gobelin tapestries. There's also a palace museum, with bits of the previous palace, other historical finds, and the collection of classical sculpture brought from Italy by King Gustav III in the 1780s. The Royal Treasury, in the old vaults, can now be visited.

Diagonally across the street from the south side of the palace, and intimately associated with it, is the Great Church, the Stockholm cathedral and, in a sense, the national church. You would hardly guess from the well-kept exterior that it is believed to be the oldest building in the city, dating from about 1250. Many Swedish kings have been crowned here (until Gustav V gave up the custom when he ascended the throne in 1907), and it is still used for solemn celebrations attended by the king. There are a number of art treasures, of which perhaps the oldest, best known, and most distinguished is the statue carved in wood of St. George and the Dragon by Bernt Notke of Lübeck, which was presented to the church in 1489 to commemorate a Swedish victory over the Danes some 18 years earlier. A sound and light show is performed here for a few weeks during summer.

You are in the heart of the Old Town now and there are several ways of continuing your look about. Here are two good suggestions immediately at hand. The first is to walk downhill on the lane called Storkyrkobrinken, to the right of the main entrance of the Great Church as you come out. This lane, like practically all those of the Old Town, follows the same route it did in the Middle Ages. Everywhere around you are buildings centuries old, living history. At the base of the hill you step out in a little square called Riddarhustorget. The two dominating buildings, across the square from where you enter, both date from the 17th century. One is Riddarhuset, House of the Nobility, in which you will find the crests of Swedish noble families. The white palace to its right was once a private possession, became the city courthouse in the 18th century, and is now occupied by the Supreme Court.

STOCKHOLM

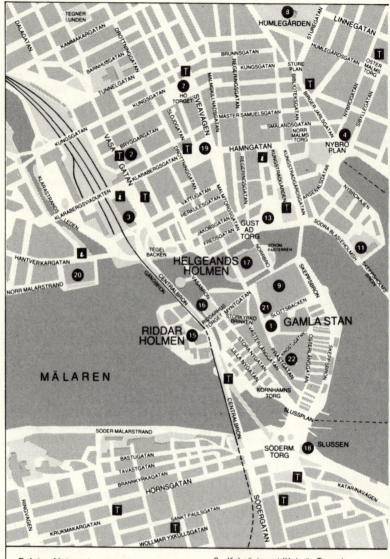

Points of Interest

1. Börsen (Stock Exchange)
2. Centralpostkontoret (Central Post Office)
3. Central Rail Station
4. Dramatiska Teatern (Royal Dramatic Theater)
5. Historiska Museet (Museum of National Antiquities)
6. Kaknästornet (Kaknäs Tower)
7. Konserthuset (Concert Hall)
8. Kungliga Biblioteket (Royal Library)
9. Kungliga Slottet (Royal Palace); Livrustkammaren (Royal Armory)
10. Moderna Museet (Museum of Modern Art)
11. Nationalmuseet (National Museum)

STOCKHOLM

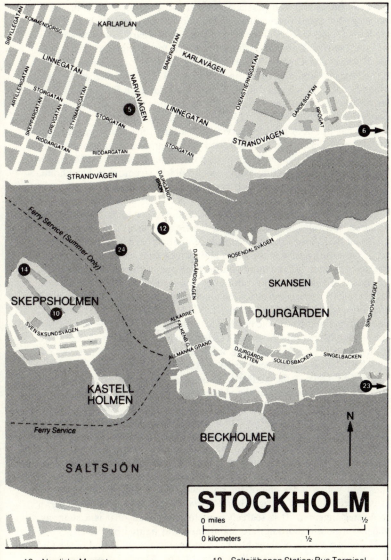

12 Nordiska Museet (Nordic Museum)
13 Operan (Royal Opera House)
14 Östasiatiska Museet (Museum of Far Eastern Antiquities)
15 Riddarholmskyrkan (Riddarholm Church)
16 Riddarhuset (House of Nobility); Supreme Court
17 Riksdag (Parliament)
18 Saltsjöbanan Station; Bus Terminal
19 Sergels Torg
20 Stadshuset (Town Hall)
21 Storkyrkan (Cathedral)
22 Tyska Kyrkan (German Church)
23 Waldemarsudde
24 Wasavarvet (Wasa Museum)
T Subway Stations
i Tourist Information Offices

From here you will see the weathered red brick and openwork spire of Riddarholm Church. This is the Swedish Pantheon, burial place of Swedish kings for about four centuries. The most famous figures buried here are King Gustavus Adolphus, hero of the Thirty Years' War, and Charles XII (in Swedish, Karl XII), who is renowned for his signal victories over the Russian and Continental armies, with inferior forces, until the tide turned against him and he fell in Norway in 1718. Two medieval kings, Magnus Ladulås, who died in 1290, and Karl Knutson Bonde, some 180 years later, are also buried here. The latest king to be put to rest was Gustav V, on November 9, 1950. Except for the funeral of a king, the church has not been used for services for a long time. The sarcophagi of the various rulers, usually embellished with their monograms, are clearly visible in the small chapels given over to the various dynasties. The church building itself is interesting as the second oldest structure in Stockholm. It is a former monastery church completed about 1290, with many additions since.

Take five minutes to continue past the church down to the quay on Lake Mälaren. It's well worth it. You get a fine view of the lake, the magnificent arches of the West Bridge in the distance, the southern heights, and above all the imposing profile of the Town Hall, which appears to be almost floating on the water. At the quay you may see one of the Göta Canal ships.

The second alternative to continuing your stroll from the Great Church is to turn left as you come out of the main entrance and walk up Trångsund to a little square called Stortorget, the oldest square in Stockholm. The dominating building, on the north side, is the Stock Exchange. This is also the headquarters of the Swedish Academy, which awards the Nobel Prize in literature. The other buildings are also old; note the tall, narrow, red merchant house and its sculptured portal from the 17th century.

The Old Town is the perfect kind of place to wander around without any decided aim, looking at the old portals, poking about in crowded antique shops, savoring the Bohemian atmosphere and the sense of age, peeking into doll-sized courtyards, making your way through curving, narrow lanes. There is little auto traffic, and the passages are too narrow to provide both streets and sidewalks. Go along Skomakaregatan to the German Church (Tyska Kyrkan), turn right for a few meters, then left again on Prästgatan. Keep your eyes open as you near the end of Prästgatan, on the right you will see one of the narrowest thoroughfares in the world. It is called Mårten Trotzigs Gränd (*gränd* means lane), and leads down to Västerlånggatan. It is scarcely a meter wide, half of it is a stairway, yet it is a public thoroughfare maintained and lighted by the city.

It's only a couple of short blocks from here to the south end of the Old Town. You should really stroll on to that point. Above you are the southern heights, connected with the Old Town by an intricate cloverleaf of bridges and streets at about four levels, called Slussen. Katarina elevator—you see it poking up all by itself on the other side of the channel—takes you up to a platform with a fine view of Stockholm.

Though the Old Town is, of course, the most ancient and historic part of the city, you will have noticed by now that it is by no means lacking in modern chic. In fact it is very definitely the trendiest area of the city, both for shopping and eating, with a veritable surfeit of expensive and glamorous restaurants and shops: there are some 300 restaurants alone.

Skansen

After the sophistication and history of the Old Town, the open-air amusement park of Skansen, founded in 1891, provides a striking contrast. It is situated on the large island of Djurgården, located to the east of the city. The park contains a museum, a zoo, numerous restaurants and cafés, a circus, an aquarium, a theater, a concert hall and much else besides, all combining to make it one of the enduring highlights of the city. One of its principal delights are the buildings—farm houses, windmills, barns, whole estates almost—that have been brought here from all parts of the country, giving even the most casual visitor a taste of traditional rural Sweden. There is even an 18th-century church that is still used for divine services and weddings. But many of the other buildings are in use too. Geese cackle near the entrance to the farm houses from southern Sweden; glass blowers blow glass—you can help blow it if you want to—in the old-time glass blower's hut.

Here also are moose, wolves, foxes and other Nordic animals; Sweden's largest aquarium with Cuban crocodiles; and nocturnal bush-babies, pygmy kangaroos and other strange animals in the Moonlight Hall. Many activities designed especially for children include a children's zoo.

You can walk to Skansen from the statue of Charles XII in about 30 minutes. It is a long walk, but it will take you through much of Stockholm's most gracious and substantial waterfront areas, past elegant apartment blocks and smart shops, with yachts and ferry boats ever-present, particularly on the broad expanse of Strandvägen.

Djurgården is also home to three outstanding museums: the Nordiska Museum, the Waldemarsudde and the *Wasa*. The *Wasa* is a 17th-century warship, once the pride of the Swedish navy, built at vast expense and the most powerful fighting ship of her day in the Baltic. Launched amid great pomp, she set out on her maiden voyage on August 10, 1628 in full view of the population of Stockholm, including of course the King himself. She had sailed less than a mile when a gust caught her, and she heeled over and unceremoniously sank—the *Titanic* of her day. Her precious guns were immediately salvaged, but with the passage of time the *Wasa* faded from memory.

However, in 1956 her position was rediscovered and it was found that, remarkably, the briny waters of the harbor had all but preserved her intact. A complex and difficult salvage operation was begun and in May 1961 the *Wasa* was raised to the surface. Painstaking restoration has returned the ship almost to her original condition, providing the visitor with an unparalleled experience of life afloat in a great warship of the past. The site where she had been displayed for many years was closed in 1988 and a new museum a few hundred meters away is scheduled to open in June 1990.

The Nordiska Museum (the Nordic Museum), housed in a splendid late-Victorian pile, is located just by the Djurgårdsbron, the bridge leading to Djurgården. It contains a vast collection of exhibits that chart Sweden's progress from 1500. Of particular interest are some magnificent fabrics, costumes and rugs, a lovely collection of bridal gowns and the charming gold and silver coronets traditionally worn by Swedish brides.

Finally, visit Prince Eugen's "Waldemarsudde," the former home of "the Painter Prince," brother of the late King Gustav V, which was bequeathed to the people on the prince's death. The many paintings, some by Eugen himself, constitute a fine collection of Swedish art, and the mansion, art gallery, and beautiful grounds are well worth seeing.

Treasures of the City Hall

The Stockholm City Hall, one of the great architectural works of the 20th century, is another appropriate excursion that you can manage in a couple of hours—more if you like. Starting at the statue of Charles XII, turn to the right and merely follow the waterfront until you arrive at its massive portal. The distance is less than a couple of kilometers.

Superlatives have not been lacking in describing the structure. It has sometimes been called "the most beautiful building of this century in Europe." This opinion is not unanimous, of course; some people have reacted violently against it, but even this sharp reaction is a measure of the strength of the total impression. The building was completed and dedicated in 1923, and has become a symbol of the city. It is the seat of the city council and central administration.

The building is certainly unusual—a massive square tower rising from the corner of a graceful central block, the whole built of dark and delicately worked brick and topped by pale-green roofs with spires, domes and minarets abounding. It successfully synthesizes elements of traditional Swedish architecture, notably in the tower, which is derived from the massive castles of 16th-century Sweden, with classical elements, the resulting mixture spiced by Oriental and Byzantine windows and spires. It is difficult to decide finally whether the end-product is beautiful or kitsch—it is undoubtedly impressive.

You can go inside and look around. Among the highlights are the Golden Hall, whose walls are decorated lavishly with mosaics; the Blue Hall, confusingly named perhaps, as the only blue visible is the sky glimpsed through the windows ranged around the top of the walls; and the Prince's Gallery, with large murals by Prince Eugene. You can also go up the 106-meter (348-foot) tower (don't worry, there's an elevator) for a predictably spectacular view. At noon and 6 P.M. the carillon plays the medieval war song of the Swedes that helped gird their loins at the Battle of Brunkeberg in 1471. The adjoining Maiden Tower is surmounted by a bronze St. George and the Dragon. Finally, visit the Terrace, a formal garden on the banks of Lake Mälaren with wonderful views of the Old Town and the southern heights rising beyond it.

Other Sights

Depending on the amount of time you have available and your special interests, there are many other places and institutions well worth a visit. Among the dozens of museums, these are particularly recommended: The National Museum, just a few doors down the quay from the Grand Hotel, which is home to the largest collection of paintings and sculptures, by both Swedish and foreign artists, in the country.

A few minutes' walk from here on the island of Skeppsholmen are the Museum of Modern Art and the Museum of Far Eastern Antiquities, both with fine collections, the latter a pleasing spot to explore or simply from which to admire the view of the Old Town.

The National Museum of Antiquities and Royal Cabinet of Coins, located to the east of the city on the spacious boulevard of Narvavägen, contains a veritable mass of historical finds dating back well into the Stone Age.

Although not a museum, there is a further attraction on Djurgården—the 155-meter (508-foot) high Kaknäs Tower. The fastest elevators in Europe hurtle you up to the observation deck, from where an unparalleled view of the city and the Stockholm archipelago stretches before you.

Music and Markets

The Concert Hall, at Hötorget, is the center of Stockholm's musical life. The building, designed by Ivar Tengbom, was completed in 1926. In front is Carl Milles' huge sculptured group of Orpheus calling up the spirits. It is in this hall that the awarding of the Nobel Prizes takes place.

It's well worth your while to get to one of the market squares fairly early in the day—9:00 A.M. will do—which are masses of color whatever the season of the year. One is just in front of the Concert House, another on Östermalm. Flowers, fresh fruits and vegetables are the principal stock in trade. Look in at the indoor markets which adjoin these squares—there you can fill your whole grocery basket from the little shops of independent dealers, and have a snack in one of the small restaurants. This is a unique aspect of Stockholm life. Incidentally, the outdoor markets operate right through the winter.

Excursions from Stockholm

Immediately outside the city limits of Stockholm proper are a number of popular attractions which you can reach within an hour by public transportation, or half an hour by car.

The sculptor Carl Milles, who was perhaps better known as an inhabitant of Cranbrook, Michigan, had his permanent home on the island of Lidingö, a Stockholm suburb, where he collected not only some of his own works, but also other outstanding pieces from several eras and countries. It was here at Millesgården that he died in September 1955, still hard at work at the age of 80, and the collection is now open to the public year-round.

The royal palace of Drottningholm is located on a little island in Lake Mälaren—the name means "Queen's Island"—a few kilometers from Stockholm. The trip is a pleasant experience, particularly by boat. If you have seen Versailles, you will be reminded of it at once when you arrive at Drottningholm, for it was clearly inspired by the French style. The palace was built by Nicodemus Tessin the Elder, and his son, Tessin the Younger, completed the gardens in the style of Le Nôtre.

Drottningholm is one of the most delightful of European palaces, embracing, as it does, all that was best in the art of living practiced by mid-18th-century royalty. In the grounds, a kind of Trianon, is the China Palace, conceived in Chinoiserie terms, a lovely little palace, hidden in the trees, where the royal family could relax and entertain their friends. Also in the grounds is the Theater. This fascinating building slumbered like the Sleeping Beauty undisturbed for well over a century, the settings and stage machinery of the 18th century in perfect condition and working order. It now houses a theater museum and delightful productions of baroque opera are once again staged in the auditorium that saw the efforts of Gustavus III to create a Swedish Golden Age. The Royal Family occupies one wing at the palace.

STOCKHOLM

Haga Palace, formerly the home of the late Crown Prince Gustav Adolf, is located only a few minutes from downtown, right on the city limits of Stockholm. A more interesting building located on the same grounds is Haga Pavilion. It is a miniature summer palace built by Gustav III (late 18th century), exquisitely furnished.

The resort of Saltsjöbaden is a residential suburb the year round. During the summer it is a rendezvous for yachtsmen and motorboat enthusiasts, and the harbor is excellent. In winter there is skating, skate-sailing, ice-boating, and skiing. The modern Stockholm observatory is located here. You can reach Saltsjöbaden from Slussen on an electric train. In the same general direction, but to the north, is Gustavsberg, where the noted ceramics works may be visited in groups by previous appointment.

PRACTICAL INFORMATION FOR STOCKHOLM

GETTING TO TOWN FROM THE AIRPORT. Buses from Arlanda Airport to the city, a distance of 45 km. (28 miles) are frequent. The trip takes about 40 minutes and the bus takes you to the City Terminal above the Central Station in the center of town. The Sheraton, Royal Viking, Terminus and Continental hotels are all within two minutes' walk. The fare is approximately SEK 30, payable to the driver. You can also buy a ticket at special ticket offices at the airport and the air terminal. A scheduled bus service to Brommaplan from the airport is also available, with stops at Kista and Sundbyberg subway stations.

A taxi to the city from the airport will cost you about SEK 350. However, SAS Scandinavian Airlines operates a limousine service on a shared-taxi basis, which takes you direct to your hotel or any other address in the Greater Stockholm area for about SEK 185 or 230 according to distance. The limousine can be booked on arrival at Arlanda Airport; for the return journey ask your hotel to make a reservation well in advance—the previous day, if possible. If two or more passengers take the limousine to the same address, only the first pays the full fare; the others pay 50%.

TOURIST INFORMATION. The Tourist Center is located in the middle of the city in Sverigehuset (Sweden House), opposite the large department store *Nordiska Kompaniet*, or *N.K.*, in Kungsträdgården (789 20 00). There you will find information about interesting sights and events, one-day tours and so on and you can make bookings for sightseeing excursions. It also sells maps, postcards, books and souvenirs. The Tourist Center is open every day.

A useful publications is *Stockholm This Week* which you can get from most hotels and all tourist centers. From a kiosk on Norrmalmstorg you can buy last-minute tickets at reduced prices to concerts and theaters.

USEFUL ADDRESSES. Embassies. *American Embassy*, Strandvägen 101 (783 53 00). *British Embassy*, Skarpögatan 6–8 (667 01 40). *Canadian Embassy*, Tegelbacken 4 (near the Sheraton) (23 79 20).

Travel Agents. *American Express*, Birger Jarlsgatan 1 (23 53 30). *Wagons-Lits/Thomas Cook*, Vasagatan 22 (762 58 27).

Car Hire. *Avis*, Sveavägen 61 (34 99 10); *Hertz*, Mäster Samuelsgatan 67 (24 07 20); *Europcar*, Birger Jarlsgatan 59 (23 10 70); *Interrent*, Hotel Sheraton, Tegelbacken (21 06 50). All the major car-rental companies also have desks at Arlanda Airport.

TELEPHONE CODES. The telephone codes for Stockholm is 08. To call any number in this chapter from outside Stockholm, unless otherwise specified, this prefix must be used. Within the city, no prefix is required.

STOCKHOLM

HOTELS. It is recommended that your reserve hotel rooms well in advance, especially from September to November. If you arrive in Stockholm without a reservation, consult the Hotellcentralen in the Central Station. This room-booking service is open daily 8 A.M.—9P.M. June through Sept. For the rest of the year it is open daily Mon. to Fri. 8.30–11.30 and 1–5, and, in May only, Sat. 8–5, Sun. 1–9. A charge is made for each room reserved. Most hotels have smoke-free rooms and rooms for the handicapped. Breakfast is usually included in the room rate. In general, Stockholm hotels are comfortable, but prices are fairly high.

More than 40 hotels offer the "Stockholm Package" at weekends throughout the year and daily during the summer months, with accommodations for one night costing between SEK 195 and SEK 430 per person including breakfast and a "Key to Stockholm" card, which gives free transportation within the city plus free entrance to museums and discounts on sightseeing. For details, write to Stockholm Information Service, Excursion Shop, Box 7542, S-103 93 Stockholm or phone The Hotel Center (08–24 08 80). The "Stockholm Package" is also bookable through travel agents.

Deluxe

Amaranten. Kungsholmsgatan 31 (54 10 60). 415 rooms. Contains the *Amaryllis* restaurant, the *Travellers'* piano bar and a nightclub called *Cindy*. It also boasts a Japanese-style recreation area and an "executive tower" with a roof garden and luxurious accommodations. Refurbished in 1988. (SARA). AE, DC, MC, V.

Anglais. Humlegårdsgatan 23 (24 99 00). 211 rooms. One of the leading hotels in Stockholm, conveniently situated near shopping districts and the subway. Popular restaurant, own video channel, garage. (RESO). AE, DC, MC, V.

Continental, Vasagatan (24 40 20). 250 rooms. Opposite the railway station. Currently being renovated. Special low rates available in summer. *Nike* restaurant. *Bistro Chez Charles, Cafeteria Concorde.* (RESO). AE, DC, MC, V.

Diplomat. Strandvägen 7C (663 58 00). 130 rooms. On the waterfront, within walking distance of Djurgården Park and Skansen as well as the city center. Turn-of-the-century atmosphere. Popular tea-house. AE, DC, MC, V.

Grand. Blasieholmshamnen 8 (22 10 20). 330 rooms, front rooms face the Royal Palace and the waterfront. A distinguished European deluxe hotel. Splendid ballroom, famous restaurant. *Thé dansant* on Sun. AE, DC, MC, V.

Lady Hamilton. Storkyrkobrinken 5 (23 46 80). 35 rooms. A gem of a hotel. Built in 1470 and converted to an hotel in 1980. A large collection of antiques including one of George Romney's portraits of Lady Hamilton. The Storkyrkan (the cathedral) and the Royal Palace are neighbors. Cafeteria. AE, DC, MC, V.

Lord Nelson. Västerlånggatan 22 (23 23 90). 31 small rooms. Small hotel right in the middle of the Old Town and twinned, naturally enough, with the nearby Lady Hamilton. Atmosphere throughout is decidedly nautical, even down to the cabin-sized rooms. However, standards of comfort and service are high. Sauna; no restaurant. Cafeteria. Located in rather noisy pedestrian area. AE, DC, MC, V.

Mälardrottningen (Queen of Lake Mälaren). Riddarholmen (24 36 00). 59 cabins on what was formerly American heiress—and wife of Cary Grant—Barbara Hutton's luxury yacht (built 1924). All cabins are furnished to deluxe hotel standards and the yacht has an attractive permanent berth at Riddarholmskajen, close to the Old Town. It has a restaurant and a bar on the bridge. AE, DC, MC, V.

Reisen. Skeppsbron 12–14 (22 32 60). 113 rooms. A SARA hotel built behind the facade of three 17th-century houses. Has the *Quarter Deck* restaurant and the best piano bar in town. Saunas, pool, garage. AE, DC, MC, V.

SAS Arlandia. At Arlanda Airport (0760–618 00). 300 rooms. Five minutes by bus from the airport. Restaurant, bar, nightclub, cinema, sauna, indoor pool, tennis. Close to golf and bathing. AE, DC, MC, V.

SAS Royal Viking. Vasagatan 1 (14 10 00). 340 rooms. A modern hotel of high international standard managed by SAS International Hotels. Within walking distance of the city center and shopping. Has a "sky bar" overlooking the City Hall and Old Town, a relaxation center with saunas, and a wintergarden, The *Royal*

Atrium, with a 36-meter (120-foot) high ceiling. Near airport bus, mainline trains and subway. SAS airline check-in desk. AE, DC, MC, V.

SAS Strand. Nybrokajen 9 (22 29 00). 137 rooms. Central location opposite the *Royal Dramatic Theater.* The building dates from 1912 and was completely renovated in 1984. Winter garden with a ceiling seven stories high and an outstanding gourmet restaurant. SAS airline check-in desk. AE, DC, MC, V.

Sergel Plaza. Brunkebergstorg 9 (22 66 00). 406 rooms, very central. Features trees and waterfalls in the glass-roofed lobby. It has a restaurant, saunas, solarium, bubblepool. (RESO). AE, DC, MC, V.

Sheraton-Stockholm. Tegelbacken 6 (14 26 00). 460 rooms. Near the railway station with a view of the Old Town and the City Hall. The restaurant, *Le Bistro,* is open until 1.30 A.M. Piano bar, boutiques, garage. AE, DC, MC, V.

Terminus. Vasagatan 20 (22 26 40). 155 rooms. Handy down-town location, if possibly noisy, opposite Central Station and close to airport buses. Popular restaurant, *Kasper.* AE, DC, MC.

Victory. Lilla Nygatan 5 (14 30 90). 48 rooms. In the Old Town near its sister hotels, Lady Hamilton and Lord Nelson (see above). Building dates from 1640 on site of the Lion's Tower which burnt down in 1625. Rooms with nautical decor. Restaurant on ground floor under separate management. AE, DC, MC, V.

Expensive

Birger Jarl. Tulegatan 8 (15 10 20). 252 rooms. Unlicensed. Quiet location within walking distance of Stureplan and the city center. Connected with neighboring church; has weekly services in English. Keep-fit area with a sauna and pool. Cafeteria. AE, DC, MC, V.

Bromma. Brommaplan (25 29 20). 142 rooms. 15 minutes by subway downtown, ten minutes by bus to Drottningholm Palace. Direct bus to Arlanda Airport. Restaurant, garage, small garden (RESO). AE, DC, MC, V.

Clas på Hörnet. Surbrunnsgatan 20 (16 51 30). 10 rooms. Arguably the most exclusive hotel in Stockholm, in an elegant 200-year-old town house. Excellent restaurant. AE, DC, MC, V.

Esplanade, Strandvägen 7A (663 07 40). Within walking distance of Djurgården, Skansen and the city center. A turn-of-the-century atmosphere. Breakfast only. AE, DC, MC, V.

Karelia. Birger Jarlsgatan 35 (24 76 60). 103 rooms. A few minutes' walk from Stureplan. Finnish sauna and pool. Restaurant with Finnish and Russian specialties, dancing, nightclub. A bit of Finland in the heart of Stockholm. AE, DC, MC, V.

Mornington. Nybrogatan 53 (663 12 40). 141 rooms. Near the indoor market at Östermalmstorg, within walking distance of theaters and shopping. Elegant fish restaurant. AE, DC, MC, V.

Palace, St. Eriksgatan 115 (24 12 20). 218 rooms. Sauna, garage. (RESO). AE, DC, MC, V.

Park Hotel. Karlavägen 43 (22 96 20). 202 rooms. Quiet, central location next to Humlegården Park, within walking distance of the city center. Restaurant, garden café, garage. (RESO). AE, DC, MC, V.

Moderate

Adlon. Vasagatan 42 (24 54 00). 62 rooms, all with bath. Central. AE, DC, MC, V.

August Strindberg. Tegnérgatan 38 (32 50 06). 19 rooms in a building dating from 1890. Near a park, quiet, central. No elevator. AE, MC, V.

City. Slöjdgatan 7 (22 22 40). 300 rooms. Central. Close to the Hötorget market. Many smoke-free rooms; seven rooms specially equipped for the handicapped. Run by the Salvation Army. Unlicensed. Elegant restaurant. Magnificent indoor wintergarden. AE, DC, MC, V.

Eden Terrace. Sturegatan 10 (22 31 60). 61 rooms, some with balconies. On two top floors of an office building. Breakfast room with a summer terrace overlooking Humlegården Park. Central. AE, DC, MC, V.

STOCKHOLM 15

Flamingo. Hotellgatan 11, Solna (83 08 00). 130 rooms. Ten minutes by subway from the city. Restaurant, dancing, grillroom. Solna has a large shopping center. AE, DC, MC, V.

Flyghotellet. Brommaplan (26 26 20). 68 rooms. By subway, ten minutes from the city; by bus, ten minutes to Drottningholm Palace. Direct airport bus. AE, DC, MC, V.

Gamla Stan. Lilla Nygatan 25 (24 44 50). 51 rooms, all with bath. In the Old Town. Run by the Salvation Army. Breakfast only. No alcohol. AE, MC, V.

Kom. Döbelnsgatan 17 (23 56 30). 91 rooms. Central, quiet. Kitchenette with refrigerator in most rooms. Sauna. Breakfast only. Near the subway. AE, DC, MC, V.

Kristineberg. Hjalmar Söderbergsväg 10 (13 03 00). 98 rooms, all with bath. Near a subway station, seven minutes from the city. Free sauna. Popular restaurant suitable for motorists. AE, DC, MC.

Scandic Hotel. Järva Krog, Uppsalavägen, Solna (85 03 60). 204 rooms, of which 102 are smoke-free. North of the city on E 4. The airport bus stops here on request, and there's a regular bus service to the city. The *Rotisserie Musketör* on the 11th floor has a fine view of Brunnsviken Lake. AE, DC, MC, V.

Stockholm. Norrmalmstorg 1 (22 13 20). 92 rooms, all with baths. The hotel is on the top floor of an office building with Kungsträrden ården Park and the *N.K.* department store just around the corner. Breakfast only. AE, DC, MC, V.

Inexpensive

Alexandra. Magnus Ladulåsgatan 42 (84 03 20). 90 rooms. In the heart of Södermalm (south of Slussen). Five minutes to the city by the nearby subway. No restaurant. Renovated in 1988. AE, DC, MC, V.

Anno 1647. Mariatorget 3 (44 04 80). 42 rooms, 30 with baths. Also some higher priced and elegant rooms. Located in a centuries-old building close to Slussen. Historic surroundings. A few steps from the subway and the ferry to Skansen. Breakfast and lunch only. AE, DC, MC, V.

Domus. Körsbärsvägen 1 (16 01 95) 78 rooms. Near subway. Family apartments with pantry available. Restaurant. AE, DC, MC, V.

Jerum. Studentbacken 21 (15 50 90 and June through Aug. 63 53 80). 120 rooms, all with showers. This student hostel is only open June 1 to Aug. 31. Close to Gärdet subway station, five minutes to the city. Cafeteria. AE, DC, MC, V.

Zinken. Zinkensväg 20. (58 50 11). 28 rooms. The hotel consists of a number of pavilions near Zinkensdam subway station. Large garden with play area, access to washing machine and kitchen. Also youth hostel. Sauna. AE, DC, MC, V.

Camping

Ängby Camping. (A3) Bromma (37 04 20). West of Stockholm at Södra ängby. A 2-star camping site. Beach on Lake Mälaren. Rates approximately SEK 55 per night. Summer only.

Bredäng Camping. (A4) Skärholmen (97 70 71). A 3-star camping site at Ålgrytevägen in Sätra, ten km. (six miles) south of Stockholm. Follow the signs from E4. 500 meters (about 500 yards) to the subway, bathing, canoe rentals and so on. Rates approximately SEK 80 per night. Open all year.

Youth Hostels

af Chapman. Skeppsholmen (10 37 15). 136 beds. A 100-year-old sailing ship with the same view as the Grand Hotel in the historic heart of the city. Open Mar. to Dec. Stay limited to five nights.

Columbus Hotel. Tjärhovsgatan 11 (44 17 17). 120 beds. Open all year.

Gustaf af Klint. A ship at berth 153, at Stadsgården quay near Slussen (40 40 77). 85 beds. Open all night and all year except Christmas/New Year.

Mälaren River Boat. Söder Mälarstrand 6 (44 43 85). 28 beds. Old ship converted into a privately run hostel. Near Slussen subway station.

STOCKHOLM

Skeppsholmen Hostel. Västra Brobänken (20 25 06). Behind af Chapman. 152 beds. Open all year except Christmas/New Year period.

Zinken. Zinkensväg 20 (68 57 86). 275 beds. Near Zinkensdamm subway station. Open all year.

There are also hostels at Gällnö, Möja, Arholma and Fjärdlang—all in the archipelago.

HOW TO GET AROUND. By subway and bus. The transport system is divided into zones. Tickets may be bought as coupons from ticket counters or from drivers. The basic fare is SEK 7 for journeys within one zone. Your ticket entitles you to unlimited transfers within one hour of the time your ticket was punched. Senior citizens and young people under 18 can travel for half fare.

It is cheaper to buy a special discount coupon which gives a saving of SEK 18 compared with buying separate tickets each time you travel. Alternatively, a special one-day tourist card is available at SEK 22 which gives you unlimited travel on buses and the subway within the inner city area, including the ferries to Djurgården. There is also a one-day tourist card costing SEK 40 which gives unlimited travel for the whole of the Greater Stockholm area. A similar three-day pass costs SEK 76. All these tickets are available at Pressbyrån newsstands, where you can also get maps of the bus and subway systems.

The Key to Stockholm card *("Stockholmskortet")* provides unlimited free transport on subway trains, suburban railway services and local buses throughout Greater Stockholm (except on airport bus services) and also offers free admission to 50 museums in the city plus free sightseeing trips by boat or bus. Cards valid for durations up to four days can be purchased at prices ranging from about SEK 70 to 280 (children under 18 half-price). It can be bought at a number of outlets, including the Tourist Center at Sweden House and the "Hotellcentralen" accommodations bureau at the central railway station.

By taxi. For a taxi ring 15 00 00 (15 04 00 for advance bookings). English-speaking drivers are available on request if you want to go sightseeing by taxi. You can also hail a taxi on the street—the sign *Ledig* indicates that the cab is for hire. They are not so readily available as, for example, in London, but the telephone booking service is very efficient, although it costs SEK 25 just for the taxi to get to you. Taxis are fairly expensive in Stockholm, and more so at night. Tip about 10-15%.

TOURS. A number of sightseeing tours around Stockholm are available, and the boat trips are particularly good value. A two-hour "Under the Bridges of Stockholm" trip which takes you into the fresh water of Lake Mälaren and back into the salt water of the Baltic gives you a vivid impression of the maritime influence which has dominated the city's history. Numerous boat trips take you further out into the archipelago, most leaving from the quay outside the Grand Hotel, normally at 8 A.M. Meals are often available on these trips. There is an information kiosk outside the Grand and details are also available from the tourist office. In addition, there are walking tours around the Old Town every evening from the end of May to mid-September. Authorized city guides may also be hired through the tourist office; call 789 20 00, but book well in advance.

For excursions, further afield, try Sandhamn, a yachting center reached by boat from Stockholm, where races are held during July and August. A one-hour boat trip from Stockholm will take you to Vaxholm, where an ancient fortress which is now a military museum guards the channel. A trip by boat or bus to the Gustavsberg porcelain factory might be worthwhile for reduced-price bargains. The porcelain museum is open weekdays only. A fascinating trip on Lake Mälaren can be made on the classic steamer S/S *Mariefred* (daily; approximately SEK 100). Also of interest is the university town of Uppsala, 45 minutes north of Stockholm by train. The cathedral here is the seat of the Archbishop of Sweden. Some tours combine Uppsala with a visit to Sigtuna, Sweden's oldest town, with its 11th-century fortified church ruin and other monuments of Swedish history.

STOCKHOLM 17

MUSEUMS. The visitor to Stockholm has a wide choice of museums to see. The entrance fee is from SEK 5 to SEK 20, with children at half price or less but admission is free at most museums to holders of the Key to Stockholm card. Many museums are closed on Monday; they also tend to close earlier on Saturday and Sunday.

Armémuseum (Royal Army Museum). Located behind the Royal Dramatic Theater at Riddargatan 13. Exhibits from crossbows to automatic rifles and missiles. Equipment of the Swedish Army from many centuries. Open daily except Mon. 11–4.

Biologiska Museet (Biological Museum). Next to Skansen. An old museum showing Nordic animals against panoramic natural backgrounds. Open daily 10–4 Apr. through Sept.; 10–3 rest of the year.

Etnografiska Museet (Ethnographical Museum). Djurgårdsbrunnsvägen 34. Famous collections from Third-World cultures. A newly-built museum. Bus 69. Open Tues. to Fri. 11–4, Sat. and Sun. 12–4; closed Mon.

Hallwyl Museum. Hamngatan 4, near Norrmalmstorg. A palatial building dating from around 1900. Fine collections of painting, sculpture, furniture, ceramics, arms etc. Guided tours only, in English at 1.15 P.M. daily June 1 to Aug. 31, except Sat. Closed Mon. Sept. to May.

Historiska Museet (Museum of National Antiquities). Narvavägen 13–17. Treasures of the Vikings and their ancestors. In same building as the **Royal Cabinet of Coin**, which includes the world's largest coin. Bus 44 and 47. Open daily 11–4; closed Mon.

Leksaksmuseum (Toy Museum). Mariatorget 1C. Thousands of toys, dolls, dolls houses, tin soldiers etc. on four floors. Two large model railways are usually demonstrated on weekends. Subway Mariatorget. Open year-round Tues. to Fri. 10–4, Sat. and Sun. 12–4; closed Mon.

Liljevalchs Konsthall (Liljevalch Art Gallery). Djurgårdsvägen 60. Temporary exhibitions, mostly of Swedish contemporary art. Café Blå Porten. Bus 47. Open Tues. and Thurs. 11–9, Wed., Fri., Sat. and Sun. 11–5; closed Mon.

Livrustkammaren (Royal Armory). In the cellars of the Royal Palace with entrance at Slottsbacken. Swedish State collections of historical objects, such as costumes, arms and armory of Swedish royalty from 16th century on. Open Mon. to Fri. 10–4, Sat. and Sun. 11–4. Closed Mon., Sept. to Apr.

Medelhavsmuseet (Mediterranean Museum). Fredsgatan 2 at Gustav Adolfs Torg. 2,500 year-old terracotta sculptures of Cypriot warriors. Also a large Egyptian collection and an exhibition from the Islamic countries. Open Tues. 11–9, Wed. to Sun. 11–4; closed Mon.

Millesgården. Lidingö. Former residence of Swedish-American sculptor Carl Milles. He had his home at Lidingö in later years, where he collected not only some of his own work, but also other outstanding pieces from several eras. He died here in 1955 at the age of 80, still at work. Sparkling fountains and monuments with a view of Stockholm as a background. (The Orpheus Fountain outside the Concert House was made by Milles in 1936). Subway to Ropsten and then by bus. Open Apr. through Sept., 10–5 daily; Oct. through Mar., Tues. to Fri. 11–3, Sat. and Sun. 11–4.

Moderna Museet (Museum of Modern Art and Photography). On Skeppsholmen, behind the sailing ship youth hostel *af Chapman.* Paintings by Scandinavian artists and Picasso, Dali, Matisse, Warhol and many more. Open Tues. to Fri. 11–9, Sat. and Sun. 11–5; closed Mon.

Nationalmuseet (National Art Museum). A few steps from the Grand Hotel. Great masters from 1500 to 1900. Also prints, drawings and applied art from the Renaissance to the present day. Cafeteria and good shop. Concerts every Tues. in July and Aug. Open Tues. 10–9, Wed. to Sun. 10–5; closed Mon.

Nordiska Museet (Nordic Museum). Djurgården. Largest collection of objects showing the progress of civilization in Sweden since 1500. Magnificent specimens of rural art. Lovely collection of bridal crowns and much more. Bus 47. Open July and Aug., 10–5 daily except Mon.; rest of year 10–9 Tues., 10–5 Wed. to Sun.

Sjöhistoriska Museet (National Maritime Museum). Djurgårdsbrunnsvägen 24. Collections illustrating history of Swedish navy and merchant marine. Unique ship models. Bus 69. Open daily 10–5.

Stockholms Stadsmuseum (City Museum). At Slussen subway station. The history of Stockholm, illustrated by many archeological finds. Models of the former palaces "Tre Kronor" (Three Crowns) and "Non Pareil." Pleasant cafeteria. Open June through Aug. Mon., Fri. to Sun. 11–5, Tues. to Thurs. 11–7. Sept. through May open till 9 P.M. Tues. to Thurs.

Strindbergmuseet. Blå Tornet, Drottninggatan 85. Home of author August Strindberg. Open Tues. to Sat. 10–4, Sun. 12–5.

Tekniska Museet (Science and Technology Museum). Museivägen, on the way to the Kaknäs Tower. Models of machines illustrating developments in technical engineering and industry. Vintage aeroplanes, cars' engines; computers, telecommunications. A mine with shafts etc. Cafeteria. Bus 69 from Karlaplan. Open Mon. to Fri. 10–4, Sat. and Sun. 12–4.

Thielska Galleriet (Thiel Art Gallery). Djurgården near Blockhusudden. Private collection of Scandinavian and French art from around 1900. Beautiful surroundings. Bus 69 from Karlaplan. Open daily 12–4 (from 1 on Sun.).

Waldemarsudde. Djurgården. Former home of Prince Eugen, a great-granduncle to the present King. He was a well-known painter and many of the Prince's own works are displayed here. Also Nordic collections. The turn-of-the-century house is surrounded by a beautiful garden on the shores of the Baltic. Cafeteria. Bus 47. Open Tues. to Sun. 11–5 and on Tues. and Thurs. evenings from 7–9. Closed Mon. Winter opening 11–4, closed Mon.; weekends only in Dec.

Wasavarvet (Wasa Museum). On Djurgården, on the way to Skansen. The salvaged 17th-century man-of-war, *Wasa*. She sank in Stockholm harbor on her maiden voyage in 1628. Rediscovered in 1956, she was raised and drydocked in 1961 and has been painstakingly restored. This is the oldest preserved warship in the world. A new museum to house *Wasa* is being built and will come into operation in June 1990. Opening times were not available at the time of going to press.

PARKS, ZOOS AND GARDENS. Djurgården (Royal Deer Park) and Skansen. A beautiful island covered in pathways, meadows and trees. Also a marina, many museums, Gröna Lund Tivoli amusement park, Skansen and its zoo, aquarium, open-air theater and various displays, and much more. Rent a bike near the bridge or take a leisurely stroll. You can also rent canoes. In summer most of the roads are closed to cars. Bus 47 or ferry from Slussen or Nybroplan (summer only).

Fjällgatan. To get a good view of the Old Town and the harbor, take the subway to Slussen and walk up on Katarina Bangatan to Fjällgatan. Most sight-seeing buses stop here for a short time.

Kungsträdgården (King's Garden). Easy to find, just across the rushing water from the Royal Palace. It contains the striking statue of King Charles XII (Karl den Tolfte) with his arm raised pointing east. On the right is the Royal Opera House, and behind that the elm trees, once threatened to make way for a new subway station, but saved by city-wide protests in 1971. The station was built elsewhere. Have a sandwich under the elms at the teahouse. The fountain in the park, built in 1873, features pictures of Nordic mythology. There are many activities in the park in summer. You can listen to music, learn to dance the Swedish *Hambo* or play chess; in winter you can skate. A meeting place for tourists and others.

Långholmsparken. Below Västerbron on the south side. Take the path to the top for the view. Some former prison buildings are still here—debate continues over the possibility of using them for a youth hostel or hotel. The little cottage is open for coffee when the flag is up. Subway Hornstull.

Skinnarviksparken. Beautiful panorama from this park. Nearest subway is Zinkensdamm. Walk towards the lake and up the mountain past some newly restored historic buildings.

HISTORIC BUILDINGS AND SITES. Drottningholm Palace. On an island in Lake Mälaren, a few kilometers from Stockholm. Reminiscent of Versailles, a magnificent 17th-century French-style building. Also in the grounds are the lovely Chinese Palace and the original court theater, with its 18th-century settings and stage machinery in perfect working order. Theater museum. Subway to Brommaplan and

STOCKHOLM

bus or boat from Stadshusbron. The Palace, Court Theater, and Chinese Palace are open daily May through Aug. 11–4.30 and 1–3.30 during Sept. (from 12 on Sat. and Sun.).

Gamla Stan (Old Town). Follow a lane called Storkyrkobrinken from the Great Church, past buildings that are centuries old, to a square at the base of the hill called Riddarhustorget. The two dominating buildings in the square, Riddarhuset (House of Nobility) and the white palace to its right, both date from the 17th century. The latter now houses the Supreme Court.

Haga Palace and Haga Pavilion. On the city limits of Stockholm, in Haga Park near Brunnsviken. Former home of the late Crown Prince Gustav Adolf. The Pavilion is the more interesting building—a miniature summer palace built by Gustav III in the late-18th century. Bus 515 to Haga Air Terminal. Guided tours every hour. Open mid-June through Aug., 12–4 daily except Mon.

Kaknästornet (Kaknäs Tower). Djurgården. T.V. tower, 155 meters (508 ft.) high. Indoor and outdoor platforms with breathtaking view. Cafeteria and restaurant, tourist bureau and souvenir shop. Bus 69. Open Oct. through Mar., daily 9–6; Apr. and Sept., daily 9 A.M.–10 P.M.; May to Aug., daily 9–12 midnight.

Kungliga Slottet (Royal Palace). Completed 1760. Hall of State (contains the King's silver throne), the Chapel Royal (Sunday service open to the public), the Apartments of State and of King Oscar and Queen Sophie, as well as the Guest Apartments are all open to the public daily. Also the Palace Museum (classical sculptures and antiquities), the Royal Treasury, with its collection of Crown Jewels, and the Royal Armory. All or part of the palace may be closed when state visits, royal dinners etc. are held. Changing of the guard, June through Aug., Mon. to Fri. at 12.10 P.M., Sun. at 1.10 P.M. Jan. through May, Wed., Sat. and Sun.; Sept. through Dec., Wed. and Sun. There is no band playing in the winter.

Mårten Trotzigs Gränd (Yard-wide Lane). In the Old Town, at the end of Prästgatan, leading down to Västerlånggatan. One of the narrowest thoroughfares in the world, scarcely a yard (a meter) wide.

Riddarholm Church. On Riddarholm Island. This is the Swedish Pantheon; burial place of 17 Swedish kings over about four centuries. Subway Gamla Stan. Open May through Aug., daily 10–3, Sun. 1–3; Sept., daily 12–3 except Mon. and Fri.

Stadshuset (City Hall). Completed 1923, it is the symbol of Stockholm and of considerable architectural interest. The tower, with a magnificent view, is open May through Sept., daily 10–3. Guided tours of the City Hall, Mon. to Sat. year-round at 10 A.M.; Sat., Sun. and holidays at 10 A.M. and 12 noon.

Storkyrkan (Great Church). Across the street from the south side of the Royal Palace. Believed to be the oldest building in the city, dating from about 1250. Contains Ehrenstal's *Last Judgement,* one of the world's largest paintings, and other art treasures. As Stockholm's cathedral, this is a living church with a congregation and sightseeing during services is not allowed. Occasionally there are sound and light performances.

Swedish Academy. North side of Stortorget, near the Royal Palace. Historic building, the headquarters of the Swedish Academy, which awards the Nobel Prize in literature.

SPORTS. Tennis. There are a number of indoor tennis courts as well as outdoor courts at: Hjorthagen, in Jägmästaregatan; Smedslätten, in Gustav Adolfs Park; South Ångby, in Färjestadsvägen; Enskede, Mälarhöjden, and Älvsjö sports grounds.

Golf. Golfing enthusiasts have a choice of 14 18-hole courses. Among the best are: Stockholm Golf Club, Kevinge, train from Östra Station or underground to Mörby Centrum; Djursholm Golf Club, Eddavägen Station, train from Östra Station; Drottningholm Golf Club, bus from St. Eriksgatan; Lidingö Golf Club, Sticklinge, underground to Ropsten thence bus; Saltsjöbaden Golf Club, Tattby Station, train from Saltsjöbanan Station, Slussen (change at Igelboda); on Wermdö, at Hemmestavik (bus from Slussen).

Swimming. Långholmsparken or Smedsuddsbadet. It's quite something to be able to swim in the center of a big city these days.

Fishing. You may fish free of charge from the bridges of Stockholm; the water is cleaner today than 50 years ago and salmon have been caught just in front of the Royal Palace. Up-to-date information on fishing, licenses, and equipment rental is available from the tourist office at Sweden House.

Winter sports. There are a number of ski trails in the vicinity of Stockholm and in the Södertörn and Roslagen areas. The track at Nacka is floodlit for night skiing. Both Fiskartorpet and Hammarby have slalom runs, lifts and ski jumps. For ice skating, there are the Stadium, Östermalm Sports Ground, Tennis Stadium and Johanneshov Rink at Sandstuvägen; many parks, including central Kungsträdgården, have winter rinks.

You can rent downhill skiing equipment and cross-country skis at Skid och Brädoktorn, Sturegatan 20 (63 75 75).

Spectator sports. If you want to be a spectator, call 22 18 40 and Miss Frida will tell you about the sporting events of the day in a tape recorded message.

Biking and canoeing. Bikes and canoes are available for rent at Djurgården bridge.

MUSIC, MOVIES AND THEATERS.

Music. Stockholm's two musical centers are the *Royal Opera House* and the *Stockholm Concert House*. The Royal Opera, located just across the bridge from the Royal Palace, has a season running from mid-August until about June 10. The Ballet Festival is in the first week of June.

The concert season lasts from about the middle of September to about the middle of May. The Stockholm Concert Association Orchestra is in regular service at the Concert House and is fully up to international standards. But of even greater interest perhaps is the veritable parade of top international virtuosos and guest conductors, representing the cream of European, British and American talent.

Every day during the summer, concerts and other kinds of entertainment are held in the open air at *Skansen*. Also, the *Gröna Lund Tivoli* amusement park, open mid-April to mid-September, has daily open-air performances with Swedish and foreign artists. Between June 15 and the end of August, there are free concerts in the city's many parks. In the *Kungsträdgården* there are daily recorded concerts and, three evenings a week at least, free entertainment on the outdoor stage, often featuring leading variety artists.

A unique experience is to attend a concert at the *National Museum* (Art Gallery), held four times during August. Occasionally there are also concerts in the *Royal Palace*.

For information about concerts and theaters (including English-speaking theaters), call at the kiosk on Norrmalmstorg where you can also buy reduced price tickets for same-day performances.

Movies. English and American movies dominate. They are shown with Swedish sub-titles and are often released at the same time as they appear in London or New York. See the evening papers for programs. The advertisements usually mention the English as well as the Swedish title.

Theaters. Several theaters specialize in light opera—playing classics and modern musicals. It's great fun hearing and seeing a familiar perennial in a strange theater and a strange language (though many may find the language barrier insuperable). Season: Sept. to mid-June.

The *Royal Dramatic Theater*—scene of the debuts of Greta Garbo and Ingrid Bergman—actually consists of two theaters, one for major performances and a smaller one for those of more limited public interest. A number of the plays presented here and at other Stockholm theaters are hits still running in New York or London. Season: Sept. through May.

Particularly recommended is the *Court Theater* of Drottningholm Palace, a few minutes to a half-hour from downtown Stockholm by car or bus (or 50 minutes by boat). This is an 18th-century theater which was somehow lost sight of, closed up for years, and when reopened a few decades ago was found to be in its original condition. The repertoire consists almost entirely of operas and ballets contemporary with the theater: in other words, of works written for that kind of stage. Seeing a performance there is a unique theater event. Performances during May, June,

STOCKHOLM

July, August and September, two to four evenings a week. Again, call at the kiosk on Norrmalmstorg for information and tickets.

SHOPPING. Shopping in Stockholm tends to be expensive, but you can be sure of the quality. You can also take advantage of the tax-free shopping system, under which a part of your sales tax will be refunded at the airport. Ask for details at the shop; you need special receipts to present at the airport, harbor or on board ship. See also "Shopping" in *Facts at Your Fingertips.* When you see the word REA, it means there's a sale in progress. The best REAs are after Christmas and midsummer.

First shopping stop in Stockholm should be the *Nordiska Kompaniet,* known as N.K., at Hamngatan 18–20. This store is a sort of combination Neiman-Marcus and Harrods, with a few specialties of its own thrown in; you can find almost anything you might want to buy here. Opposite the N.K. is the *Gallerian shopping arcade,* where you can find shoes, clothing, books, antiques, perfume, cameras and much more. On the other side of the fountain is *Åhléns City,* a huge department store near Sergels Torg, Drottninggatan and Hötorget. Both N.K. and Åhléns are open Sundays. Here also is the *P.U.B.* department store, in buildings on both sides of Drottninggatan with a tunnel connection. P.U.B. also has an extensive range, but is less luxurious and lower-priced. It faces on to Hötorget and the Concert Hall, in an area where shops of all kinds can be found.

In Gamla Stan many specialty shops can be found on Västerlånggatan. If you walk towards Slussen and to the right on Hornsgatan, you come to a hill called Puckeln, where many small and interesting art galleries are to be found. Handicrafts are on sale at *Svensk Hemslöjd,* Sveavägen 44, the *Stockholm Handicraft Shop* at Drottninggatan 14, *Adolphson Wadle's Present* at Västerlånggatan 55 and *Brinkens Konsthantverk* at Storkyrkobrinken 1.

There are shopping malls in suburbs such as Vällingby, Kista and Skärholmen, where you can also find the huge furniture store *IKEA,* and an indoor flea market which is open on Saturdays and Sundays. Best bets for glassware include *Nordiska Kristall,* Kungsgatan 9 or *Rosenthal Studio-Haus,* Birger Jarlsgatan 6. *The Crystal Showrooms* at Drottninggatan 25 and Norrmalmstorg 4 cater mainly to U.S. visitors with all price tags in U.S. dollars.

RESTAURANTS. Since restaurants play such an important part in Stockholm life, a fairly extensive list is given here. Most have liquor licenses, though do remember that alcohol is very expensive. Some of the downtown establishments close for three or four weeks during the summer. As in all big cities, there are many types of restaurant in Stockholm, such as Greek, Japanese, Chinese, Korean. All the main hotels have their own restaurants. If you are on a budget, look for bargains such as Sunday Specials, happy hours, inclusive menus etc. You'll find details in the newspapers next to the entertainments section.

Expensive

Aurora. Munkbron 11 (21 93 59). Located in a beautiful 300-year-old house in the Old Town with pleasant small rooms in vaults. Charcoal grill. Excellent food and service. AE, DC, MC, V.

Clas på Hörnet. Surbrunnsgatan 20 (16 51 36). One of the most unusual settings in Stockholm—on the ground floor of an elegant restored 200-year-old town house which is also an exclusive hotel. Excellent international and Swedish cuisine. AE, DC, MC, V.

Coq Blanc. Regeringsgatan 111 (11 61 53). Was once a theater; stage and stalls intact. Excellent food. Budget-priced lunch menu. AE, DC, MC, V.

Coq Roti. Sturegatan 19 (10 25 67). A gourmet restaurant run by professionals; French cuisine in sophisticated setting. AE, DC, MC, V.

Eriks Fisk. On quay-berth 17, Strandvägskajen (660 60 60). This former sand barge has been converted into a *de luxe* seafood restaurant. In summer enjoy the view from the deck. Choose your own fish. AE, DC, MC, V.

L'Escargot. Scheelegatan 8 (53 05 77). As the name implies, snails are a specialty of the house, but it is more popular for its daily six-course gastronomic menu. AE, DC, MC, V.

Fem Små Hus. Nygränd 10 (10 04 82). In the Old Town. Its name means "five small houses." Many small rooms in vaults. Excellent international cuisine and Swedish specialties. AE, DC, MC, V.

Garbo. Blekingegatan 32 (40 12 07). It was here that Greta Garbo was born in 1905 so the atmosphere is very movie oriented. AE, DC, MC, V.

Gourmet. Tegnérgatan 10 (31 43 98). Lives up to its name: one of the best French restaurants in town. Pleasant atmosphere. AE, DC, MC, V.

Grand Hotel. S. Blasieholmshamnen 8 (22 10 20). Excellent restaurant (terrace outside in the summer) with marvelous views of the Royal Palace and the Old Town. This is the place for *Smörgåsbord* in relaxed and sophisticated surroundings. AE, DC, MC, V.

K.B. or Konstnärshuset. Smålandsgatan 7, near Norrmalmstorg (11 02 32). Eat and drink in intimate surroundings in the heart of town. Murals by Swedish artists who paid for their drinks with paintings. AE, DC, MC, V.

Latona. Västerlånggatan 79 (11 32 60). Cavernous cellar-restaurant in the heart of the Old Town, by Järntorget. Scores for atmosphere, service and excellent food. AE, DC, MC, V.

Mälardrottningen. Riddarholmen (24 36 00). Floating restaurant and hotel on Barbara Hutton's former private yacht. Seafood specialties. Reservation essential. AE, DC, MC, V.

Operakällaren. In the Opera House facing Kungsträdgården, the waterfront and the Royal Palace (11 11 25). World-famous for international cuisine and the atmosphere. AE, DC, MC, V.

Riche and Teatergrillen. Birger Jarlsgatan 4 (10 70 22). The *Riche* side has a veranda on the street. Fine paintings create an elegant ambience. Roast beef—not perhaps one of the most obvious things to expect in Stockholm—is served from a silver trolley every day. The *Teatergrillen,* or *Theater Grill* (tel. 10 70 44) is more intimate and lives up to its name in attracting some of the theater crowd. Good for a quiet dinner. The grill is closed in July. AE, DC, MC, V.

Solliden. Skansen (660 10 55). On the heights at Stockholm's favorite pleasure grounds, ten minutes from the center of town. Open May to Aug. Wonderful view of the city and harbor. Also self-service on the ground floor and a big outdoor restaurant in summer. AE, DC, MC, V.

Stallmästargården. Norrtull (24 39 10). Historic inn with view of Brunnsviken Lake. Coffee in the courtyard, with a lovely garden, after a good meal on a summer evening is a delightful experience. AE, DC, MC, V.

Stortorgskällaren. Stortorget 7 (10 55 33). Charming medieval cellar in the Old Town near the Cathedral and the Royal Palace. Adjoining a fish restaurant with the same management. AE, DC, MC, V.

Ulriksdals Wärdshus. In a fine park near Ulriksdal Palace (85 08 15). 15 minutes by car or bus 540 from Humlegården Park. Old Swedish inn with famed *Smörgåsbord.* AE, DC, MC, V.

Moderate

Berns Salonger. Berzelii Park, next to Norrmalmstorg (24 12 80). Recently renovated restaurant with an authentic 19th-century atmosphere. AE, DC, MC, V.

Birger Bar. Birger Jarlsgatan 5 (20 72 10). Popular restaurant specializing in Italian cuisine. AE, DC, MC, V.

Cattelin. Storkyrkobrinken 9, in Old Town (20 18 18). Seafood a specialty, but there's also a bistro. Members of Parliament meet here. AE, DC, MC, V.

Colibri. Corner Drottninggatan and Adolf Fredriks Kyrkogatan (10 81 20). Plank steak.

Daily News Café. Kungsträdgården in Sverigehuset (21 56 55). Good food. Swedish and foreign newspapers to hand (but not on the menu). AE, DC, MC, V.

Gondolen. (40 22 22). Suspended under the gangway of the Katarina elevator at Slussen. View of the harbor and the Old Town. AE, DC, MC, V.

STOCKHOLM

Hamngatan 1. Hamngatan 1 (20 01 36). Modern decor; open-air service on sidewalk in summer. Good food and large portions. Closed Mon. AE, DC, MC, V.

Hard Rock Café. Sveavägen 75 (16 03 50). Similar concept to its namesakes in New York and London, offering hamburgers against a rock-music background. AE, DC, MC, V.

La Grenouille. Grev Turegatan 16 (20 10 00). French-style establishment with three separate restaurants in different price brackets. AE, DC, MC, V.

Matpalatset. Hamngatan 15 (20 91 95). Was Stockholm's 1986 "Restaurant of the Year". Five small restaurants in one building. AE, DC, MC, V.

N.K. Department Store. Opposite Sverigehuset. A shoppers' favorite, with a restaurant, salad bar and coffee shop. AE, DC, MC, V.

Östergök. Kommendörsgatan 46 (61 15 07). Specializes in fish, but there's also a steakhouse and a pizzeria here. Popular. AE, DC, MC, V.

Rodolfino. Stora Nygatan 1 (11 84 97). Italian specialties, though not exclusively, in small, chic spot in the Old Town, by the Riddarhuset. Popular with the younger crowd; good food and service. AE, MC, V.

Stadshuskällaren. Stadshuset (City Hall), (50 54 54). Rustic atmosphere in the cellar of the City Hall overlooking Lake Mälaren. No meals in main restaurant during the summer. AE, DC, MC, V.

Sturehof. Stureplan 2 (14 27 50). A fairly large, unpretentious restaurant, which makes fish its business. Pub in old English style. Quieter in the back of the restaurant. Just in the middle of town. AE, DC, MC, V.

Vau-de-Ville. Hamngatan 17 (21 25 22). French-bistro atmosphere. Excellent food at reasonable prices. Chosen as Stockholm's 1986 "Restaurant of the Year." AE, DC, MC, V.

Inexpensive

Gröna Linjen. Mäster Samuelsgatan 10, second floor (11 27 90). Good for lunch. Vegetarian. No credit cards.

Tehuset (the tea house). Under the elms in Kungsträdgården Park. Lively and chic outdoor place. Have a hot sandwich there at noon and watch the Royal Guard march by. Summer only. No credit cards.

Zum Franziskaner. Skeppsbron 44 (11 83 30). German-style restaurant on the waterfront in the Old Town. Food is reasonable and service very friendly. Popular. AE, MC, V.

In the **Gallerian shopping arcade** there are several good places to eat, including *Glada Laxen* (M), a café specializing in fish, but often with lines waiting at lunchtime. Also the *Pizzeria* (I), with a salad table and other dishes besides pizza. On the balcony, you can find *Edelweiss*, with a choice of salads and cakes.

The indoor market at *Östermalmshallen* has many food shops. At this 100-year-old indoor market visit *Gerdas* fish shop, where you can get an excellent lunch at a reasonable price in unusual and noisy surroundings. In the same building, on the second floor, you can find the biggest salad table in town. It's called *Örtagården* (the Herb Garden) (I) (662 17 28).

Look out for the special lunch offers available at almost all restaurants Mon. to Fri. 10–2. A main course plus drinks, salad, bread and butter costs about SEK 30–40.

NIGHTLIFE. Stockholm has a wide range of nightspots to choose from, the names and ownership of which change fairly frequently. See the last page in the daily papers for what's on and where. There are no real nightlife bargains and you should expect a supper in one of these nightspots to cost you between SEK 200 and 300. When there is a show it could cost you more. It's also a good idea to book in advance.

Entry to a pub with live music would be about SEK 25–45. Also many restaurants have dancing a few nights a week.

Aladdin. Barnhusgatan 12 (10 09 32). Oriental decor. Big dance floor.

Atlantic. Teatergatan 3 (21 89 07). Mixed, elegant crowd.

STOCKHOLM

Bacchi Wapen. Järntorgsgatan 5 (11 66 71). As well as the restaurant, there's a disco, piano bar and café.

Börsen. Jakobsgatan 6 (10 16 00). Stockholm's biggest "show restaurant," with international artists.

Café Opera. Operakajen 9 (11 00 26). Very popular, so get there as early as possible.

Club Alexandra. Birger Jarlsgatan 29 (10 46 46). Most famous nightspot in town, located in Stockholm Plaza Hotel.

Cindy's Bar. Amaranten Hotel (54 10 60).

Daily News Café. Kungsträdgården (21 56 55). Central, near the N.K. department store. Restaurant, bar and disco.

Engelen. Kornhamnstorg 59 (10 07 22). In an old pharmacy in the Old Town. Long lines and mixed crowd, but more for the younger set.

Fasching. Kungsgatan 63 (21 62 67). Stockholm's biggest jazz club.

Gamlingen. Stora Nygatan 5 (20 57 86). Again, for the younger set.

Kaos. Stora Nygatan 21 (20 58 86). In the Old Town. Wide range of music. Young, mixed crowd.

King Creole. Kungsgatan 18 (24 47 00). Some evenings features "old-time" dancing.

Melody. Birger Jarlsgatan 27 (21 21 00). Popular disco, restaurant and bar.

Stampen. Stora Nygatan 5 (20 57 93). Old Town. A pub with "trad" jazz music.

Bars

There are piano bars at the Hotel Sheraton, Amaranten, Reisen, Continental, Sergel Plaza and Malmen.

If you want something to eat after midnight, there are a few places near Norrmalmstorg such as **Collage**, Smålandsgatan 2 (10 01 95), **Café La Clé**, Hamngatan 6 (20 87 00) and **Monte Carlo**, Sveavägen 23 (11 00 25).

COPENHAGEN

Scandinavia's Fun Capital

The center of Danish fun is Copenhagen, biggest and happiest of the Scandinavian capitals and by almost unanimous agreement one of the liveliest cities of Europe. More than a million Danes, a quarter of the country's population, live and let live here. The city, on the island of Zealand, is just as flat as the sea that embraces it, as flat as the rest of Denmark, which averages only 98 feet above sea level. (This is why every second inhabitant has a bicycle.)

When is the best time to come? Denmark is lovely in summer, fall and spring. In winter, well, let's just say that while Copenhagen is as welcoming as ever, it can be a little chilly. However, there is a special atmosphere in Copenhagen in winter, which the Danes call *hyggelig*—the nearest translation they can give is "warm and cozy." There is an intimate and welcoming ambience in the warm, candle-lit cellar bars and restaurants, and with far fewer visitors shopping is much easier—hotel prices are often lower too. The first sign of the approach of spring is the opening of the oldest amusement park in the world, Bakken in the Klampenborg forest just outside Copenhagen.

By May, however, Denmark has escaped from the bonds of the long Nordic winter, a fact neatly underlined by the opening of the world-famous Tivoli Gardens on May 1. Celebratory candles flicker in the windows of every home too, in commemoration of Denmark's liberation on May 4, 1945, while the next day there are celebrations in every Danish town from southern Jutland to the far reaches of Bornholm. The circus arrives in May. At the end of June, the world's largest yacht race, known as "Round Zealand" attracts between 1,500 and 2,000 participants annually. The Royal Danish Ballet end their season, and June comes to a climax on 23 June with Midsummer's Eve, a night of outdoor dancing, singing, feasting, bonfires and fireworks, transforming the whole nation into one big carnival. Try to celebrate this night along the Sound. You'll never forget the unreal summer twilight, streaked with rockets edged with a thousand fires along the shores of Sweden and Denmark.

With the end of June, everyone enjoys the long, sunflooded days and short balmy nights in Denmark. Make your reservations early; the Danes will do the rest.

The Lie of the Land

Many visitors find it odd that Denmark's capital should be on the extreme eastern edge of one of the country's larger islands, only a few miles from Sweden. But the reason is simple. Historically, Copenhagen was the capital not only of Denmark in its modern form, but also of Norway and southern Sweden and other Baltic territories. As a well-sheltered port with immediate access to the high seas—large ships still sail from the city center—Copenhagen in days gone by was an ideally situated capital.

Being on the coast, Copenhagen is a cleaner capital than most. Though it lacks a background of mountains to set it off, viewpoints from which it can be admired, hills to which its houses can cling, and though much of it has had to be rebuilt, Copenhagen remains a charming city.

Exploring Copenhagen

If you suggest to someone that, although Copenhagen has a history stretching back to the 11th century, the city really doesn't look very old, you are likely to get the reply, "Considering it's been bashed about by the Swedes a few times, ravaged by a number of fires and bombarded by the British, that's hardly surprising." Strategically located on the Sound connecting the Baltic with the Kattegat and the North Sea, Copenhagen was just a small village ceaselessly harassed by Wendian pirates until the middle of the 12th century. But in 1167 Bishop Absalon, warrior and politician as well as priest, like many contemporary clerics, decided to protect the infant village by building a castle on the small central island known as Slotsholmen, today the very heart of the old city.

Shortly thereafter the town adopted the name of Køpmannaehafn (Merchants' Haven), and proceeded to grow apace within its protecting walls. In the 15th century, the king came to live in Copenhagen and a university was started. Increasing in both size and importance little by little, the prosperous city entered upon a great period of expansion with the accession of King Christian IV (1588–1648) to the throne. This man of extraordinary energy was possessed with a passion for building. Whenever he could take time off from waging wars, he started some new project, and even today so many of his works remain that whenever there's a question about who erected what, Christian gets the credit. Rosenborg Slot (Rosenborg Castle), the Runde Tårn (the Round Tower) and the Børsen (Stock Exchange) with its exotic dragon spire, were all built by him. He also gave the town an arsenal and a naval dock, and put up the "Nyboder," or rows of small houses which are still inhabited by naval personnel and pensioners.

COPENHAGEN

In 1659, when the Swedish King Carl Gustaf tried to put an end to the continual Dano-Swedish wars by the simple strategy of conquering Denmark outright, Copenhagen found itself in a difficult situation. The town was besieged and everyone, including Frederik III, the then king, took a hand at defending it. After attempting to take the city by storm, the Swedes were routed and driven back to their own shores. This same Frederik thereupon built the Kastellet (Citadel) near Langelinie, which served the reverse of its intended function in 1940 when the Germans initiated their occupation of Denmark by capturing the old fortifications.

Back in 1728 and 1795, fires swept Copenhagen and destroyed vast portions of it. The devastation had scarcely been repaired when a British fleet twice bombarded the city during the Napoleonic Wars in 1801 and 1807. Fortunately the palaces survived—Amalienborg, Christiansborg and Rosenborg—and the vacant sites undoubtedly provided opportunities for rebuilding that might not otherwise have been undertaken. After the Napoleonic Wars, Denmark enjoyed relative peace and Copenhagen expanded far beyond the ramparts and water fortifications. Industries such as brewing, shipbuilding and manufacturing hardware became immensely profitable, and the city grew from a population of 130,000 in 1850 to its present size of well over a million inhabitants, suburbs included.

Strolls About Town

With this partial introduction to the Copenhagen scene, the time has come to sally forth into the bewildering jumble of winding streets, unexpected canals and multitudinous buildings which are the distinguishing features of the Danish capital. The average visitor from abroad, as he steps out of the Central Station into the warm sun of a summer morning, is likely to be a bit baffled at the start. As we've already pointed out, there is a serious scarcity of distinguishing landmarks by which the new arrival can easily chart his course through this intricate city. While it's true that Copenhagen a few years back seemed to be largely a collection of charmingly distinctive spires, there are now so many tall modern buildings that you can no longer see them. And to top it off, about the time you are at last getting yourself oriented, you are so unnerved by the sudden appearance of a platoon of bicyclists bearing down upon you that all idea of where you are or where you intended to go is just as precipitously driven from your head. Watch out too for the special bicycle lanes; the Danes take their cycling seriously and most major roads have bicycle lanes on either side.

Any attempt to plot out some interesting tours for the person bent on discovering the "real" Copenhagen is difficult. Assuming that you master your fear of two-wheeled traffic and have provided yourself with a suitable map, it's more than possible that you'll start off in the wrong direction and be so captivated by what you see that you won't detect your error until you've gone several blocks out of your way. Don't be alarmed, however—before you've had a chance to get the points of the compass properly unscrambled, it's more than likely that a friendly Dane will stop and politely offer to show you the way.

So let's plunge in and start at the Rådhus Pladsen, or Town Hall Square. Dominating the square is the Town Hall itself, an immense and impressive redbrick building surmounted by a tall tower. It was completed in 1905. High above the main entrance is the figure of Bishop Absalon, founder of the city. Inside you see first the World Clock invented and built by Jens

28 COPENHAGEN

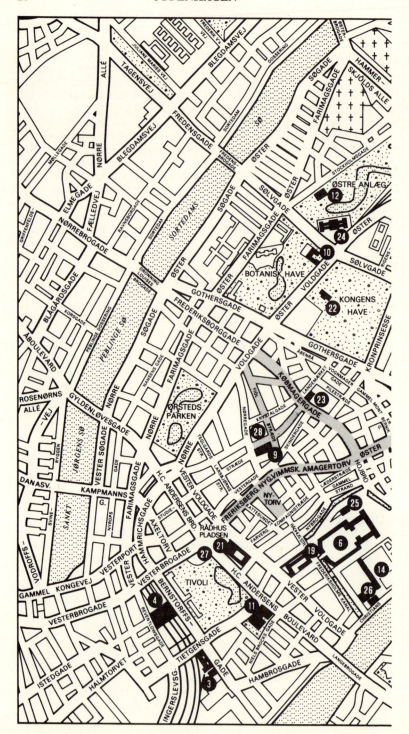

COPENHAGEN

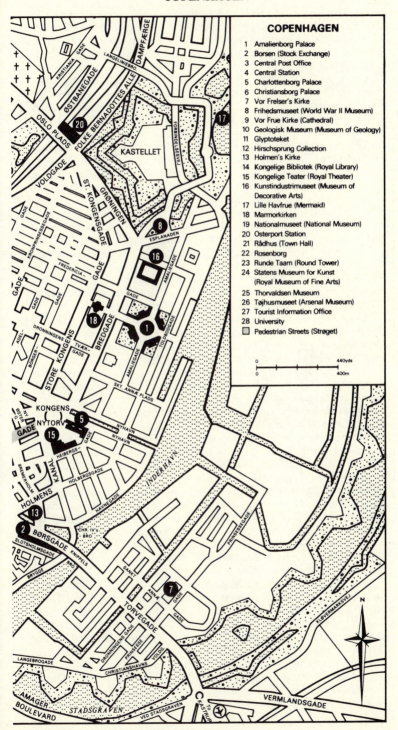

Olsen. They you come to a large hall surrounded by a balcony, which is used for official functions. Here there are marble busts of Hans Christian Andersen, poet, playwright and writer of the famous stories for children, of Bertel Thorvaldsen, the noted sculptor, and of Martin Nyrop, the building's architect.

Above, on the first floor, are the council chamber and the municipal reception room. You can climb up the 105-meter (350-foot) tower, but only on one of the official guided tours. From its top there are fine views of the city and the surrounding countryside.

As you emerge from the Town Hall, a turn to your left would take you up Vesterbrogade, and in a moment you would come to the main entrance of the famous Tivoli Gardens. Just down from here, on Hans Christian Andersens Boulevard, is the city tourist office. Hardly anyone comes to Denmark without first having heard of the Tivoli Gardens. These date back to 1843, when Georg Carstensen, Danish architect and man of letters, persuaded Christian VIII to let him lay out an amusement park on the site of Copenhagen's old fortifications. "If only people are allowed to amuse themselves," he argued, "they will forget to talk politics." Within a few months Tivoli, patterned after London's now long-extinct Vauxhall Gardens, was a reality. In 1951 the wheel turned a full circle when the Festival of Britain organizers used Tivoli as a model for the Festival Gardens in London's Battersea Park. During its short season from May to September, Tivoli welcomes an average of 4 million visitors.

Whatever you happen to be doing in Tivoli, on a Saturday or Sunday you will enjoy the appearance of the Tivoli Guard. This is a group of toy-town soldiers (age limit 17) dressed in the style of the Queen's Guard, who march through the Gardens to the music of their own band.

On certain nights, the Gardens close with a magnificent display of fireworks. As rockets fly to meet the moon and colorful set pieces vie with the electric brilliance of the Chinese Pagoda, the illuminated fountain, and the fairy-like lights among the trees, you will begin to appreciate something of what Tivoli means to the Danes.

At the southern end of the Gardens, again on Hans Christian Andersens Boulevard, is the Glyptotek. It is a rather fanciful neo-Classical building, but contains an excellent collection of French sculpture, with fine pieces by Degas, Gauguin, and other Impressionists. There is also an outstanding collection of Egyptian works, including a famous statue of a hippopotamus, and much Greek and Roman statuary, all well-displayed. A gift to the municipality from Carl Jacobsen, founder of the Carlsberg breweries, the museum is maintained by the Carlsberg Foundation, which has done much to further cultural and scientific activities in Denmark. The winter garden outside contains Kai Nielsen's *Watermother* sculpture, serenely watching the 14 marble babies who tumble over her.

Back again on Vesterbrogade, you'll find the newly opened Scala center, with three floors of shops, cinemas, even a gym and swimming pool. Down the street you'll find the SAS building, one of the city's few skyscrapers. It also contains the Royal Hotel. Opposite is the Central Station, and in the same building, though the entrance is on Bernstorffs Gade, is the Air Terminal. There is an obelisk in front of the station commemorating the freeing of the Danish peasants from the feudal yoke in 1788. Just beyond, in the black Vesterport building, is Den Permanente, The House of Danish Design, where the best of modern Danish arts and crafts are displayed and sold. Ten minutes' walk from here along Vesterbrogade brings you to the Bymuseum, the City Museum. Outside is a model of medieval Copenhagen, while inside are exhibits depicting the city's history. Absalonsgade, a little street running down one side of the Museum, has been returned to its 19th-century appearance.

Up Strøget to Slotsholmen and Christianshavn

The next part of our exploration of the city, again using Rådhus Pladsen as a jumping-off point, takes us to the "Strøget," a series of narrow streets running eastwards from Rådhus Pladsen. The principal street here is Frederiksberggade, a pedestrian-only shopping street that more than any other in Copenhagen is the city's answer to Fifth Avenue or Bond Street. Not far along Frederiksberggade, we come to a double square, the northern half of which is called Gammeltorv and the southern, Nytorv. The most interesting thing about these twin squares is the splendid fountain in the middle of the former. On April 16, the Queen's birthday, children are brought here to see the "golden apples dance." These golden apples are gilded metal balls which "dance" on the jets of water.

Looking to the right from the Nytorv half of this square, you may be able to see a spot of water to the south. A few steps in this direction bring you to Rådhusstraede and then to Frederiksholms Canal, where you'll find the entrance to one of Copenhagen's most fascinating places, the National Museum, built in the 1740s for Crown Prince Frederik, who later became King Frederik V. Inside you can see the world's finest collection of Stone Age tools and runic stones dating from the Viking period. Note particularly the beautiful Hindsgavl Dagger, fashioned and used several thousand years before the birth of Christ. You can also get some idea of Viking camp life, the ships with which they traveled all over the world, and their unusual burial mounds in which it was the custom to put a jug of liquor beside the body of the deceased to assure him happiness in heaven.

One of the featured exhibits in the Historical Music section is a number of Bronze Age *lur*, unusual musical instruments between four and six feet in length, which were popular 3,000 years ago; 36 lurs or fragments have thus far been found in peat bogs all over Denmark. The museum offers for sale interesting silver and bronze replicas of certain of the exhibits.

Directly across the bridge from the National Museum is the Christiansborg Slot, seat of the Folketing, or Danish parliament, and the Supreme Court. It's an imposing building that dominates the little island—Slotsholmen, the very heart of the city—on which it stands. And appropriately, this is where Bishop Absalon built his first fortress in 1167. Its ruins can be visited under the present building, which is the sixth on this site. From 1441 until the fire of 1794 Christiansborg was used as a royal residence.

On the same island with the palace are clustered a number of other important buildings. Set in an idyllic garden is Det Kongelige Bibliotek, the Royal Library, with Denmark's largest collection of books, newspapers, incunabula and manuscripts, including the earliest records of Viking expeditions to America and Greenland. On one side of the library is Tøjhuset, Copenhagen's arms museum, with outstanding displays of uniforms, weapons, and armor, in an arched hall nearly 180 meters (200 yards) long.

On the other side of the library is the low, red-brick Børsen, former Stock Exchange. This fine example of Renaissance architecture is claimed to be the oldest stock exchange in the world still used for its original purpose, though the main part of the business has now been moved to other premises. The Børsen stands in tribute to the skill and originality of Christian IV. Indeed, it is said that he lent a hand in the twisting of the tails of the four dragons that form its spire. The spire, as unusual as it is beautiful, is certainly the most distinctive feature of the Børsen, but the entire structure is one of the city's greatest architectural treasures.

Still on Slotsholmen and on the island side of Christiansborg Slot, we come to the Thorvaldsen Museum. Here the great sculptor is buried, surrounded by the originals or casts of all his works. Beyond and to the north of this museum we recross the canal over Højbro, or High Bridge.

To the left is a delightful row of houses bordering the northern edge of Slotsholmen. The quays in front of them were for long Copenhagen's fish market, and a sadly much-diminished market is still held here regularly. The fishy theme is reflected too by the presence of two excellent and long-established fish restaurants hard by the site of the market.

Let's stand in the middle of Højbro for a moment and look back down the canal to the right. Just across from Børsen is Holmens Kirke, where two of Denmark's greatest naval heroes are entombed. One is Niels Juel, the man who shredded the Swedish fleet at Køge in 1677, and the other is the almost legendary Tordenskjold, who defeated Charles XII of Sweden during the Great Northern War. At the far end of the canal you see Knippelsbro, the big drawbridge leading to the island of Christianshavn. That green and gold spire with the curious spiral staircase winding around it is part of Vor Frelsers Kirke (Our Saviour's Church). After a look inside, you'll find that the excellent view from the tower is well worth the climb.

Christianshavn is one of the oldest quarters of Copenhagen. Though somewhat dilapidated now, and haunt of more than its fair share of low-life types, the area has retained some of its Left Bank charm, not least along the canals that thread through it where old houses lean out over houseboats and yachts. Row boats are available for hire; particularly attractive on a moonlit night. Those nostalgic for the 1960s can get a taste of counter-culture at Christiania, a community founded in 1971 when students occupied army barracks. The giant cartoons and grafitti covering the buildings preach drugs and peace. Up to 1,400 people live here during the summer; the winter population is smaller.

The Runde Tårn and the University

Alternatively, head north from Højbro along Købmagergade. Continue past the equestrian statue of Bishop Absalon and the charming brick Nikolaj Kirke (actually part restaurant and exhibition center today, but still one of the principal landmarks of the city, not least for its towering spire). Cross over the Strøget and continue north. A couple of hundred meters up on the right you'll come to the Runde Tårn, the Round Tower, which Christian IV built as an observatory, not as part of the church to which it is attached, though this, with a handsome interior, is well worth a visit. If you are energetic, you can climb to the top of the Runde Tårn up the internal spiral ramp. Peter the Great of Russia, so the story goes, drove up in a horse-drawn carriage.

Perhaps this is the place for a few more words about Denmark's amazing warrior-architect-scholar-king. Vitally alive to every new idea, Christian IV was much more than a builder. During his busy life he found time to revolutionize farming, reform the administration of his Norwegian kingdom, create seven new chairs of learning at the University and start trading companies to exploit the fabled riches of the East and discover a Northwest Passage. Even when he went for a walk, he would pull a ruler out of his pocket and check the workmanship of local masons and carpenters.

Across the road from the Runde Tårn is the Regensen, since 1628 a residential college for university students. It is worth pushing aside the heavy door and taking a quick look at the courtyard. The old lime tree there celebrates its birthday with a private May lunch, after which the students "shake hands" with a pair of gloves hung up in its branches.

From the Regensen, continue along Krystalgade to the University and, on Nørregade, the Vor Frue Kirke, the Church of Our Lady. The University celebrated its 500th anniversary in 1979, but the bulk of its buildings, including the main university, dates from the period of Copenhagen's great expansion in the 19th century. The growth of the University has lately been such, however, that many departments have had to be moved to more spacious quarters outside the city center.

The Vor Frue Kirke has been Copenhagen's cathedral since 1924. Bishop Absalon is believed to have built a chapel here in the early-13th century. Ravaged by fire in 1728 and hit during Nelson's bombardment in 1807, it was rebuilt in stern neo-Classical style in the early-19th century. The entire structure was extensively restored between 1977 and 1979. Bronze statues of Moses and David flank the entrance, and Thorvaldsen's marble sculptures of Christ and the Apostles can be seen inside. The ruins of the first church (1320) can now be seen in the basement, and a small historical collection has been opened on the first floor. On coming out take a turn to the left down Nørregade and, before you know it, you are back at the twin squares of Gammeltorv and Nytorv, our first stop.

Kongens Nytorv to Langelinie

Thus far we have described a large circle in the older part of town. The trip we are about to start upon will take us pretty much in a straight line. It begins at Kongens Nytorv, which lies at the opposite end of Strøget from Rådhus Pladsen. Strøget, you will recall, is the series of streets with different names that comprise Copenhagen's principal shopping district. The better stores are at the end from which we are about to set out.

In the center of Kongens Nytorv is a mounted statue of Christian V. Near the end of June every year, newly matriculated students arrive here in horse-drawn wagonettes and dance around the silent figure of the king. The southern side of the square is flanked by the Kongelige Theater, featuring ballet and opera as well as classical drama. Next door stands the Theater's annex, popularly called the "Starling Box". The Dutch Baroque building of Charlottenborg, which has housed the Danish Academy of Fine Arts since 1754, is also in Kongens Nytorv.

The stretch of water you see running up to Kongens Nytorv is the Nyhavn Canal. Picturesque 18th-century buildings crowd both sides. Today the area has become fashionable, with one restaurant opening after another. A veritable fleet of old-time sailing ships normally lines the quays along Nyhavn, and on one side the *Fyrskib XVII,* a stout old lightship dating from 1893, permanently moored, is seeing out her days as a floating museum. The far end of Nyhavn is the departure point for the hydrofoil to Malmö in Sweden, while beyond, the passenger ships to Norway and the Baltic dock.

Our path, however, is down Bredgade, a wide street leading north from Kongens Nytorv, to the first turning to the right, Sankt Annae Plads, then the next left into Amaliengade.

Before you stands an imposing colonnade. Although it looks like stone, it is actually made of wood—if you don't believe us, try tapping it. When you've gone through the arches, the square you are in contains the four residences that comprise Amalienborg Palace. The one immediately to the right is used by Queen Margrethe and her family, the following (facing you on the right) is occupied by dowager Queen Ingrid. During the fall and winter, when the Queen lives in Copenhagen, the guards, complete with bearskins and headed by their band, march through the city from the barracks adjoining Rosenborg Slot every day, to relieve the Amalienborg sentries at noon. Colorful, too, is the sight of a royal coach with its scarlet-coated drivers giving the team some brisk trotting exercise through the busy streets.

Turning left out of the palace square we come back to Bredgade. Directly in front of us broods the Marmorkirken, the Marble Church, a somewhat topheavy building with an enormous dome several sizes too large for it. Its ponderous Baroque exterior contrasts a little painfully with the delicate facades of the Amalienborg Palace. Perched around the outside are 16 statues of various religious leaders from Moses to Luther, and below them stand other sculptures of outstanding Danish ministers and bishops. The building was completed in 1894, after having lain in ruins since 1770.

We turn right into Bredgade and continue past the three brilliantly-gilded onion domes of the Russian Church before arriving in front of the Museum of Decorative Arts, the Kunstindustrimuseet, a fine Rococo building that was originally a royal hospital. Today, it contains an excellent collection of artefacts—ceramics, silverware and Flemish tapestries—from the Middle Ages to the present day, as well as a collection of musical instruments.

A few steps more take us up to Esplanaden, where there is a small museum, the Frihedsmuseet, documenting the heroic efforts of the Danish resistance in World War II. Close by, you will see the Gefion Fountain. Powerfully and dramatically this commemorates the legend of the goddess Gefion, who was promised as much of Sweden as she could plough around in one day. Changing her four sons into oxen, she carved out the island of Zealand. Perhaps there may be an element of truth in the story, for if you look at a map of Sweden you'll see that Lake Vänern is much the same size and shape as Zealand itself.

The park in front of us, alongside Esplanaden, is graced by the English Church standing at its entrance. In the center, surrounded by two rings of moats, is the Kastellet, or Citadel. It dates from the late-17th century when it was begun by Frederik III. Much work, renovating and expanding it, was also carried out in the 18th century, by which time it was the principal fortress of the city. The grounds are open to the public. Stretching straight ahead of us is the Langelinie Promenade, where foreign navies moor their ships, and all of Copenhagen meets on Sunday afternoon. About halfway along it, the Little Mermaid of Hans Andersen's famous fairy story perches on a rock by the water's edge and gazes wistfully across the harbor.

Jewels, Flowers and Old Masters

The last of our three excursions begins in Kongens Have, the King's Gardens, where little children play around the statue of Hans Christian Andersen. Our objective is the Renaissance-style Rosenborg Slot, now a museum containing not only a breathtaking display of all the Danish crown jewels but also a fine collection of furniture, together with the personal effects of Danish kings from the time of Christian IV, including that monarch's precious pearl-studded saddle.

Just opposite the palace are some 25 acres of botanical gardens, as well as an observatory and mineralogical museum. Across the street from the north end of these gardens we come to Statens Museum for Kunst, the national art gallery, whose liveried doorkeeper sports buckle shoes and a cocked hat on chilly days. An imposing late neo-Classical facade hides an excellently modernized interior, with a good, though cramped cafeteria. With few exceptions, the collections are generally dull, consisting mainly of second-rate Old Masters and endless rooms of 19th-century Danish pictures. However, the contemporary works should at least provide some light relief. There is also a good collection of works by Matisse. Behind the main building is the Hirschsprung Collection, containing more Danish 19th-century works.

We have now been through most of the better-known parts of the heart of Copenhagen, but it would be an error to forget that the real heart of any city is the living one. The red-coated postmen, the bear-skinned, not over-military-looking Royal Guard, the spirited Tivoli Guard, the cyclists, the little fat man who sells fruit in the street all week and then blossoms out as a racehorse owner on Sundays, Queen Margrethe: all these are the real sights of Copenhagen.

Short Excursions Out of Town

When the sun is shining, whether there is spring in the air or snow on the ground, and the Copenhagener wants a few hours in the country the chances are he will go to Dyrehaven, the Deer Park near Klampenborg. Here nearly 2,000 of these timid, graceful animals wander about at complete ease. A golf course, a summer fun-fair (open mid-April to late August) and several all-year-round restaurants occupy the rest of the 3,500 acres of forest, paths and ponds that make up this lovely park. Near the entrance to the park is the Bellevue bathing beach. Farther along the seaside drive from the capital to Elsinore (Helsingør) are a host of luxurious villas and charming places to stop. Also near Elsinore is Denmark's only casino, the Marienlyst Hotel.

Even closer to Copenhagen than Klampenborg is the fashionable suburb of Charlottenlund. It is a lovely walk from the S-station to Strandvejen where the Akvarium is. Across the road is the beach, popular though less fashionable than the one at Bellevue, and nearby are the picturesque Chalottenlund Fortress and an unofficial, though good, campsite for foreigners only.

Starting from either Lyngby or Holte, you can go for a walk in the woods close by, or else stroll around lakes Lyngbysø and the much larger Furesø. At Lyngby, near Sorgenfri station, you'll find the open-air museum known as Frilandsmuseet. In a park covering 40 acres is a collection of reconstructed old Danish farms, several windmills, and country houses moved here from the other parts of Denmark and southern Sweden.

The Hareskov woods can be reached from Svanemøllen station (train B). From Hareskov you may ramble through the forest to Fiskebaek and have lunch there. Afterwards you might vary your return journey by riding the motorboat to Lyngby or Holte station.

A shorter trip which many enjoy is to Dragør on the island of Amager. This quaint old fishing village, where geese still roam in the crooked streets, has a charm of its very own. The oldest house contains a museum of furniture, costumes, drawings, and model ships. Its chimney is twisted to prevent the Devil finding his way through. The museum in Store Magleby, an old, half-timbered farmhouse, displays Amager furniture, dresses, and needlework.

Another haunt you might enjoy, as much for the trip out as for what you find at your destination, is to Grundtvigs Kirke. Consecrated in 1940 and built in a style based on the typical Danish village church, this building, with its organ-like façade stands in memory of the poet, clergyman and founder of the Folk High School, whose name it bears.

PRACTICAL INFORMATION FOR COPENHAGEN

GETTING TO TOWN FROM THE AIRPORT. There is a frequent bus service from the airport to the Central Station. Airport buses leave every 15 minutes, the journey takes 25 minutes and costs Dkr. 24 (tickets are purchased on the bus). Buses also run to the airport from the station. The bus calls at the Hotel Scandinavia (for information tel. 33–25 24 20). Public buses are half the price and run just as often: routes 32, 32H for Rådhus Pladsen, route 9 for Kongens Nytorv and Østerport, route 38E for Valby Station.

Taxis are expensive, costing around Dkr. 75, but may be practical for groups.

TOURIST INFORMATION. The Tourist Information Office, run by the Danish Tourist Board, is at H.C. Andersens Blvd. 22 (33–11 13 25).

For students and young people "Use it" (*Huset*) at Rådhusstraede 13 (33–15 65 18), has useful information and an accommodations service. Open Mon. to Fri. 10–4 (Tues. and Thurs. 10–6); 15 June to 15 Sept., daily 10–8.

USEFUL ADDRESSES. Embassies. *British Embassy,* Kastelsvej 36–40 (31–26 46 00). *Canadian Embassy,* Kristen Bernikowsgade 1 (33–12 22 99). *U.S. Embassy,* Dag Hammarskiölds Allé 24 (31–42 31 44).

Travel Agents. *American Express,* Dagmarhus, Amagertov 18 (33–12 23 01). *Wagons-Lits/Cooks,* Vesterbrogade 2B (33–14 27 47). *Spies Rejsebureau,* Nyropsgade 41 (31–23 35 00). *Tjåereborg Rejser,* Rådhus Pladsen 75 (33–11 11 00). Charter flights and accommodations in most European destinations can be arranged by the last two companies. *SAS Airlines,* Hammerichsgade 1 (33–13 72 77) for Europe, (33–13 62 66) within Denmark and (33–13 82 88) out of Europe.

Car Hire. *Avis,* Vester Sogade 10 (33–50 42 99). *Hertz,* Ved Vesterport 3 (33–12 77 00). *Inter-Rent,* Jernbanegade 6 (33–11 62 00) offer lowest rates and are highly recommended. *Share-a-Car,* Studiestraede 61 (33–12 06 43), is cheaper and also hires out campers and tents. *Europcar,* Gammel Kongevej 70 (31–24 66 77).

TELEPHONE CODE. The telephone codes for Copenhagen vary according to the area of the city. To call any number in this chapter, including Copenhagen numbers within the city, the prefixes we've included must be used unless otherwise specified.

COPENHAGEN

HOTELS. Hotels in Denmark's capital are numerous and range from the luxurious down to the very plain and modest side-street hotel. During the season (May through Oct.) it is advisable to book your room well in advance, either directly or through your local travel agent. If you happen to come without a reservation, go to the "Room Service" at Kastrup Airport or at the Central Station. Young people may go to "Use it" (*Huset*), Rådhusstraede 13 (33–15 65 18), where there is also a noticeboard indicating room availability outside opening hours.

The accommodations service at the Central Station is at Kiosk P and it is open daily to personal callers from 1 May to 15 Sept. 9 A.M. to midnight (Nov.–Mar. 9–5). There's a Dkr. 13 deposit per person for rooms in private homes, which cost about Dkr. 110 for a single and Dkr. 220 for a double. Telephone inquiries can be made on 33–12 28 80, Mon. to Fri. 9–5. The postal address is *Hotelbooking Copenhagen*, Hovedbanegården, DK-1570 Copenhagen V. There's also a booth at the airport, which is always open.

Many listed hotels do not fall squarely into our price categories (see *Facts at Your Fingertips* for Denmark). In particular, *Moderate* rates for an hotel at the pricier end may overlap into *Expensive*, or at the lower end may stretch into *Inexpensive*. Take special care and always ask. During the off-season (Nov. to Apr.) many hotels, especially the new ones, lower their rates considerably. It is therefore advisable when reserving to have the prices confirmed. Hotels designated (BE) charge for breakfast. The budget hotel area is near the Central Station, around Colbjørnsengade/Helgolandsgade.

Deluxe

D'Angleterre. Kongens Nytorv 34 (33–12 00 95). 189 beds. A classic, ranking first among Copenhagen hotels. It has recently been renovated but retains an Old-World charm. Suites available. Sidewalk terrace café is a popular meeting place all year round. Widely regarded as one of the best hotels in Europe. Bar, restaurant with music, beauty salon, barber shop. (BE). AE, DC, MC, V.

Kong Frederick. Vester Voldgade 23/27 (31–42 59 02). 97 comfortable rooms with private facilities, and good restaurant. English-style "pub." AE, DC, MC, V.

Nyhavn 71. (33–11 85 85). A Romantik Hotel. 113 beds. One of the most charming and atmospheric hotels in Copenhagen, in converted 200-year-old storehouse. Most of the rooms have view of the harbor. Some suites. Excellent restaurant serving Danish Cold Table at lunchtime and *à la carte* in the evenings. AE, DC, MC.

Plaza. Bernstorffsgade 4 (33–14 92 62). Now under the joint banner "Royal Classic Hotels," with the *d'Angleterre* and *Kong Frederik*. 82 rooms. This group offers special weekend winter rates and various off-peak bargains. AE, DC, MC, V.

SAS Royal. Hammerichsgade 1 (33–14 14 12). 447 beds, all rooms with bath. This modern hotel has the best of Danish architecture, art and furniture. Every comfort. Sauna, restaurant, bar. (BE). AE, DC, MC, V.

SAS Scandinavia. Amager Blvd. 70 (33–11 23 24). 1,046 beds. Enormous tower block mid-way between the airport and the city facing the old city moats. Pool, restaurant, bar, coffee shop, sauna. (BE). AE, DC, MC, V.

Sheraton Copenhagen. Vester Søgade 6 (33–14 35 35). 846 beds, 34 suites, all rooms with T.V. Liberal use of blond wood, gray and pink in the decor. Sauna. (BE). AE, DC, MC, V.

Falkoner Hotel. Falkoner Allé 9 (31–19 80 01). 166 beds, and just coming into the lower end of the Deluxe category, so good value. In the Frederiksberg section. Good bus connections and parking facilities. AE, DC, MC, V.

Expensive

Hotel City. Peder Skrams Gade 24 (33–13 06 66). An individually owned tourist hotel, in an old city-center building, newly refurbished to keep traditional atmosphere. Popular with Americans. All rooms have full facilities; telefax and telex services. Breakfast only (included in room price) but many restaurants close by. Good value. AE, DC, MC, V.

Savoy Hotel. Vesterbrogade 324 (31–31 40 73). 67 rooms, all with bath. A surprising oasis of peace in a small garden courtyard off Vesterbrogade. The 1906 building was renovated in 1985. Rooms have all facilities. Breakfast-only restaurant (BE) but affiliated to a first-class restaurant nearby. AE, DC, MC, V.

Sophie Amalie. Sankt. Annae Plads 21 (33–13 34 00). 117 rooms, all with bath, some suites. Completely renovated. Bar. Guests use restaurant of adjoining Copenhagen Admiral. Good value, quiet; some rooms with harbor view. (BE). AE, MC, V.

Hotel Vestersøhus. Vestersøgade 58 (33–11 38 70). 53 large rooms with balconies, all recently redecorated. Recommended is the two-room suite with kitchen and balcony. Also the 15 apartments with bathroom and kitchen are good value for long stays. A family hotel, patronized by the U.S. Embassy, and facing the lakes. Breakfast restaurant. AE, DC, MC, V.

Webers Hotel. Vesterbrogade 118 (31–31 14 32). 80 rooms, all with private facilities. AE, DC, MC, V.

Moderate

Alexandra. H.C. Andersens Blvd. 8 (33–14 22 00). 63 rooms, all private facilities. Close to the Rådhus Pladsen, the center of the capital. Quiet, restaurant. AE, DC, MC.

Ascot Hotel. Studiestraede 57 (33–12 60 00). An attractive old building, with a wrought iron staircase and original features. Centrally located. Popular with Americans, who like facilities such as same-day laundry and dry-cleaning services, and extended room service; all rooms with private facilities. Many have been newly renovated; a few have kitchenettes. Good breakfast buffet in restaurant with bright decor. AE, DC, MC.

Bel Air. Løjtegardsvej 99 (31–51 30 33). 346 rooms, all with bath. Near airport; bus 34 to Copenhagen takes 25 minutes. Restaurant, bar, sauna. DC, MC, V.

Copenhagen Admiral Hotel. Toldbrogade 27/28 (33–11 82 82). A happy surprise to find this interesting conversion of a 1787 granary in the *Moderate* category (overlapping top price end) with a very high standard of facilities. Some two-story suites (Expensive) and restaurant, lobby bar, sidewalk café, shop, sauna. Business and tourist guests from America. MC, V.

Hotel Excelsior. Colbjørnsgade 4 (31–24 50 85). 55 rooms, comfortably furnished in Scandinavian style, 42 with private facilities, in recently renovated building. Bold interior color scheme; the lobby is like a child's post-modern playroom. Pleasant plant-filled atrium for drinks. AE, DC, MC, V.

Hotel Marina. Vedbaek Strandvej 391 (42–89 17 11). At Vedbaek, a residential area 30 minutes north of the city. 100 rooms, all with private facilities, also apartments for 2, 4, and 6, with modern kitchens. Near forest, beach, and yachting harbor. Good restaurant, excellent value. AE, DC, MC, V.

Hotel Neptun. Skt. Annae Plads 18 (33–13 89 00). 66 comfortable rooms, all furnished in mahogany and with private facilities. A classic hotel with 140 years of tradition. Restaurant and café, travel agency. AE, DC, MC, V.

SAS Globetrotter. Envej 171 (31–55 14 33). Near airport. 196 rooms, all with private facilities. Modern, with restaurant, bar and cafeteria, bowling, and sauna. Bus 9 to Børsen takes 15 minutes. AE, DC, MC, V.

Scandic Hotel. Kettevej 4 (31–49 82 22). 210 rooms, all with private facilities. The place to go if you want an indoor pool and sauna. At Hvidovre, western Copenhagen. AE, DC, MC, V.

Triton. Helgolandsgade 7–11 (31–31 32 66). 123 rooms with bath. Streamlined and modern, with large rooms in blond wood and warm tones. Exceptional buffet breakfast. Restaurant, bar. AE, DC, MC, V.

Hotel Østerport. Oslo Plads 5 (33–11 22 66). 73 rooms, 50 with bath. Modern Scandinavian design building, 15-minutes' walk from center, attracting many American summer guests. Meeting room, bar serving light meals. Gourmet restaurant, *Saison,* open for lunch and dinner. AE, DC, MC, V.

Inexpensive

Amager. Amagerbrogade 29 (31–54 40 08). 26 rooms, 16 with private facilities. On the way to the airport but still central. DC, MC.

COPENHAGEN

Missionhotellet Ansgar. Colbjørnsgade 29 (31-21 21 96). 87 rooms, 44 with private facilities. AE, DC, MC, V.

Dragør Faergegård. Drogdensvej 43, Dragør (31-53 05 00). 23 rooms. An idyllic setting in old fishing village, near beach and airport. Buses to Rådhus Pladsen take 40 minutes (BE). DC, MC.

Esplanaden. Bredgade 78 (33-13 212 75). 50 rooms, all with private facilities. Centrally located near Langelinie and Kastellet. Bus and train connections. Good value. DC, MC, V.

Gentofte. Gentoftegarde 29 (31-68 09 11). 71 rooms, all with shower and toilet. Quiet, on the outskirts: bus 24 to Norresport (25 minutes) or train A. AE, DC, MC, V.

Skovshoved. Strandvejen 257, Charlottenlund (31-64 00 28). A charming hotel, about five miles from the center, among old fishing cottages beside the yacht harbor. 20 rooms, all with private facilities, and rooms vary from very large ones overlooking the sea, to smaller rooms overlooking a courtyard. Licensed since 1660, it has retained its Old-World charm, though fully modernized. Gourmet international restaurant (E) attached. (BE costs Dkr. 45). AE, DC, MC, V.

Hotel Viking. Bredgade 65 (33-12 45 50). One hundred-year-old former mansion close to Amalienborg Castle, Nyhaven, and the "Little Mermaid," in an area of palaces and mansions. 90 comfortable and spacious rooms, 19 with private facilities (no TV/radio, which you may find an asset!). Restaurant in same building but not part of Viking. Well managed. Closed to public transportation. AE, DC, MC.

West. Westend 11 (31-24 27 61). 24 rooms. A simple, reasonably priced hotel with few facilities. (BE).

Youth Hostels

Copenhagen Hostel. Sjaellandsbroen 55 (32-52 29 08). 448 beds in 2- and 4-bed rooms. Open all year, 3 miles from center, bus 37 from Holmens Bro near Holmens Kirke.

Vesterbro Ungdomsgård. 8 Absalonsgade (31-31 20 70). Open 5 May-Aug., near Central Station, membership card not required.

Danish Tourist Board list of Youth Hostels available free of charge. Official guide: *Danmarks Vandrehjem,* Vesterbrogade 39, Copenhagen V (32-52 29 08). Dkr. 25 plus postage.

Camping

Absalon Camping. Korsdalsvej 132, Rødovre (31-41 06 00). West of Copenhagen.

Bellahøj Camping, Hvidkildevej (31-10 11 50). In northwest Copenhagen area.

Strandmøllen. DK-2942 Skodsborg (01 80 38 83). North of Copenhagen.

Leaflet with locations, opening times and rating available from Danish Tourist Board free of charge. Complete Guide published by *Campingradet,* Olof Palmes Gade 10, Copenhagen Dk. 2100 (price Dkr. 32 plus Dkr. 20 postage).

HOW TO GET AROUND. By bus and train (S-train). A joint fare system, with optional transfers, covers buses and trains in Copenhagen city and environs. A one-hour ticket for three zones costs Dkr. 8; get it from bus drivers and rail stations. You can save money by buying a packet of 10 basic tickets for 70 Dkr. This system covers an area that stops south of Køge, west of Roskilde, and includes these towns, and Hillerød and Elsinore. Buses and S-trains start as early as 5 A.M. (Sunday 6 A.M.). The last bus and S-train leaves central Copenhagen around half past midnight, but night buses cover certain city routes. Get Zone system details from the 24-hour enquiry service (33-14 17 01).

In and around Copenhagen you can save by buying a *Copenhagen Card,* a ticket valid for one, two, or three days, which costs Dkr. 80, 140, and 180, respectively. It also provides free admission to more than 40 museums and other places of interest, including Tivoli Gardens, and gives a reduction of up to 50% on the ferry crossing to Sweden. You can buy the card at rail stations, tourist offices, travel agents, and some hotels. The card has a 50% discount for children aged 5–11.

By taxi. Taxis are expensive but all are metered. The basic charge is 12 Dkr. plus Dkr. 8–10 per kilometer (including waiting time at traffic lights, etc.). Tipping is optional and rarely expected, although a 4 Dkr. tip is charged for taking baggage to the 2nd floor, or for accompanying less mobile or elderly passengers. Cabs available for hire have the *Fri* sign. They may be hired at taxi stands, en route, or by telephone on 31–35 35 35.

By bicycle. Bicycles may be hired for about Dkr. 30 to 50 per day, deposit Dkr. 100 to 200, from *Danwheel-Rent a Bike,* Colbjørnsensgade 3 (31–21 27 27); *Rent a Bicycle, Jet-Cycles,* Istedgade 71 (31–23 17 60); *Københavns Cyclebørs-Velonia,* Gothersgade 157–159 (33–14 07 17); *Urania Cykler,* Gammel Kongevej 1 (31–21 80 88); *Cykeltanken,* 247 Godthåbsvej, near Bellahøj Camping (31–87 14 23). and from Helsingør, Hillerød, Klampenborg and Lyngby rail stations, Apr. through Oct., (33–14 17 01).

By horse-drawn cab. For romantics there are horse-drawn cabs in the famous Deer Park (Dyrehaven), and in the city center. Expensive.

TOURS. From May to October there are various bus tours around the city and beyond. Here we outline the tours of Copenhagen: for further details and tickets contact tourist information offices, travel agents and some hotels. All sightseeing buses depart from Lur Blower Column on Rådhus Pladsden. Although tickets may be purchased from the guide at the point of departure, to be sure of a seat buy them in advance.

The "Grand Tour of Copenhagen" covers all the major sights, with stops at the Gefion Fountain, den Lille Havfrue (the Little Mermaid) and Grundtvigs Kirke. It lasts two and a half hours, and runs twice daily, Apr. through Oct.; in winter, once a weekday, twice on Sat.

The "Royal Tour of Copenhagen" covers Christiansborg Palace with the Royal Reception Rooms, Rosenborg Castle (crown jewels), passes by other royal buildings, and ends at Amalienborg Slot. It takes two and three quarter hours and is available June through Sept. 11, Tues, Thurs., and Sat.

The "City and Harbor Tour" starts by coach and includes a motor boat tour of the charming canals of Christianshavn. Duration is two and a half hours and it takes place from May 1 to Sept. 11 at 9.30 daily.

The "Industrial Art Tour" includes visits to a porcelain factory (either Bing & Grøndahl or Royal Copenhagen Porcelain), the Kunstindustrimuseet (Museum of Decorative and Applied Arts), and Den Permanente, the Danish design center. This tour lasts two and a half hours and runs from May 15 to Sept. 15, every Thurs.

"An Afternoon of History and Romance" includes a visit to an old village in a Copenhagen suburb, a river cruise, the Frilandsmuseet (Open-Air Museum) and the Dyrehaven (Royal Deer Park). Coffee and Danish pastry is included in the price. This tour lasts four hours and runs June 15 to Aug. 31, every Sat.

"Under Sail on the Sound." On the Isefjord, Denmark's oldest schooner. May–Sept. about four hours. Lunch or dinner on board. Departs from Amalienhaven (behind the Copenhagen Admiral Hotel, Toldbodgade 24). For information, tel. 01–15 17 29.

To join a motor boat tour (with or without guide) go to Gammel Strand or Kongens Nytorv. The boats also stop at Den Lille Havfrue and some go to Christianshavn. A fine way to experience Copenhagen.

There are guided walking tours, lasting two hours, with various starting points and routes, July through Aug. Consult the Copenhagen dailies or ask for information at the Tourist Information Office.

Guided tours of the Carlsberg Brewery, Ny Carlsbergvej 140, are on Mon. to Fri. at 9, 11 and 2.30. Meet at Elephant Gate. To make arrangements for groups, tel. 31–21 12 21, ext. 1312. The Tuborg Brewery, Strandvejen 54 (buses 1 and 21) provides tours on weekdays at 10, 12 and 2.30, or by arrangement for groups (tel. 31–29 33 11).

COPENHAGEN

MUSEUMS. Copenhagen is a fine city to stimulate a sense of history and it certainly has its fair share of museums and art galleries. We list here the major museums plus a few smaller ones of special interest, together with opening times. Opening hours and admission fees are subject to change.

Although admission to many museums is free it could pay you to invest in a *Copenhagen Card*, a tourist ticket giving unlimited bus and rail travel in Copenhagen plus free admission to sights including Tivoli. Valid for one, two or three days at Dkr. 80, 140, and 180, respectively, it can be bought from rail stations, the Tourist Information Office, hotels and travel agents.

Davids Samling (C.L. David Collection). Kronprinsessegade 30. Medieval Islamic pottery. European decorative art from 18th cent. Open all year, Sept. 16 through Apr., Tues. to Sun. 11–3; closed Mon.; May through Sept. 15, Tues. to Sun. 10–4, closed Mon. Adm. free.

Frihedsmuseet (Liberty Museum). Churchill parken, Esplanaden. Exhibits detailing the efforts of the Danish Resistance in World War II. Open all year: Tues. to Sat. 10–4, Sun. 10–5; closed Mon. Adm. free.

Fyrskib XVII. Nyhavn 10. Lightship dating from 1895. Open all year, when the gangway is down.

Geologisk Museum (Geological Museum). Øster Voldgade 5–7. Open all year, Tues. to Sun. 1–4. Closed Mon. Adm. free.

Glypotek. Dantes Plads. Egyptian, Greek, Etruscan and Roman collections, 19th-cent. French and Danish art. Open May through Aug., Tues. to Sun. 10–4; closed Mon. Sept. through Apr., Tues. to Sat. 12–3, Sun. 10–4, closed Mon. Adm. Dkr. 15, children free, Wed. and Sun. free.

Den Hirschsprungske Samling (Hirschsprung Collection). Stockholmsgade 20. 19th-cent. Danish art. Open all year, Wed. to Sun. 1–4; closed Mon. and Tues. Also open Wed. eve. 7–10, Oct. through Apr. Adm. free.

Jagt- og Skovbrugsmuseet (Hunting and Forestry Museum). Hørsholm. Train to Holte then bus to Hørsholm, or bus 84 or faster 75E (weekdays only). Open Feb. to Nov. 10–4 Tues. to Sun., closed Mon. Closed Dec. through Jan. Adm. Dkr. 5.

Kobenhavns Bymuseum (Copenhagen City Museum). Vesterbrogade 59. Guild relics, costumes, paintings and engravings illustrating the history and appearance of the capital through the ages. Also Søren Kierkegaard reliquae. Open May through Sept., Tues. to Sun. 10–4; closed Mon. Oct. through Apr., Tues. to Sun. 1–4. Adm. free.

Kunstindustrimuseet (Museum of Decorative and Applied Arts). Bredgade 68. European and Oriental handicrafts. Open all year, Tues. to Sun. 1–4; closed Mon. Adm. free on weekdays, except July and Aug.; 12 Dkr. on weekends, July and Aug.

Nationalmuseet (National Museum). Frederiksholms Kanal 12. Exhibits illustrate Danish civilization from Stone Age to recent times; also, ethnographical and coin collections. The Prehistoric and Greenland collections are outstanding. Opening times of the different sections are complex (tel. 33–13 44 11), but most sections are open Sun. 10–4, some Tues. to Sun. 10–4, and other 1–4. General admission times are as follows: Sept. 16 through June 15, Tues. to Fri. 11–3, Sat. and Sun. 12–4; June 16 through Sept. 15, Tues. to Sun. 10–4. Closed Mon. Adm. free, except for the special collection *Jugenzeit Interior*—elegant rooms in *fin de siècle* style (1890), adm. Dkr. 10, children Dkr. 3.

Ordrupgårdsamlingen (Ordrupgård Collections). Vilvordevej 110, Charlottenlund. 19th-cent. French paintings, especially Impressionists. Bus 160 from Klampenborg or Lyngby S-stations. Open all year, Tues. to Sun. 1–5; Wed. 7 P.M.–10 P.M.; closed Mon. Adm. Dkr. 5.

Statens Museum for Kunst (National Gallery). Sølvgade Sølvgade 48–50. Danish and European paintings, including Matisse collection. Open all year, Tues. to Sun. 10–5; closed Mon. Adm. free.

Teaterhistorisk Museum (Theater Museum). Christiansborg Ridebane 18. Open June through Sept., Wed., Fri. and Sun. 2–4; Oct. through May, Wed. and Sun. only 2–4. Adm. Dkr. 10, children Dkr. 5.

Thorvaldsens Museum. Porthusgade 2, Slotsholmen. Works by Danish sculptor (1770–1844). Open Tues. to Sun. 10–5. Closed Mon. Adm. free.

COPENHAGEN

Tøjhusmuseet (Royal Arsenal Museum). Tøjhusgade 3. Collection of weapons and uniforms in Royal Arsenal built around 1600. Open May through Sept., Tues. to Sat. 1–4, Sun. 11–4; Oct. through Apr., Tues. to Fri. 1–3, Sat. 1–4, Sun. 11–4. Closed Mon. Adm. free.

Zoologisk Museum (Zoological Museum). Universitetsparken 15. Open Tues. to Sun. 11–5. Closed Mon. Adm. free.

TIVOLI GARDENS. This world-famous amusement park is open daily from Apr. 26 to mid-September, 10 A.M. (amusements all in operation by 2.30 P.M.) to midnight. It covers an area of 850,000 square feet. In May, amusements are cheaper, and on some Wednesdays children get free afternoon tickets for a few amusements.

Concert Hall: Not only does Tivoli lie in the heart of Copenhagen, but during the summer months it is the city's musical center as well. Symphony concerts are given every evening at 7.30 and 9 (sometimes free). Also free daily "proms".

Pantomime Theater ("Peacock Building" to left of main entrance). Performances every evening except Sun., pantomimes 7.45, ballets 9.45. Pantomime came to Denmark from Italy via France and England about 150 years ago. This is the only place in the world where traditional pantomime is still performed.

Open-air Stage (in middle of gardens). International variety acts every evening at 7 and 10.30, weekends 5, 7, and 10.

Amusements. In the farthest righthand corner of the gardens ("The Fun Corner") and in "The Alley" behind the scenic railway; open from 2 to 4 until midnight.

Variety Theater Glassalen has a varied program with Danish revues during the summer.

Tivoli Boy Guards. Parade every Sat. and Sun., 6.30 and 8.30.

Fireworks. Weds. and Sats. at 11.45 P.M. on lake and open-air stage. Sun., stage fireworks at 11.30 P.M.

Restaurants. Eating places of all categories; open daily 9 A.M.–midnight. *Divan I* and *Divan II* are noteworthy but by no means inexpensive. Of greater gastronomic interest but no cheaper is *Belle Terrasse.* Over beer and sausages at *Ferry Inn* (*Faergekroen*) you can join in the folk singing. Also *Perlen, Balkonen, Grøften* and *Nimb.*

Dancing. Every night from 10–midnight at *Taverna.*

Jazz, Folk. *Slukefter* and *Vise Vers Huset.*

PARKS AND ZOOS. In the **Botanisk Have** (Botanical Gardens), Gothersgade 28 (tel. 33–12 74 60). Gardens open May to Aug. daily 8.30–6. Sept. to April daily 8.30–4. Palmhouse with tropical plants open all year 10–3 daily. Cactus house open all year Sat. and Sun. only 1–3. Adm. free.

Danmarks Akvarium is at Strandvejen, Charlottenlund. Take the S-train and walk, or bus 1 or 27. 90 tanks with about 3,000 fish and other marine animals from all over the world. Open daily Mar. through Nov. 10–6; Dec. through Feb. Mon. to Fri. 10–4, Sat. and Sun. 10–5. Adm. Dkr. 23, children Dkr. 10. The **Zoologisk Have** (Zoo) is at 32 Roskildevej. Founded in 1859, it is the largest and oldest zoo in Scandinavia. Open Apr. through May, Sept. through Oct., daily 9–5; June through Aug., daily 9–6; Nov. through Mar., daily 9–4. Adm. Dkr. 35, children Dkr. 16.

The **Dyrehaven** (Deer Park) is near Klampenborg and can be reached by S-train or bus 27. At Hellerup is the World War II Resistance memorial park, **Mindeparken Ryvangen,** reached by S-train or bus 21, and open 10 A.M. to sunset.

HISTORIC BUILDINGS AND SITES. Devastated over the centuries by war and fire, Copenhagen has been re-built many times. Its surviving genuine Renaissance buildings are therefore especially worthy of attention; however architects of later centuries also put up exceedingly handsome buildings. You may wish to take a trip out of town to see rather more homely historic buildings at Sorgenfri and Dragør. See *Copenhagen This Week* for comprehensive list.

Amalienborg (Amalienborg Palace). Four identical mansions (1740–50) creating a delightful Rococo square. Queen Margrethe sometimes in residence. Changing of the Guard at noon. The equestrian statue in the center is of King Frederik V.

COPENHAGEN

Børsen (Stock Exchange). Slotsholmen. Built by King Christian IV around 1640. Fine Dutch Renaissance building with remarkable dragon-tail spire. Still in use but not open to general public.

Christiansborg Slot (Christiansborg Palace). Slotsholmen. State apartments, knights' hall, palace ruins. Royal Family residence since 1794. Conducted tours in English June to Aug. at 11, 1 and 3, except Mon. Oct. to Apr. at 2 (except Mon. and Sat). Adm. Dkr. 18, children Dkr. 7.

Dragør. Amager. Seaside village settled by Dutch immigrants. Museum open May through Sept., Tues. to Fri., 2–5; Sat. and Sun. 12–6. Closed Mon. Adm. Dkr. 5. Bus 30 or 33 from Rådhus Pladsen.

Folketing (Parliament). Christiansborg Slot. Open June to Sept., Sun. to Fri. 10–4. Closed Sat. Guided tours also Sun. year-round on the hours, 10–4. Adm. free.

Frilandsmuseet (Open-air Museum). Sorgenfri. Original old Scandinavian buildings in natural surroundings. Bus 84, or S-train. Open mid-Apr. through Sept., daily 10–5; closed Mon.; Oct. 1 to 14, 10–3; Oct. 15 to Apr., Sun. only, 10–3. Adm. Dkr. 10.

Grundtvigs Kirke. På Bjerget. Modern cathedral in village-church style. Bus 10, 16, 19, 43. Open Mon. to Sat. 9–4.45; Sun. 12–4, winter 12–1. Except during services (tel. 31–81 54 42). Adm. free.

Holmens Kirke. Holmens Kanal. Royal chapel and naval church, built 1619. Open 15 May to 15 Sept., Mon. to Fri. 9–2; winter Mon. to Sat. 9–12. Closed Sun. Adm. free.

Kastellet (Citadel). At Langelinie: 17th-cent. fortifications. Open year-round daily 6 A.M. to sunset. Adm. free.

Det Kongelige Bibliotek (Royal Library). Christians Brygge 8. Enter from Christiansborg courtyard. National Library of Denmark, topical exhibitions, exquisite gardens. Open all year Mon. to Sat. 9–6. Closed Sun. Adm. free.

Rådhuset (Town Hall). Tel. 33–15 38 00. Open all year. Mon. to Fri. 10–3. History of local city administration. Reception rooms for councillors. 346 ft. tower. Guided tours Mon. to Fri. at 1, Sat. at 10. Tower tours Mon. to Fri. at 11 and 2, Sat. at 11.

Rosenborg Slot (Rosenborg Castle). Øster Voldgade 4a. Built by Christian IV, 1606–17. Crown Jewels. Open May through Sept. 25, daily 10–4; Sept. 26 through mid-Oct., daily 11–3; treasury open Oct. 24 through Apr., Tues. to Sun. 11–3, closed Mon; castle open Oct. 24 through Apr., Tues., Fri., Sun. 11–1. Adm. Dkr. 20, children Dkr. 7.

Runde Tårn (Round Tower). Købmagergade. Christian IV's observatory, built 1642. Open Dec. through Mar., daily 11–4; Apr. through May, Sept. through Oct., daily 10–5; June through Aug., daily 10–8. Adm. 5 Dkr. Observatory open Sept. 15–Apr. 15, Wed. only 7–9.45 P.M. Adm. Dkr. 10, children Dkr. 4.

SPORTS. Copenhagen is a paradise for active sports people. The Tourist Information Office and Copenhagen Idraetsparks Information Office, P. H. Lings Allé 2, DK-2100 (tel. 33–12 68 60), open Mon. to Fri. 8–4, are good sources of information. **Jogging** may be practised in the parks and woods, and there is a fitness-testing course at Brøndbyskoven. For information on **squash** courts and rackets for hire at *Svanemøllehallen* tel. 31–20 77 01. The Copenhagen Squash Club (Vestersøhus, Vester Søgade, tel. 33–11 86 38) charges Dkr. 75 an hour.

Swimming. The nearest sandy beach is at Charlottenlund. More popular is the artificial beach a little further north at Bellevue. Go to Klampenborg by S-train C or bus 27 (from Hellerup). Other good beaches include Amager Strandpark (bus 12) and Dragør Sydstrand (bus, 30, 31). Beaches free. There are several indoor swimming pools around Copenhagen and its suburbs. Details from Tourist Information. Swimming pools, open during the summer are: Frederiksberg Swimming Baths, 29 Helgesvej; Kildesovshallen, 25 Adolphsvej, Gentofte; Vesterbro Swimming Baths, 4 Angelgade; Øbro Hall, Idraetsparken. South of Dragør (bus 30 or 33) are low meadows alongside the beach, with shallow water (the cleanest near Copenhagen): ideal for children. A 5-mile man-made beach is now open to the public at Køge Bugt Strandpark, south of Copenhagen. It is fine, sandy and clean. Bus

121 from Valby Station, or by S-train A to Ishøj or Hundige station and from there by the beach bus (season only) direct to the beach. You can windsurf along most of the coast of North Sealand. Contact local tourist offices for board hire etc.

Sailing is popular in Copenhagen, and the waters are ideally suited to it. Visitors can obtain assistance through the big clubs, especially the *Royal Danish Yacht Club* (33–14 87 87) and the *Copenhagen Amateur Sailing Club,* Klubhuset Svanemøllehavnen (31–20 71 72). Sailing boats and motor boats can be hired from *Maritim Camping* at Jyllinge (31–38 83 58) or *Holiday Charterboat,* Falkonercentret, Copenhagen (31–19 09 00).

Fishing. Freshwater fishing for rainbow trout, river trout, carp tench, and eel, at Søllerud Naturpark, Langkaerdammen, Attemosevej, Holte. Information on day fishing licenses is available from local tourist offices. You must provide your own equipment. **Sea fishing in the sound** for cod, herring, garfish, mackerel, contact the following: *m/s Kastrup,* Kastrup Industrihavn (31–50 54 38); *m/s Skipper,* Kalkbraenderihavn (42–84 69 53); *m/s Hanne Berit,* Rungsted Havn (42–57 07 24).

Golf. Visiting golfers have a choice of around a dozen nine- or 18-hole golf courses within some 20 miles of the city center. Details from Tourist Information.

Horse riding. This is popular in the Dyrepark at Klampenborg. Experienced riders lead groups and prices (Dkr. 50–95 an hour) vary according to the mount.

Skating from October to the end of March. Copenhagen has five skating rinks. Details from Tourist Information.

Tennis. The following clubs accept guest members for day-time play only: *Boldklubben of 1893* (31–38 18 90); *Hellerup Idraetsklub* (31–62 14 28); *Kobenhavns Boldklub* (01–71 41 80); *Kobenhavns Boldklub* (31–30 23 00).

Sports Events. You can find out about sporting events, and have other sports queries answered at Københavns Idraetsparks Information (as above).

Horseracing is accompanied by totalizator betting in Copenhagen. Flat racing takes place between the latter part of Apr. and mid-Dec. at the Klampenborg Race Course. Bus 27 or S-train C to Klampenborg, then bus 160 or bus 176 from station. Trotting events are held year-round, Sun. and Wed., at Charlottenlund Race Course; S-train C or bus 1 to Charlottenlund. **Cycle races** take place on the Ordrup track at Charlottenlund, usually Mon. and Tues. **Soccer** is played at the Idraetsparken at Østerbro or Valby, Sun. afternoons or evenings, except July.

THE ARTS. For a list of future events in music, theater, film, exhibitions, etc. *Copenhagen This Week* is an excellent source of information. You can also get details on concerts, festivals, etc. from *MIC* (*Dansk Musik Informations Center*), Vimmelskaftet 48, DK-1161 Copenhagen (31–11 20 86), open from 9–4 (personal callers 1–4). The main theater and music season is from September through May, and tickets can be obtained either direct from theaters or concert halls, or from ticket agencies such as *Wilhelm Hansen* (31–15 54 57) except for Tivoli. Details from Tourist Information.

Concerts and Guest Performances. The Radiohuset Concert Hall has weekly concerts by the Danish Broadcasting Service's three orchestras. The Sealand Symphony Orchestra is resident and gives more than 150 concerts every summer, with Danish and foreign soloists. You can hear new music at Ny Carlsberg Glypotek, the Royal Museum of Fine Arts, and the concert hall of the Louisians Museum in North Sealand.

Theater, Opera and Ballet. The Royal Theater is one of the few in the world to have theater, ballet and opera in the same buildings. Performances on the two stages alternate between all three. The *Mermaid Theater* is the only one in Copenhagen to give its performances in English.

Movies. The Danes rarely dub films; they use subtitles instead. This means that you can often see original British and American films in your language. The same applies to television.

SHOPPING. Copenhagen is something of a shopper's paradise. Prices are high, but then so is the quality. At the same time, many shops offer tax-free shopping— look for the sign; it's always prominently displayed. Note, however, that you can

COPENHAGEN

claim back tax only when your total purchases from any one shop exceed Dkr. 1,200 (U.S. residents) or Dkr. 2,300 (U.K./other EEC residents).

The first place to head for on any shopping expedition in Copenhagen are the Strøget, the pedestrians-only streets—all lined with shops—that lace the heart of the old town.

Design. Near the Central Station (10 Frederiksborgade), at *Den Permanente* (The Permanent Exhibition of Danish Arts and Crafts, all exhibits for sale) there is a comprehensive selection of the finest handwork from all over the country.

A store where you'll find a beautiful and large display of Scandinavian design, plus the best of handicrafts from other countries is *Illum,* Østergade 52, the local Harrods. There are over 70 departments, including porcelain, the best names in Danish and Scandinavian furniture, fabrics and Finnish Rya rugs; a tax-free shipping service, two restaurants, a hairdresser, and credit cards are accepted. A shopper's delight.

Illums Bolighus, Amagertorv 10 (not to be confused with the above store), is *the* Center of Modern Scandinavian Design. If you are interested in some of the most attractive and yet practical things that are being marketed today, this is the spot to visit. Many items on sale here are made by famous Scandinavian designers and artists, some of whom have works exhibited in the New York Museum of Modern Art. A wonderful shop for browsing and picking up ideas for decor, entertaining, etc.

Ikea, Mårkaervej 15, Tåstrup (bus 119 from the station), is a huge furniture store with own, often cheaper, designs.

Silver. *Georg Jensen Silver* is at Østergade 40. Here you will find the largest collection of Jensen hollowware in the world. Browse among extensive offerings of gold and silver jewelry and study the permanent exhibit of tables laid with many of the famous patterns in sterling silver and stainless steel. There is also a small museum with original Jensen pieces, exhibits and photographs relating to his life and work. Antique and second-hand items for sale.

Danish design achieves beauty by classic lines and graceful forms, and centuries of sensitive craftsmanship are reflected in every piece of contemporary silver. *Hans Hansen* at Amagergade 16 features stunning flat ware, cigarette boxes, and such.

Peter Hertz, Købmagergade 34, is one of the oldest silversmiths in town and makes most of his pieces to order. He specializes in marvelous place settings and delicate jewelry.

But moderns must first visit *A. Michelsen,* Bredgade 11—their prize-winning cigarette container and silver pitcher, their graceful tubecluster candelabra and the enameled anniversary and enameled Christmas spoons designed each year, are all collectors' items. The 1984 spoon was designed by Queen Margrethe.

A bit further along Bredgade, at number 36, is *A. Dragsted,* whose jewelry and tableware are favorites with the Royal Court.

Porcelain and Glass. The *Royal Copenhagen Porcelain Manufactory* (actually a shop on the original factory site) at Amagertorv 6. Three floors of beautiful displays from Flora Danica hand-painted dinner services to figurines. Second quality items also available, at reduced prices.

Bing & Grøndahl porcelain is next door and ranks equally high in quality and design. Second quality available from factory at Vesterbrogade 149. *Rosenthal,* Frederiksberggade 21 has a choice of porcelain and glassware primarily by Scandinavian artists such as Bjørn Wiinblad and Tapio Wirkkala. *Match,* Vimmelskaffet 42 (on Strøget) displays of glass and porcelain from Scandinavia, kitchen to table top.

Holmegaard glassware is on display at Østergade 15, offering everything in Danish design from snaps klukflaske to beautiful opalescent vases. A permanent glass exhibition/museum has been opened. Visits can be made to glassworks in Fensmark to see glass being made, also second quality on sale at reduced prices.

Arts and Crafts. At Ny Østergade 11 is the *Bjrn Wiinblad House,* with a sales display of the artist's own products.

For native crafts, see *Håndarbejdets Fremme,* Vimmelskaftet 38, which has embroideries, handprinted fabrics, and trinkets in impeccable taste. Every article is handmade; patterns and materials are also sold.

Clara Waever at Østergade 42 features special embroidery, lace, and linen.

Elling, at Bredgade 24, features materials of fanciful design together with bright printed pieces amusing for a child's room.

In the 1785 Potter's House at Torvegade 38, *P. Brøste* displays modern Danish and foreign arts and crafts.

Form & Farve, Nicolaj Plads 3, offers a host of characteristic Scandinavian designs, from notebooks to clothes.

At Bredgade 47, the captivating wooden toys, bowls, and plates of *Kay Bojesen* are on display.

Department Stores. *Magasin du Nord,* a huge, modern department store at Kongens Nytorv is the biggest of its kind in Denmark, with particularly good buys in silver, ceramics, and furs.

Illum, Østergade 52, see above, under *Design.*

Daells Varehus, Nørregade 12, is a smaller store, but offers good quality at extremely reasonable prices. Cash only sales.

RESTAURANTS. Copenhagen is reputed to have over 2,000 restaurants, and most of the city's hotels have good dining rooms. Prices are high, however, for the most part, so always be sure to check the menu, which by law much be displayed outside, before going in. A number of restaurants, even the more expensive, offer good-value fixed-price menus, usually of three courses. In addition, look out for restaurants displaying the *Dan-Menu* sign, where a two-course meal—either lunch or dinner—will cost Dkr. 75. Lunch is often the Danes' main meal. In many restaurants and cafés, a salad is included in the price of the main dish, and the second cup of coffee is often free, thereby halving the cost of what may seem an expensive cup. Always ask. Most Expensive and Moderate restaurants take credit cards; many Inexpensive only take cash. Service is always included in all bills.

Further budget bets are the many foreign restaurants that have appeared in recent years. You'll also find all the familiar fast food chains here. There are many pizzerias, particularly in the old city, and American-style burgers are sold all over town at **Burger King, McDonalds** and elsewhere. There are cafeterias in the **Magasin, Anva, Daells Varehus** and **Favør** department stores, which close half an hour before the shop. Cheapest of all are sausages and hamburgers from sidewalk vans (*poølsvogn*) which provide excellent, filling fare.

Expensive

L'Alsace. Ny Østergade 9 (33–14 57 43). Braques and Chagalls deck the walls of this elegant restaurant, set in an ancient courtyard; specializes in fish and French cooking. Book ahead; closed Sun. AE, DC, MC, V.

La Brasserie. Hotel d'Angleterre, Kongens Nytorv 34 (33–32 01 22). The place where Copenhagen's see-and-be-seen set goes to eat. French-inspired food in bistro surroundings. AE, DC, MC, V.

Den Sorte Ravn. Nyhvn 14 (33–13 12 33). French/Danish cuisine. 18th-century building on "gentleman's" side of Nyhavn. Specialties include fresh local seafood, sauces. Book ahead. AE, DC, MC, V.

Els. Store Strandstraede 3, off Nyhavn (33–14 13 41). Menu changes daily; gourmet food using fresh produce. Original 1853 decor. Book ahead. AE, DC, MC, V.

Den Glyde Fortun Fiskekaelderen. Ved Stranden 18 (33–12 20 11). Menu includes two meat dishes, otherwise all seafood in delicious sauces. Specialties of the day written on blackboard. Closed Sun. lunch. Book ahead. AE, DC, MC, V.

Gilleleje. Nyhavn 10 (33–12 58 58). Decorated with fascinating antiques from old spice-trading, sailing-ship days. Interesting spicey recipes. Open lunch and dinner except Sun., July. Book ahead. AE, DC, MC, V.

Kong Hans Kaelder. Vingardsstraede 6 (33–11 68 68). Luxury, gourmet food; top prices for highest quality. Closed lunch, Sun. and mid-July to mid-Aug. Book ahead. AE, DC, MC, V.

Langelinie Pavillonen. Langelinie, near Little Mermaid (33–12 12 14). Superb harbor views. Open lunch, tea and dinner; dancing most evenings. International menu. AE, DC, MC, V.

COPENHAGEN 47

Pakuskaelderen. Nyhavn 71—basement restaurant of hotel (33–11 85 85). Best Cold Table in town, lunch only. International menu and grills in evening. Old restored warehouse in charming area. Book ahead. DC, MC, V.

Le Restaurant. In Hotel d'Angleterre (33–12 00 95). International menu, pleasant atmosphere, lush decor. DC, MC, V.

Skovshoved. Strandvejen 267, Charlottenlund (31–64 00 28). 15 minutes' drive out of town. Gourmet restaurant with idyllic conservatory dining room. Superb food. Book ahead. AE, DC, MC, V.

St. Gertruds Kloster. Hauser Plads 32 (33–14 66 30). Fascinating ancient building with cloisters and antique church artifacts, lit by 1,200 candles. International menu; special children's dishes. Open daily from 4 P.M. Book ahead. AE, DC, MC, V.

Moderate

Bof & Ost. Gråbrødretorv 13 (33–11 99 11). Basement in ancient square. Closed Sun. Informal bistro with Caviar-Vodka Bar. Open 11.30 A.M.–11 P.M.

Café Royal. In SAS Royal Hotel, Hammerichsgade (33–14 14 12). Open 6.30 A.M.–midnight. Light meals and snacks.

Café Victor. Ny Ostergade 8 (33–13 36 13). Open 10 A.M.–11.30 P.M. Very smart, fashionable clientele. International food.

Copenhagen Corner. Rådhus Pladsen (33–91 45 45). Modern, good international food. 11.30 A.M.–midnight.

Havfruen, Nyhavn 39 (33–11 11 39). Copenhagen natives love the maritime-bistro ambience at the "Mermaid", and are drawn by French-inspired fish specialties. Closed Sun.

Hereford Beefstouw. Large restaurant at Vesterbrogade 3 (33–12 74 41) and smaller, more intimate one at Åbrenå 8 (01–11 91 90). Best steaks in town, cooked to your order. Mix-your-own salads with good dressings. Closed for lunch Sat. and Sun. AE, DC, MC, V.

Ida Davidsen. Store Kongensgade 70 (33–91 36 55). Traditional Danish lunch restaurant with very best open sandwiches and specialties. Closed Sat. and Sun.

Mongolian Barbecue. Store Kongensgade 64–66 (33–14 64 66). Also at Stormgade 35 and Strandvejen 26. Hearty all-you-can-eat menus. New and popular.

Peder Oxe. Gråbrødretorv 11 (33–11 00 77). Steaks and salads. Charming area; can be crowded. 11.30 A.M.–10.30 P.M.

Queen's Rib. In Kong Frederik Hotel, Vester Voldgade 23–27 (33–12 59 02). French and Danish cuisine. Open-air eating from May to Sept. Pub for light meals. AE, DC, MC, V.

Stedet. Lavendelstraede 13 (33–15 66 25). Good cooking; relaxed, casual atmosphere. Open 11.30–3, 5–10.30, Sun. 5–10.30. Closed June and July.

Inexpensive

Amagertorv 8. In Royal Copenhagen Porcelain Shop. Open shop hours, closed Sun. Delicious pastries and light meals.

Café Asbaek. Ny Adelgade 8. In modern art gallery. Light meals and specialties. Open 11–3.30. Closed Sun.

Café Nikolaj. In old Nikolaj Church. Good Danish food. Open noon–midnight except Sun. and Mon.

Café Smukke Marie. Knabrostraede 19. Specializes in buckwheat pancakes with various fillings. Open 1 P.M.–midnight Mon. to Fri.; 4 P.M.–midnight Sat. and Sun.

The Cedars. Lavendelstraede 6. Lebanese buffet. Good value. Open 5–12 P.M.

Chico's Cantina. Borgergade 2. Very popular Mexican restaurant. Good atmosphere and excellent value food. Open noon–3 P.M. and 5 P.M.–midnight.

Green's. Grønnegade 12–14. Vegetarian; popular buffet. Classical music plays, chic bohemians chat, and friendly staff serve.

Krasnapolsky. Vestergade 10. Interesting salads, pasta, snacks. Near the university: there's a brooding youth at every table. Lunch only. Open 11.30 A.M.–midnight; 3 P.M.–midnight on Sun.

Mama Rosa. Østergade 59 (Strøget). Italian specialties, pizza and fresh pasta. Open 11 A.M.–midnight.
Mexicali. Åboulevarden 12. Mexican specialties. Open Tues. to Fri. 5 P.M.–midnight; Sat. and Sun. noon–midnight. Closed Mon.
Peppe's Pizza. Gothersgade 101, Rødhus Pladsen 57, Falkoner Allé 17, Frederiksberg and Skt. Pedersvej 1, Hellerup. Open noon–midnight; Fri. and Sat. to 3 A.M. Excellent freshly made pizzas of all types. Good house wine. Take out too.

NIGHTLIFE. Still feeling strong? There's a long way to go before exhausting the city. All-night membership clubs are now things of the past. About 35 restaurants are permitted to stay open until 5 A.M. (ask your hotel porter or see the newspaper). For shows, see the *Ekstrabladet* newspaper advertisements. For the young, many discos have been opened in recent years. Bohemians in general might like to make their way to the district around Nikolaj Kirke, locally known as "The Minefield." Here are dozens of small music and dance spots, and a beer is the price of admission.

The nightspots listed below are moderate to expensive and usually have an admittance fee.

Clubs and Discos

Compass Club. Amager Blvd. 70. In Scandinavia Hotel. Thurs., Fri. and Sat. only, 10 P.M.–5 A.M.
Fellini Nightclub. Hammerichsgade 1. In SAS Royal Hotel. 10 P.M.–4.30 A.M. Closed Sun.
La Fontaine Jazz Club. Kompagnistraede 11. 11 P.M.–6 A.M.
Jazzhus Montmartre. Nørregade 41. Reputed to be one of the best places for modern jazz in Europe. 8 P.M.–1 A.M. (Fri. and Sat. to 5 A.M.).
New Daddy's/Café Rio. Axeltorv 5. Largest disco in town. Mon.–Thurs. 10 P.M.–4 A.M.; Fri. 10 P.M.–7 A.M.; Sat. 10 P.M.–8 A.M.
Penthouse Club. Sheraton Hotel. 10 P.M.–5 A.M.
Privé. Ny Østergade 14. Hot place for the younger crowd. 10 P.M.–5 A.M. Closed Sun.
Slukefter. Tivoli. May to Sept., 8 P.M.–2 A.M.
Three Musketeers. Nikolaj Plads 25. Best place for traditional jazz, dancing. 8 P.M.–2 A.M., Fri. and Sat.–3 A.M. Closed Sun.
U-Matic. Vestergade 10. Mon.–Wed. 9–2, Thurs. 9–3, Fri. and Sat. 9–5.

Bars with Entertainment

After 8. In Hotel Scandinavia. 8.30–4.
Café Royal/Laurits Betjent. Ved Stranden 16. 10 P.M.–5 A.M. Closed Sun.
Kakadu Bar. Colbjørnsensgade 6. 8 P.M.–5 A.M. Popular.
King's Court Piano Bar. In Sheraton Hotel. 5.30 P.M.–2 A.M.
Musikcafé'n. Rådhusstraede 13. Fri. and Sat. 9 P.M.–2 A.M.
Purple Door Music Theater/Club Bluestime. Fiolstraede 28. Thurs. to Sun. only, 8.30 P.M.–1 A.M.
Rådhuskroen. Løongangsstraede 21. 12 P.M.–4 A.M.
Universitetscafeen. Fiolstraede 2. 10 P.M.–5 A.M.; Sun. 5 P.M.–5 A.M.
Vin & Olgod. Skindergade 45. Viking dinners, fanfare on Viking Lures (musical instruments), dancing and singing. 8 P.M.–2 A.M. Closed Sun.
Vinstue. Kongens Nytorv 19. English pub atmosphere. 10 P.M.–1 A.M.
Wonder Bar. Studiestraede 69. Singles bar. 9 P.M.–5 A.M.

OSLO

The Countryside Capital

The bright, breezy and outdoorsy capital of Norway is an hospitable city of some 450,000 people located at the head of the long, low Oslo fjord. Here is a world capital with nature at its very doorstep, a perfect place to adjust from the frenetic, over-civilized existence of some Western countries to the simpler, more wholesome values of Norwegian life.

Oslo is not a city of great architecture, sweeping boulevards and imposing buildings, yet in the somewhat haphazard arrangement of the streets there is a certain charm. And if you really go looking, you will certainly find buildings both old and modern of distinction. But, as every Oslonian says, "The surroundings!" Yes, they are magnificent, and the view of the town from any of the easily-reached heights that surround it is superb. But do not jump to the conclusion that the first thing to do is to rush out of town. That's only part of the program—there is plenty to do in Oslo before you head for the hills.

But hills, forests, fjords and farms, mountains and meadows there are aplenty, all encompassed within the nominal city limits of Oslo. The city is in fact the tenth-largest in the world in total area, but this statistic is really no more than a bureaucratic convenience. The built-up area of Oslo is small and in no way compares even with Stockholm and Copenhagen, let alone the likes of London, Paris or Rome. Thus the presence of a fairly rumbustious Nature close at hand is more than any other the most distinctive feature of this little capital.

So be warned. Anyone coming to Oslo in pursuit of sophisticated urban high-living is liable to be somewhat disappointed. Indeed, it should also be added that the rather puritanical Norwegians actively frown on anything that might be considered high living, principally by imposing stinging taxes and strict regulations on the sale of alcohol. However, those in search of gentle relaxation, with the accent on the great outdoors, though perhaps with just a dash of sophistication to spice up the mixture, will find the Norwegian capital very much to their liking.

By Way of Background

Oslo is an ancient city, founded in 1050 by King Harald Hardraarda (or Hard Counsel), yet in contrast to most European capitals, very little remains that is more than a couple of hundred years old at most. The reasons for this apparently paradoxical state of affairs are not so hard to find, however.

Despite its antiquity and despite having been capital of Norway since the middle ages, for much of its history Oslo has really been no more than a bit-part player on the European stage, and an unfortunate one at that. With Norway falling under the influence and rule of first Denmark and then Sweden, Oslo was little more than a pawn, intermittently besieged, conquered, traded-off and reconquered. The city, or more exactly the Akershus Fortress that was its strategic heart, was attacked first by Duke Erik of Sweden in 1310—no more than 10 years after it had been completed by Haakon V. It was subsequently besieged (successfully) by Christian II of Denmark in 1531-2 and by the Swedes again in 1537 and 1716, who on both occasions were attempting to wrest it from the Danes. As if this was not enough, the old wooden city was also periodically ravaged by fire, culminating in the disastrous fire of 1624 when practically the whole town was burned to the ground. Thus in contrast to Stockholm, for example, which has rarely been seriously attacked, Oslo's tempestuous past has seen the repeated destruction of much of the city, explaining the relative scarcity of older buildings today.

1624 in fact marks the beginning of the development of the modern city. Following this second fire, Christian IV, Danish ruler of Norway, decided to rebuild the town about a mile to the west of its original location so as to bring it closer to the protecting walls of the Akershus Fortress. He also decreed the houses be built of stone or brick and that the streets be a certain width. As a final flourish, he then renamed the city Christiania.

For the next two hundred years or so the little capital enjoyed a reasonable degree of prosperity, though it also suffered further severe fires in 1686 and 1708. But its growth was never more than steady and was in any case punctuated by regular political and economic setbacks, chiefly the result of Norway's continued domination by Denmark. During the Napoleonic Wars, for example, Norway was forced by the Danes to commit herself to the French cause, despite the close ties that by that point existed between Norway and Great Britain. The inevitable result was a British blockade of Norwegian ports with grave consequences for Norwegian trade.

On May 17, 1814, a Norwegian constitution was formulated at Eidsvoll (just north of Oslo at the southern end of Lake Mjøsa), and later a Norwegian king was proclaimed. It was only after 1814 that Norway finally achieved her independence from the Danes (though at the cost of renewed domination by Sweden) and the little city began to grow significantly. And it is from the middle years of the 19th century that the majority of Oslo's principal buildings date: The Royal Palace, the Stortinget (or Parliament) and the University were all constructed between about 1820 and 1860, while Karl Johans Gate, still the principal thoroughfare, was laid out between 1818 and 1848. The 19th century also witnessed a considerable increase in both trade and population (in 1855 Oslo's population was still less than 40,000, by 1900 it was 150,000; similarly, by the same date Oslo had overtaken Bergen as Norway's principal port). The growth of the city also gave rise to a considerable housing shortage, with the result that many small wooden houses were built, outside the then city limits, by workers flooding into Oslo from elsewhere in Norway. A number of these little buildings can still be seen in areas such as Valerengen, Kampen and Rodeløkka, many of them now modernized, expensive, and much sought-after private homes.

Following Norway's emergence into total independence in 1905, when King Haakon VII was crowned as the first king of Norway since the Middle Ages, the city continued to grow (and, on January 1 1925, reverted to its original medieval name of Oslo), but it was the immediate post-war period that witnessed the greatest period of expansion. The striking and monumental City Hall, completed in 1950, is the most obvious symbol of this growth and the spurt of building that accompanied it. Similarly, much of suburban Oslo dates from this period. Today, though still something of a toy town, Oslo is an harmonious, stable and civilized capital, that has put its troubled history behind it.

Exploring Oslo

The heart of Oslo is Karl Johans Gate, a spacious street (much of it now for pedestrians only) about a mile long that runs east to west from the Sentralstasjon or Oslo-S (Central Station) to the Slottet (Royal Palace). About half-way along is a little park, Studenterlunden, which for the sake of argument we'll use as the starting point for our exploration of Oslo. The most obvious feature here is the late-19th-century Nationalteatret (National Theater), an attractive classical building at one end of the little park. It's one of the focal points of the capital's cultural life and, appropriately, twin statues of Henrik Ibsen and Bjørnstjerne Bjørnson, Norway's most distinguished men of letters, flank the entrance. The theater has been newly renovated after a backstage fire in 1982 closed its main stage and auditorium. Its intimate amphitheater carried on as usual. No performances, however, are given in the summer. (On either side of the theater, by the way, are the city's principal bus stops and the entrance to the electric tram that runs up to Holmenkollen).

Immediately to the north of the National Theater is the handsome neo-Classical facade of the University of Oslo, built from 1811. In fact, most of the University's departments have long since been moved to more spacious quarters at Blindern, to the north of the city. But the building remains the administrative center of the University and examinations are still conducted here in the *Aula,* or Central Hall, which is famous also for the murals of Edvard Munch that cover its walls. The Aula is also the venue for the presentation of the Nobel Peace Prize.

The forecourt of the University is the scene every fall of the inmatriculation of new students to the University every year. But it's also an excellent vantage point from which to watch the procession on May 17, Constitution Day, of thousands of schoolchildren, marching behind brass bands

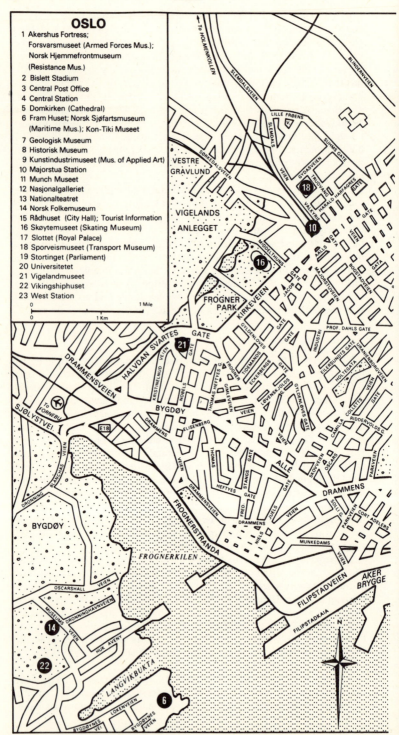

OSLO

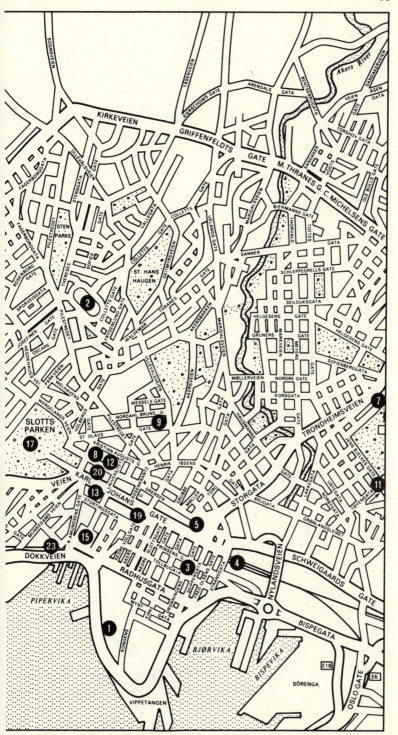

banners, as they wend their way along Karl Johans Gate before climbing the hill to the Palace to greet the royal family.

From the University, in fact, it's no more than a few hundred yards up to the Palace, standing in its fine park (which unfortunately is very much less salubrious at night). The Palace is not open to the public, but you can watch the changing of the guard every day at 1.30. The band plays when the King is in residence (all year round except mid-May to October when he moves out to his country home at Bygdøy). The statue on the parade in front of the Palace is of King Karl Johan, a Swedish king of Norway after whom the city's main street is named. To the west is another statue, this time of Queen Maud, daughter of Edward VII, King of England, and mother of the present king, Olav. Across the road is a third statue. This is Haakon VII, who was Norway's king from 1905 to 1957 and presided over his country's independence in 1905. He is still regarded with great affection by the Norwegians, not least for keeping alive the hopes of his beleaguered people during World War II when Norway labored under the Nazi occupation. His son Olav today enjoys the same deep hold on the affection of his people.

Again using the park by the National Theater as a base, this time head east away from the Palace and towards the Stortinget, Norway's Parliament. It's quite a striking building, heavy and sturdy, in parts more like a cathedral than a Government building. Inside, it has been richly decorated by modern Norwegian artists. It can be visited during the summer recess. (July and August, Monday to Saturday 12–2; admission free). Leave the Storting to the right and continue up Karl Johans Gate, here paved over and a bustling shopping center, towards the Domkirken, the Cathedral. Just before you reach the Cathedral, you pass through Stortorget, a busy flower market in the spring and summer. Though small, the Cathedral is an attractive church, if a little dour from the exterior. It was consecrated in 1697 and contains a fine carved wooden pulpit dating from 1699. However, it has since been substantially remodeled, notably in 1849–50 and just after the last war, when the striking ceiling frescos, by Hugo Lous Mohr, illustrating the perpetual battle between the forces of light and darkness, and the stained glass windows, designed by Emanuel Vigeland, brother of the more famous Gustav, were executed.

In the arcades behind the Cathedral, where there has been a market since the middle ages, you will today find the Arts and Crafts Center. It's a good place to potter around for an unusual souvenir. In front of the Cathedral there's another statue, this one of Christian IV, King of Norway and Denmark, who moved the site of Oslo nearer to the Akershus Fortress after the disastrous fire of 1624.

The National Gallery

The third and final exploration of the center of Oslo is to the cluster of museums behind and to the north of the University. Here you will find the Nasjongalleriet (National Gallery), the Historisk Museum (Historical Museum) and the Kunstindustrimuseet (Museum of Applied Art).

The National Gallery, established originally in 1836, is Norway's foremost art collection, containing some 3,000 paintings by Norwegian artists and about 1,000 by other artists. In addition, there are large collections of engravings, drawings, prints and water colors, the whole amounting to a very creditable 40,000 catalogued works. Though the emphasis is perhaps not surprisingly on Norwegian works from 1800 onwards, there are also many works dating from the Renaissance to the 19th century by both Norwegian and foreign artists. However, perhaps the highlight of the collection are the paintings by Edvard Munch, by some way Norway's most famous and influential painter. In spite of its all round excellence, however, the National Gallery, in common with many leading museums around the world, is severely handicapped by a lack of display space. The modern collections in particular have long been crammed into inadequate galleries. But the gallery's modern works were moved to a new home in the adjacent Bank of Norway's old building at the end of 1987, which by a happy coincidence was also the gallery's 150th anniversary. The building is now an independent Museum of Modern Art.

Back to back with the National Gallery is the Historical Museum, containing the University's collection of antiquities. Of particular interest is the fine display of Viking artefacts, especially jewelry. And a visit here is a useful supplement to one to the Viking ships at Bygdøy (of which more later) on the other side of the harbor.

Finally, continue up St. Olavs Gate, which runs diagonally away from the entrance to the Historical Museum, to the fascinating Museum of Applied Art, or Kunstindustrimuseum. Here you'll find furniture, silver, china, clothes—in short all the bric a brac and clutter that help bring the past alive—from the middle ages to the present, displayed against an imaginative background of music from each period. The emphasis is on Norwegian artefacts, but there are also sizeable collections from other lands, including the Far East.

Toward the Harbor

Having by now explored much of the center of the city, head down toward the harbor and the Akershus Fortress, Oslo's most ancient and historic building. The long, low bulk of the Fortress was built by King Haakon V in the early-14th century and has seen much violent military activity during its troubled life. It's an impressive building, by turns gloomy and romantic, with many spires and unexpected jutting roofs. As befits its military status, the Nazis used it as their headquarters during their occupation of Oslo in the war, and appropriately the Fortress today houses the excellent Hjemmefrontmuseum (Resistance Museum) which graphically and imaginatively charts the progress of the occupation from 1940–45, and the heroic efforts of Norway's Resistance. The fortress also contains a stone monument honoring the memory of those Norwegians who were executed by the Nazis.

Visit the State Apartments here—tours, in English, by guides dressed in period costume—or take in one of the Sunday lunch-time concerts in the chapel. Alternatively, you may just like to wander around the attractive grounds and along the ramparts, from where there is a magnificent view over the harbor and the city. Just outside, and to the east of the Fortress is the Forsvarsmuseet (Armed Forces Museum), latest addition to Oslo's museums. It too is well worth a visit for those with a military turn of mind.

From Akershus, it is no more than a few minutes' walk, past the martial figure pointing out to sea (an impressive statue of one Peter Wessel Tordenskiold, Admiral of the Danish/Norwegian fleet from 1715–20) to the red-brick Rådhuset (City Hall), its twin blunt towers looming over Rådhusplass. Outside, on the harbor side, you'll find another statue, F.D.R. in fact, holding a copy of the Atlantic Charter. The statue was unveiled by his wife Eleanor in 1950.

The main entrance to the City Hall is on the opposite side of the building, away from the harbor. But there's a second entrance on this, the harbor side which leads to the Tourist Information office. (Similarly, city sightseeing buses leave from this side, as do the sightseeing boats from the quays just across the road). But walk around to the principal entrance on the city side. It's well worth having a look inside at the massive central hall and the other rooms—the council chamber, the anterooms and the Munch room—open to the public. The whole of the interior is commandingly impressive, but by far and away the most eye-catching features are the murals, some 2,000 square feet in all, illustrating aspects of life in and around the city. They were produced during the '30s and '40s, but the building wasn't finished until 1950—work on the City Hall actually began in 1930 but had to be suspended during the war—and not surprisingly many of them, notably that on the left hand wall of the central hall, also deal with the Nazi occupation. Some may find them gaudy and rather wooden, as well as being perhaps a little dated, but they are undeniably impressive for all that. For those who wish, there are guides on hand to show you around.

The latest attraction is Aker Brygge, only a few minutes away from the City Hall, by the harbor. In this new shopping and leisure center are a myriad of small cafés and ethnic restaurants, both indoor and outdoor, as well as several theaters and restaurants.

The Environs of Oslo

To some extent, one can fairly claim that the principal attractions outside Oslo proper are, quite simply, the hills, forests and fjords that encroach so closely on the city and are so distinct a feature of life here. But there are also five specific places of interest outside the city, none of which should be missed by anyone intent on doing justice to a visit here. These are: the Frogner Park, northwest of the city; Bygdøy, just across the fjord from the harbor; Holmenkollen, north of the city; and two museums, the Henie-Onstad Art Center, overlooking the Oslo fjord at Høvikodden, and the Munch Museum to the northeast.

Frogner, or Vigeland, Park (easily reached by tram no. 2, or bus nos. 72 and 73 from the National Theater) contains perhaps the most startling sight in Oslo. This is the 60-foot high monolith, carved from a single block of stone weighing in at 200 tons, by the sculptor Gustav Vigeland (1869–1943). But as well as the monolith, the park, which was also designed by Vigeland, contains a further 650 statues by the sculptor which took him a total of 40 years to complete and which combine to illustrate and illuminate Vigeland's central theme: the cycle of life. Thus the entire park and its accompanying statues chart man's birth, growth and inevitable decay, the whole climaxed by the giant monolith. As you walk around the park, starting at the imposing bronze gates, you follow the progress of man's life, beginning naturally with birth and progressing through childhood, adolescence, maturity, old age and death. In addition, there is a massive fountain supported by six monumental figures symbolizing man's burden. Further evidence of Vigeland's prolific output is provided by the adjoining Vigeland Museum. (There is a good open-air restaurant here to revive those whose spirits may have flagged after confronting Vigeland's work in the raw). The museum contains 1,650 sculptures, 12,000 sketches and 3,700 woodcuts, all the work of this indefatigable artist.

Opinions have long been divided as to the artistic merit of Vigeland's work. Certainly, it is hard to see Vigeland's output as part of any wider European movements or schools. Nonetheless the park as a whole can have an overwhelmingly powerful impact and many visitors have commented that it provided the high point of their stay here. See it for yourself and make up your own mind. A large outdoor swimming pool is just one of its many attractions.

The museums at Bygdøy, however, present no such problems. They're easily reached by ferry from in front of the City Hall in summer, or by half-hourly bus (no. 30 or 30X) from the side of the National Theater. The most conspicuous of the buildings at Bygdøy is not actually a museum at all; rather, it's a huge tent-like structure (the traditional shape of a Viking boathouse)—known as the Framhuset —housing the sturdy little polar ship *Fram*. Actually, "little" is possibly a misleading term—the *Fram* is by no means a large vessel, even by the standards of her day (she was built in 1892), but housed in her permanent enclosed dry dock she appears positively massive. She was built for Fritjof Nansen, earliest of the many remarkable Norwegian polar explorers of the late-19th and early-20th centuries, for his three-year drift across the permanently frozen waters surrounding the North Pole. She was subsequently used by Otto Sverdrup on his journey to map the west coast of Greenland, and then to take Roald Amundsen on the first leg of his successful journey to the South Pole in 1911. She has been beautifully preserved and the visitor can clamber all over this most famous of polar vessels. Outside, you will find another famous Norwegian polar ship, even smaller than the *Fram*. This is the *Gjoa*, built originally as a fishing boat, and subsequently used by Amundsen on his discovery of the Northwest Passage (1903–6). Like the *Fram*, the *Gjoa* spent over three years gripped in the ice of the Arctic making her slow way across the roof of the world, eloquent proof of the skills of Norwegian shipwrights. Visitors are not, unfortunately, allowed on board.

A harpoon's throw from the *Fram* building is Oslo's Sjøfartsmuseum, or Maritime Museum. It's excellently laid out and graphically charts Norway's illustrious seafaring traditions and triumphs from the Vikings to the present day. The museum contains a veritable treasure chest of models, pictures, nautical bric-a-brac, even the interior of a passenger ship from the early years of this century. An interesting annex contains a number of actual vessels, from early fishing boats to a beautifully built and finished Olympic sailing dinghy. There's a good restaurant and cafeteria in the museum (in summer the cafeteria moves outside).

Opposite the Maritime Museum is the third in this trio of nautical haunts, the Kon-Tiki Museum, home of Thor Heyerdahl's famous balsa wood raft of the same name in which he caught the imagination of the world by sailing over 5,000 miles from Peru to Polynesia in 1947. The raft, never presumably too sturdy at the best of times, is showing its age somewhat these days, but is still an impressive sight. Underneath it there's an interesting and convincing mock up of the many different types of fish that congregated under its frail balsa wood timbers during the crossing, including a splendid whale shark, almost as long as the raft itself. The museum also houses *Ra II*, the papyrus boat in which Heyerdahl sailed from Morocco to Barbados in 1970, again in an attempt to prove that ancient man undertook long ocean crossings.

A little inland from the three museums is an equally impressive museum celebrating Norway's maritime exploits, though of a very much earlier period—the Vikingshiphuset or Viking Ship Museum. The museum is some 15 minutes' walk from the Maritime Museum, but well signposted and easy to find. (Coming from the city, the no. 30 or 30X bus stops right outside). Opened in 1936, it houses three remarkable and very beautiful Viking ships dating from A.D. 800–900, all discovered at the turn of the century. Almost as interesting as the vessels themselves are the various artefacts which were found on board, for these were burial ships, buried with Viking chieftains and intended to serve them in the next world as they had in this. Thus the ships were piled high with the goods and chattels of the chieftains, all of which have helped to build our remarkably complete picture of Viking life.

Finally, visit the immense Norsk Folkemuseum, the Norwegian Folk Museum, located just up the road from the Viking ships. Principally an outdoor museum (though no more than a couple of miles from the city center, the museum is practically in the country), it contains some 150 original wooden farmhouses and other buildings from all over Norway, many dating from the middle ages, that have been reassembled here. The chief treasure is one of Norway's unique stave churches, its roofs piled high like a pagoda, dating from the 13th century.

The museum was founded originally in 1894 and moved to Bygdøy in 1902 under the patronage of King Oscar II when the king's collection, which included the stave church, was added. Over the years, collections from other museums have also been transferred here. As well as the buildings themselves, the museum has an extensive collection of interiors, notably Ibsen's study, preserved exactly as it was when he lived in Oslo. There are goings-on galore at the museum in summer, especially on Sundays when there are displays of folk dancing, puppet shows, movies, handicraft demonstrations and lectures.

Up to Holmenkollen

The next excursion out of Oslo will take you in a completely different direction, northwest out of the city in fact and up into the hills to Holmenkollen and the Tryvannshøgda observation tower. Board any Frognerseter/Holmenkollen suburban train (T-bane) from the Nationaltheateret station and disembark at Holmenkollen. (If you want to stop at the observation tower first, get off at Frognerseter and walk up—it takes about 15 minutes. Holmenkollen will be visible, and from the tower at Tryvannshøgda, it is a 20-minute downhill walk.)

Norway is generally regarded as the home of modern skiing and no single place played a more significant role in its development than Holmenkollen. Indeed, to many Norwegians, Holmenkollen possesses a near-mystic significance and is regarded almost as a symbol of Norway. This reverence reaches a peak during the annual Holmenkollen championships, normally held in March. They have been held every year since the beginning of the century—except during World War II—and grip the attention of the entire nation. The King—no mean ski jumper himself in his youth—is one of the staunchest supporters. For the visitor, however, the principal attraction of Holmenkollen is the ski jump itself, a towering ramp stretching skywards down which the intrepid jumpers (once you've seen the jump, you may not think "intrepid" quite strong enough an adjective) hurtle before hurling themselves into space. If you've got a head for heights, take the elevator to the top of the tower—the view is predictably sensational.

Blasted into the rock by the side of the jump is the little ski museum—there's a statue of Nansen outside—which illustrates the development of skiing in Norway. Highlights of the museum are a ski over 2,500 years old and a display of polar equipment used by Nansen and Amundsen on their journeys to the North and South Poles respectively (including a phlegmatic stuffed dog taken—before it was stuffed—to the South Pole).

Finally, walk down the hill again from the jump to the Holmenkollen Park Hotel, a matter of 200 yards or so, to have a look at this marvelous late 19th-century building. It's been substantially renovated and a brand new annex added, but the original wooden building, with its multitude of projecting balconies, gables and overlapping roofs, has been lovingly preserved. The hotel has a variety of cafés and restaurants, though all are pricey. Less expensive refreshments are available at the Holmenkollen restaurant a little further down the hill, where you can sit on the terrace and enjoy the view in rather more comfort than from the top of the ski jump. The tram station for the ride back into town is located just below the restaurant.

Our final two excursions—to the Munch Museum and the Henie-Onstad Senteret, the Henie-Onstad Art Center—will not take you far from the city center, but are nonetheless well outside the downtown area.

The Munch Museum lies to the northeast of the city and can be reached by subway from Jernbanetorget in front of the Sentralstasjon to Tøyen (any train) or by bus (no. 29) from the City Hall, again to Tøyen. Edvard Munch (1863–1944) is the only Norwegian painter who can be claimed to have exercised a decisive influence on the wider European stage, and his work—tormented and expressionist—remains hugely popular today. The museum, opened in 1963, the centenary of the artist's birth, is thus a fitting memorial to Norway's most famous painter. It includes all those works—some 22,000 in all—in the artist's possession at the time of his death, all of which he left to the city. Needless to say, it is not possible to display anything more than a small fraction of this vast collection at any one time, so the exhibits are changed regularly, making repeated visits here a pleasure (though the most important works are generally on view at all times). But as well as Munch's work, the museum also holds regular exhibitions of works by other artists and presents lectures, concerts and films. Guided tours in English are available. The museum has undergone a lot of alterations in order to display a larger collection of Munch's paintings.

Across the street from the Museum are the Natural History museums and the Botanical Gardens, the latter an oasis on a hot summer's day. There is also a large open-air swimming pool close by.

Finally, visit the Henie-Onstad Art Center, 20 minutes west from the National Theater by bus no. 32 or buses 151, 161, 162, 252 or 261 from Universitetplassen, overlooking the fjord at Høvikodden. It's a modern art center in the widest sense. At the heart of the complex is the collection of 20th-century paintings donated by ice skater Sonja Henie and Niels Onstad, her husband. But the center also puts on concerts, film shows, theater, ballet, lectures and the like. A good cafeteria and restaurant complete the picture.

PRACTICAL INFORMATION FOR OSLO

GETTING TO TOWN FROM THE AIRPORT. There is a regular bus service (every 15 minutes) from Oslo airport (Fornebu) stopping at the Scandinavia Hotel (opposite the Royal Palace) and at the Central Station; cost is NOK 20 and journey time is around 15 minutes; to/from Gardemoen airport, NOK 50, journey time 50 mins. There are also city buses from the airport which cost around NOK 15. A taxi from the airport to the city center will run about NOK 80 to NOK 100.

TOURIST INFORMATION. The city tourist office is located in the City Hall on Rådhusplassen (harbor side), Oslo 1 (414863). They can supply information on all aspects of the city from sightseeing trips to renting bicycles. In addition, they publish annually the *Oslo Guide,* which gives details of hotels, museums, restaurants etc., in the city, and the monthly *Oslo This Week,* which lists all current activities in the city. The excellent-value *Oslo Card* is also available from the tourist office. Valid for one, two or three days and costing 75, 110 and 140 NOK, respectively, the card gives unlimited free travel on all public transport within the city and free entry to all museums, as well as discounts on many sightseeing buses and boats and car hire, and special rates in some restaurants. It also entitles you to free parking on any city-owned parking lot. (The Oslo Card is also available from hotels, travel agents, larger stores and branches of the ABC Bank in the city center.)
The City Hall tourist office is open May 15 through Sept. 15, Mon. to Sat. 8.30–7, Sun. 9–5; Sept. 16 through May 14, Mon. to Fri. 8.30–4, Sat. 8.30–2.30; closed Sun. There is a second tourist office in the Sentralstasjon (at the eastern end of Karl Johans Gate), tel. 02–416221. It is open daily 8 A.M.–11 P.M. This office also helps tourists find accommodations. The *Landslaget for Reiselivet: Norge* (Norwegian Travel Association), Langkai 1, Oslo 1 (02–427044), is a good place for long-distance travel inquiries. All these offices close on national holidays.

USEFUL ADDRESSES. Travel Agents. *Winge Reisebureau* (agent for American Express), Karl Johansgt. 33/35 (412030). *Bennett Reisebureau,* Karl Johansgt, 3 (209090). *Mytravel International,* Karl Johansgt, 35 (412030). *Berg-Nansen Reisebureau,* Arbiensgt 3 (591901).
Embassies. *U.S. Embassy,* Drammensveien 18 (448550). *Canadian Embassy,* Oscarsgate 20 (466955). *British Embassy,* Ths Heftyesgate 8 (552400).
Car Hire. *Avis,* Munkedamsveien 27 (410060). *Europcar,* Fredensborgveien 33 (202150). *Hertz,* Wergelandsvn 1 (205212).
All the leading car hire companies also have desks at Fornebu airport.

TELEPHONE CODES. The telephone code for Oslo is 02. To call any number in this chapter, unless otherwise specified, this prefix must be used. Within the city, no prefix is required.

HOTELS. Oslo is well supplied with hotels in all price ranges, many offering excellent-value special deals at all times of year. For example, from the end of June to early August, 23 Oslo hotels give substantial discounts and this offer is also valid at weekends all year round. Similarly, two children under 15 can stay in their parents' room at no extra charge. Full details of all Oslo hotels are given in the tourist office's *Oslo Guide.*
The tourist office also runs an accommodations office at the Central Station for hotels, pensions and rooms in private houses. You must, however, apply in person

OSLO

at the office and no advance bookings will be taken. There is a fee of 10 NOK, NOK 5 for will be refunded when you check in. This office is open daily, 8 A.M.–11 P.M. Closed national holidays.

Deluxe

Ambassadeur. Camilla Collettsvei 15 (441835). 50 beds. Near Royal Palace, with indoor pool and sauna. AE, DC, MC, V.

Bristol. Kristian IV's Gate (415840). 220 beds, all rooms with bath. Quietly located on a side street, the Bristol has an excellent restaurant, the *Bristol Grill,* while *El Toro* is a Spanish restaurant with dancing and floor shows. There is also the *Leopard Grill,* plus a nightclub and disco on the second floor. The *Trafalgar* bar, the *Library* bar and the *Winter Garden* complete the picture. AE, MC, V.

Continental. Stortinsgate 24/26 (419060). 304 beds, all rooms with bath. Opposite the National Theater and with view of the Royal Palace. Its *Annen Étage* restaurant is one of the most elegant in Oslo, and produces excellent food. The *Loftet* is a beer and wine restaurant with billiards and disco. There is also the *Tivoli* grill, a modern and inexpensive restaurant, and the *Continental* bar near the lobby. However, of outstanding interest is the *Theatercaféen* on the ground floor, an elegant and hardly changed late-19th-century meeting place much frequented by Oslo high society and media folk. AE, DC, MC, V.

Gabelshus Hotel. Gabelsgt 16 (55 22 60). 85 rooms, all with bath. Only 5 mins. from city center in quiet street, this hotel is more like a large country house. Good restaurant, spacious bedrooms.

Grand. Karl Johansgate 31 (429390). 525 rooms, all with bath or shower and all with color T.V. On Oslo's main street and opposite Parliament and city park. Indoor pool, sauna and solarium. The *Speilen* restaurant is Oslo's most exclusive and has dancing; but the hotel's other restaurants include the *Étoile,* for French cuisine, the *Palmen,* a sandwich buffet, and the *Fritzner* grill, a top-grade spot. The *Grand Café* is a famous Oslo rendezvous, where Ibsen had his permanent chair, and with murals depicting life in late-19th-century Oslo; the *Bonanza* is a restaurant and nightclub with a Western theme. AE, DC, MC, V.

SAS Park Royal Hotel. Fornebuparken, 1324 Lysaker (120220). 500 beds, 10 suites, all with bath. Located near the airport; ten minutes from center. Restaurant seating 230, bar, sauna, fitness room, tennis, direct check-in to airport, executive office for hire; ample parking spaces. AE, DC, MC, V.

Expensive

Europa. St. Olavsgate 31 (209990). 285 beds, all rooms with bath and color T.V. Centrally located and modern. Special reductions for children. DC, MC, V.

Fønix. Dronningensgate 19 (425957). 98 beds, most rooms with bath or shower. Restaurant and bar—wine and beer only. Located near Central Station. AE, MC, V.

Gyldenløve. Bogstadveien 20 (601090). 30 beds. Bed and breakfast only, no alcohol. AE, MC, V.

Holmen Fjord. Slemmestadvn. 64, 1360 Nesbru (847280). 108 beds. 20 minutes west of Oslo on E18. Right on waterside with marina, sailboats, motor boats and windsurfboards for hire. Trim room, sports facilities, restaurant, nightclub.

Holmenkollen Park. Kongeveien 26 (146090). 278 rooms., all with bath and most with balconies. Magnificent old Norse-style building overlooking the city and located by the Holmenkollen ski jump. Luxurious annex added in 1981, but the original log-cabin part of the building remains the chief attraction. Facilities include gourmet restaurant, coffee shop, bar and nightclub, indoor pool, whirlpool, sauna, gym, squash court, curling rink and parking for 90 cars. AE, DC, MC, V.

KNA Park Avenue Hotel. Parkveien 68 (446970). 289 beds, all rooms with bath or shower. Run by the Royal Norwegian Automobile Club. Intimate restaurant and bar, and good bistro. AE, DC, MC, V.

Nobel. Karl Johansgate 33 (427 80). 148 beds., most rooms with bath or shower. On Oslo's main street, with bistro and bar. Special summer rates. Good restaurant. AE, DC, MC, V.

Rica Oslofjord. PO Box 160, 1330 Sandvika (545700). 486 beds, all rooms with bath, T.V., etc. 7 km. (4 miles) from Fornebu airport, 15 km. (9 miles) from center of Oslo. Shuttle bus. Restaurants, nightclub, bar. All rooms around marble atrium. Local bus and train services to center. AE, DC, MC, V.

Ritz. Fr. Stangsgate 3 (443960). 90 beds. Hotel and pension; with restaurant. Attractive place in quiet side street. 7-minute tram ride from center. AE, DC, MC, V.

Sara. Gunnerusgate 11–13 (429410). 464 beds, 100 rooms with bath. Opposite Central Station. *Crystal Garden* restaurant has both Scandinavian and international menus. *Glamrik* pub has Viking-style decor; coffee shop. DC, MC, V.

Savoy. Universitetsgate 11 (202655). 105 beds. Near the National Gallery; with restaurant. AE, DC, MC, V.

Scandic. Drammensveien, 1322 Høvik (121740). 230 beds, all rooms with bath or shower. At Høvik, 6 km. (4 miles) west of city on E18. Restaurant, cafeteria, sauna, parking. AE, MC, V.

Standard. Pilestredet 27 (203555). 72 beds. With restaurant. MC, V.

Stefanhotellet. Rosenkranzgate 1 (429250). 200 beds, all rooms with bath or shower. Centrally located, with popular 8th-floor restaurant—no alcohol but a superb lunch buffet, including traditional sour cream porridge eaten with smoked meats. AE, MC, V.

Triangel Hotel. Holbergs plass (208855). 192 beds, 103 rooms with bath or shower. Fully renovated in 1984. À la carte and buffet restaurant. Garage. No alcohol. AE, V.

West. Skovveien 15 (554030). 76 beds, all rooms with bath or shower. Renovations completed in 1987. Ideally located in West End near the Palace. Good restaurant; fully licensed. DC, MC, V.

Moderate

Anker Stiftelsens Yrkesskolens Hybelhus. Storgata 55 (114005). 500 beds, many rooms with 4 beds. Centrally located, with cooking facilities, supermarket, cafeteria, and restaurant. Open May to Aug. only. AE, DC, MC, V.

Bondeheimen. Rosenkrantzgate 8 (429530). 135 beds, all rooms with bath or shower. Located in a side street off Karl Johansgate in city center. Some family rooms. Cafeteria, no alcohol. Disabled access. AE, DC, MC, V.

Majorstuen. Bogstadun 64 (693495). 80 beds, all rooms with bath or shower. Friendly restaurant and pub—wine and beer only. Located in the busy shopping area of Oslo west. Reached by metro from the National Theater to Majorstuen. AE, DC, MC, V.

Munch. Munchsgate 5 (424275). 225 beds, all rooms with bath or shower. Restaurant with wine and beer. Located in pleasant surroundings near the Munch Museum in Oslo east. Disabled access. AE, DC, MC, V.

Norrøna. Grensen 19 (426400). 61 beds. With cafeteria, but no alcohol. AE, DC, MC, V.

Norum. Bygdøy Alle 53 (447990). 90 beds, all rooms with bath. In residential area west of the city center; bistro with good food. AE, DC, MC, V.

Inexpensive

Bella Vista. Årrundundveien 11B (654588). 18 beds, all rooms with bath or shower. Self-catering.

Blindern Studenthjem. Blindernveien 41 (461281). 300 beds, all rooms with bath or shower. Cafeteria. Located to the northwest of city center. Students' residence in winter.

Youth Hostel

Haraldsheim Youth Hostel, Haraldsheimvn 4 (155043). 4 km. (2½ miles) from city center, with 300 beds, family rooms, restaurant, lounge, T.V. Great views across Oslofjord. Take tram 1 from National Theater to Sinsen. Closed Christmas week.

OSLO

Camping

Bogstad Camp and Tourist Center, Ankerveien 117, (507680). Open all year. Take bus 41 to Bogstad. Situated by large lake in scenic surroundings. Windsurfing, swimming a few mins. from Holmenkollen.

Ekeberg Camping, (198568). 3 km. (just under 2 miles) from city center. Open June 20 to Aug. 20. Bus 24 from Jernbanetorget or 74 from Parliament.

Stubljan Camping, (612706). Bus 75 to Ingierstrand from Oslo S.

HOW TO GET AROUND. By bus and tram. The bus and tram network is generally good. The heart of the network is by the National Theater in the city center. All stops here give details of schedules, but details are also available from the tourist office. There is a flat fare of NOK 12 for all journeys, but there is an "inner circle" ticket, NOK 6, for a limited area in the center. A number of good-value discount tickets are available. Best of all is the *Oslo Card* (available from the tourist office) which gives unlimited free travel on all public transport for one, two or three days at a cost of NOK 75, 110, and 140 respectively (children half price). The *Oslo Card* also entitles you to free admission to museums, discounts on car rentals and in certain restaurants, and on sightseeing tours. Alternatively, there is a *Tourist Ticket*, again available from the tourist office, which gives 24 hours' unlimited travel on all public transport for 30 NOK. (children half price). There are also two multi-journey tickets called *maxikort* and *minikort*. The first, costing NOK 120, gives you 14 coupons, each entitling you to one hour's travel with unlimited transfers. The second, costing NOK 40, contains four coupons. Both are half price for children.

By metro. The Oslo metro, currently divided into eastern and western sectors—the western sector radiating from the National Theater and the eastern sector from Stortinget—was linked in 1986. A single ticket, valid for one hour and no transfers costs NOK 12. But the Oslo Card is also good for metro travel. The most important line for most visitors is that from the National Theater to the Frognerseter station on the Holmenkollen line high above the city. But the metro services, some supplemented by electric trains, also extend into the suburbs.

By taxi. Cabs are expensive but numerous. They can be hailed in the street if the light on the roof is on, as long as they are more than 100 yards from the rank, but there are also cab stands at the Central and West rail stations. Otherwise, call 388090 (or 388080 for an advance booking, at least 1 hour in advance). There is an additional charge for more than two passengers and at night. Tip around 10% of the fare.

By bicycle. The tourist office can supply lists of all places where bikes can be rented. Deposit NOK 200. Oslo, not least because of its small scale, is a delightful city to cycle around, though hilly in parts, and rides out into the country are easy to make.

On foot. The city is easily explored on foot and the tourist office can supply lists of suggested walks.

TOURS. *H.M. Kristiansen* provides three tours, all lasting three hours, and all starting from the City Hall harbor side. Tickets are available on the bus or from the Oslo Tourist Information Office. The "Oslo Highlights" morning tour goes to the Vigeland Sculpture Park, Holmenkollen, the Viking Ship Museum, and the *Kon-Tiki*. May through Sept., daily at 10 A.M. NOK 100 adults, NOK 50 children. The "Morning Sightseeing" tour visits Akerhus Castle, Vigeland Sculpture Park, the Munch Museum, and Holmenkollen. Apr. through Oct., daily at 10 A.M. NOK 100 adults, NOK 50 children. The "Afternoon Tour" goes to the Norwegian Folk Museum, Viking Ships, *Kon-Tiki*, and the Polar Ship *Fram*. Apr. through Oct., daily at 2.30 P.M. NOK 120.

The *Oslo Guide* brochure (free from the tourist office) has several walking tours on its map. Some go farther afield and link up with public transportation. Taxis also give sightseeing tours in English for a fee of NOK 200 per hour. Cal 02-388090 or 02-388000 to reserve a personal tour.

If you're allergic to crowds, you'll get a more authentic picture of life in Oslo's seaside suburbs by taking one of the regular passenger ferries that ply between the city and Nesodden. Travel by return boat, or get off at Nesodden to explore, and return by a later boat. Ferries start from Aker Brygge.

Or you can take the bus (starts from Grønlandstorg, but best entered outside the University), to Sundvollen, final destination Hønefoss. For the next hour you will see some of the most magnificent scenery to be found in the Oslo region as you wind and climb your way around the precipitous edges of the crystal blue Tyri Fjord. At Sundvollen you can walk up Dronningveien, or go by car, to the top of Krokkleiva with famous views from Kongens Utsikt (the King's View), one of the most beautiful in Norway. The walk is quite stiff (takes about 3 hours altogether). Alternatively, take the 36 bus to Jevnaker, where you can visit the Hadeland Glass Works, the largest of its kind in Scandinavia. Founded in 1762, the work is still performed by craftsmen and visitors may see glassblowing, cutting and etching of crystal.

Blaafarvevaerket, a former cobalt works, at Åmot, is also worth a visit, and is best reached by car or sightseeing bus. Open late May through late Sept., Mon. to Sat. 10-8.

English language guides are available from tourist office. All guides are licensed.

MUSEUMS. Most cities in the world have museums of the traditional kind, and Oslo has its share—but in addition, Oslo has a series of unique museums, particularly its "one man" and "one ship" museums.

Barnekunst Museet (International Children's Art Museum). Lille Frogner Alle 4. Children's art—drawings, paintings, ceramics, tapestries and handicrafts collected from more than 100 countries. Children's workshop. Open all year; closed Mon. and Thurs. Admission NOK 20, reduced rates for groups, families, children.

Forsvarsmuseet (The Norwegian Armed Forces Museum). Situated in the old arsenal building in the lower grounds of Akershus fortress. A new construction, when completed, will cover the history of Norwegian defence from the late Middle Ages to contemporary times. Open May through Sept., Mon., Wed., and Fri. 10-3, Tues. and Thurs. 10-8, Sat. 10-4; Oct. through Apr., Mon. to Fri. 10-3, Sat. 10-4, Sun. 11-4. Admission free.

Framhuset (The Polar Exploration Ship). *Fram* was built by the well-known designer Colin Archer for Nansen's Polar expedition 1893-96. It was also used by Otto Sverdrup 1889-1902, and later by Roald Amundsen on his expedition to the South Pole 1910-12. Open Mon. to Sat. 10-6, Sun. 11-6; closed in winter. Admission NOK 7.

Henie-Onstad Kunstsenter (The Sonja Henie-Niels Onstad Art Center). At Høvikodden, 11 km. (7 miles) from Oslo. The Center was opened in 1968 and contains a permanent collection of 20th-century art, donated by Sonja Henie and her husband Niels Onstad. Displays are changed regularly to reflect current trends and ideas in literature, film, dance, music, architecture and applied arts: other events like concerts are also staged here. Buses 32, 34, 36 and 37 leave regularly from the city center. Open all year Mon. to Fri. 9 A.M.-9.30 P.M., Sat. and Sun. 11-9.30. Admission NOK 20 adults, NOK 10 students, children, servicemen and senior citizens; NOK 40 family ticket.

Historisk Museum (The Historical Museum). Frederiksgate 2. Contains the University's Ethnographical Museum, Numismatic Collection and its Collection of Antiquities, Viking artefacts and jewelry. The collection from the Middle Ages is Oslo's richest art collection from that period. Open mid-Sept. through mid-May, Tues. to Sun. 12-3. Admission free.

Kon-Tiki Museet (The Kon-Tiki Museum). At Bygdøynes, the museum contains the raft on which Thor Heyerdahl and five companions drifted over 8,000 km. (5,000 miles) across the Pacific from Peru to Polynesia. It also houses the 14-meter (46-foot) reed boat *Ra II* and items belonging to it from Heyerdahl's 1970 expedition across the Atlantic Ocean. Open mid-May through Aug., daily 10-6; Sept. and

OSLO

Oct., daily 10.30–5; Nov. through mid-May, daily 10.30–4. Admission NOK 10 adults, NOK 4 children, NOK 6 students, servicemen and senior citizens.

Kunstindustrimuseet (The Museum of Applied Art). St. Olavsgate 1. Collections of both Norwegian and foreign applied arts from the Middle Ages through to the 20th century. Displayed are furniture, silver, glass, ceramics and textiles. Of note is the Baldishol tapestry, woven in Hedmark in the 1180s, one of the five tapestries which have been preserved from the Romanesque era. Open all year Tues. to Fri. 11–3, Sat. and Sun. 12–4; late opening Tues. 7 P.M.–9 P.M. Admission NOK 10 adults, NOK 5 students, servicemen and senior citizens, children free. Free admission in mid-winter.

Kunstnerforbundet (Artists Association). Kjeld Stubsgate 3. Contemporary Norwegian art, also handicrafts. Open July through Aug., Mon. to Fri. 10–4, Sat. 10–2; Sept. through June, Mon. to Fri. 10–5, Sat. 10–3, Sun. 12–4.

Kunstnernes Hus (Artists' Center). Wergelandsveien 17. Changing exhibitions of contemporary Norwegian and foreign paintings, sculpture and prints. Open Tues. to Fri. 10–6, Sat. and Sun. 12–4; closed Mon. Admission NOK 10 adults, NOK 5 children.

Munch-Museet (The Munch Museum). Tøyengaten 53. In 1940 Edvard Munch bequeathed the City of Oslo many of his works; paintings, drawings, water colours, prints and sculptures, books, letters and private papers. The collection has been increased by gifts from individuals. Lectures and concerts. Guided tours available. Open Tues. to Sat. 10–8, Sun. 12–8; closed Mon. Admission free during low season (mid-Sept. to mid-May); mid-May to mid-Sept. admission NOK 10.

Nasjonalgalleriet (The National Gallery). Universitetsgaten 13. Norway's largest public collection, with emphasis on Norwegian painting, sculpture and lithographs. Also has a collection of French and modern European paintings. Open Mon. to Fri. 10–4, Sat. 10–3, Sun. 12–3; late opening Wed. and Thurs. 6 P.M.–8 P.M. Admission free.

De Naturhistoriske Museet (Natural History Museum). Sarsgata 1. Botanical garden and conservatories, mineralogical and geological museum, paleontological museum with fossil plants and animals, and zoological museum. Botanical gardens open May through Aug., Mon. to Fri. 7 A.M.–8 P.M., Sat. and Sun. 10–8; Oct. through Dec., Mon. to Fri. 7–7, Sat. and Sun. 10–7; Jan. through Mar., Mon. to Fri. 7–5, Sat. and Sun. 10–5; Apr., Mon. to Fri. 7–6, Sat. and Sun. 10–6. All other museums open all year, Tues. to Sun. 12–3, except the Botanical Museum which is open Wed. to Sat. 12–3.

Norsk Arkitektmuseum (Norwegian Architecture Museum). Josefinesgt. 32. Alternating exhibitions. Library. Open Mon. to Fri. 9–3; closed Sat. and Sun. Admission free.

Norsk Folkemuseum (The Norwegian Folk Museum). Museumsveien 10 Bygdøy. Outdoor collection of 170 buildings, including 13th-century stave church. Indoor collection designed to illustrate Norway's urban and rural culture. Henrik Ibsen's study, a Lapp (Sami) collection and a pharmacy museum are also to be seen here. In summer: restaurant, folk dancing, concerts. Open mid-May through Aug., Mon. to Sat. 10–6, Sun. 11–6; Sept., Mon. to Sat. 11–4, Sun. 12–5; Oct. through mid-May, Mon. to Sat. 11–4, Sun. 12–3. Admission NOK 20 adults (NOK 10 in winter), NOK 10 children (NOK 4 in winter).

Norsk Hjemmefrontmuseum (Norway's Resistance Museum). Situated in an old building in the grounds of Akershus Fortress, close to the monument to patriots who gave their lives in World War II. Attempts to give a true picture of major events in Norway during the German occupation. Lecture hall, library, war publication archives. Open May through Sept., Mon. to Sat. 10–4, Sun. 11–4; Oct. through Apr., Mon. to Sat. 10–3, Sun. 11–4. Admission NOK 10.

Norsk Sjøfartsmuseum (The Norwegian Maritime Museum). Bygdøynes. Contains a collection of boats used along the Norwegian coast, models of sailing ships and a model shipyard. Ocean navigation is presented through models, paintings and objects. Slide projectors, radar instruments, library, restaurants, cafeteria. Open May through Sept., daily 10–8; Oct. through Dec., Mon., Wed., Fri. and Sat. 10.30–4, Tues., Thurs. and Sun. 10.30–5; Mar. and Apr., Mon., Wed., Fri. and Sat. 10.30–

4, Tues. and Thurs. 10.30–8, Sun. 10.30–5. Admission NOK 10 adults, NOK 4 children.

Norsk Teknisk Museum (Norwegian Museum of Science & Industry). Kjelsåsvn. 143, (adjoining Frysja park). Vast exhibition halls displaying industrial and technical development in Norway right up to the space age. Telecommunications exhibition with models. Open Tues. to Sun. 10–7; closed Mon. Admission NOK 10. Cafeteria, picnic area, swimming in Frysja park. Open mid-May through mid-Sept., Tues. to Sun. 10–7; mid-Sept. through mid-May, Tues. 10–7, Wed. to Sun. 10–4. Admission NOK 10 adults, NOK 5 children.

Oslo Bymuseum (The City Museum). Frognerveien 67. Situated in Frogner Hovedgård (Frogner Manor), built around 1790. Contains maps, portrait gallery, views of Oslo, rooms furnished as in former days. New display showing development of Oslo from Viking times to present day with models. Open May through Aug., Mon. to Fri. 10–6, Sat. and Sun. 11–5; Sept. through mid-Dec. and Jan. through Apr., Mon. to Fri. 10–4, Sat. and Sun. 11–4. Admission NOK 10 adults, NOK 5 children.

Oslo Kunstforening (Oslo Art Association). Rådhusgate 19. Situated in residence dating from 1626; exhibitions of paintings, sculpture, prints and etchings. Open Tues. to Fri. 11–5, Sat. 11–4, Sun. 12–4.

Postmuseet (Postal Museum). Dronningensgt. 15. Contains displays of stamps, postal accessories, and the development of communications over three centuries. Open Mon. to Fri. 10–3, Sat. 10–1; closed Sun. Admission free.

Skimuseet (The Ski Museum). Collections of skis, including the 2,500 year old Øvrebø ski and part of Nansen's and Amundsen's polar equipment. Shows history of skiing and ski jumping. A lift gives access to the 55–meter (180–foot) tower, which has a magnificent view. Open Apr., daily 10–3; May, daily 10–5; June, daily 10–7; July through mid-Aug., daily 9 A.M.–10 P.M.; mid- to late Aug., daily 10–7; Sept., daily 10–5; Oct. through Dec., daily 10–3. Admission NOK 12 adults, inclusive ticket (museum, ski jump and observation tower) NOK 23, NOK 6 children, students and servicemen for museum only.

Skøytemuseet (Skating Museum). Frogner Stadium, entrance Middelthungsgt. Focus on Norwegian speed-skating champions. Open Wed. 6–8 P.M. and Sat. 12 noon–2 P.M., or by appointment (tel. 500993). Admission free.

Sporveismuseet (Transport Museum). Vognhall 5, Slemdalsvn. 1–3. Norway's only collection of veteran trams and buses. Pictures and artifacts connected with public transport. Open Sun. all year, 12–3; Apr. through Sept., Sat. also, 12–3. Admission NOK 10 adults, NOK 5 children.

Teatermuseet (Theater Museum). Nedre Slottsgt. 1. On second floor above Gamle Rådhus restaurant. Traces the development of Oslo's theater from the beginning of the 19th century up to 1950. It is situated in one of the oldest buildings in Oslo, built around 1600. Open Wed. 11–3, Sun. 12–4. Admission NOK. 5.

Vigelandmuseet (The Vigeland Museum). Nobelsgate 32. Formerly Gustav Vigeland's studio and residence. It contains 1,650 sculptures, 3,700 woodcuts, 423 plates for woodcuts and around 11,000 sketches. Concerts in summer. Guided tours. Open May through Oct., Tues. to Sat. 12–7; Nov. through Apr., Tues. to Sat. 1–7.

Vikingskiphuset (The Viking Ships and Archeological Finds). Huk Aveny 35, Bygdøy. Remarkable relics of the Viking Age, all found near the Oslo fjord. Open May through Sept. daily 10–6; Oct., daily 11–5; Nov. and Dec., daily 11–4; mid-Jan. through Mar., daily 11–3. Admission NOK 10 adults, NOK 5 children and students.

PARKS, ZOOS AND GARDENS. Botanisk Hage (Botanical Garden and Museum). Trondheimsveien 23. Hot houses, geological and zoological collections. Open Tues. to Sun. 12–3; closed Mon. Admission free.

Dyreparken Tusenfryd (Zoo). Located in the suburb of Ås. Opened in June 1988. Animals, funfair, minigolf, cafeteria. Open daily throughout the summer. Admission NOK 90 (children 70).

Frognerparken (The Vigeland Sculptures in Frogner Park). Gustav Vigeland's gigantic work—a world of people carved in granite, iron and bronze. Open-air

OSLO

swimming pool, cafeteria, sports arena, tennis courts, restaurants. Open 24 hours a day all year. Admission free.

Gamlebyen Ruiner in park with archeological excavations, part of the center of ecclesiastical affairs in medieval Oslo. Open summer only. Admission free.

Sørenga Ruiner. Ruins of the earliest buildings in Oslo: The Royal Palace and the Maria Church from approx. 1050. This was the king's center of power. Open summer only. Admission free.

HISTORIC BUILDINGS AND SITES.

Akershus Slott og Festning (Akershus Castle). One of Oslo's most formidable buildings, first built by Haakon V around 1300. It was then rebuilt by Christian IV around 1620 and has subsequently been restored and redecorated. It contains the royal mausoleums, state apartments (16th cent.) and World War II Resistance Museum and the Armed Forces Museum. Open Mon. to Sat. 10–4, Sun. 12.30–4. Admission NOK 10.

Bogstad Gård (Bogstad Manor). Sørkedalen. Patrician manor built around 1760, once owned by prime minister Peder Anker. Landscaped garden and art treasures. Open mid-May through mid-Sept., Wed. 6–7, Sun. 12–5. Admission NOK 20 adults, NOK 5 children.

Damstredet. Picturesque wooden houses from early 19th century; many are today the homes of artists.

Domkirken (Oslo Cathedral). At Stortorvet. Built between 1694 and 1699, the exterior was restored in 1849–50. The interior was restored in 1949–50. Altar piece and pulpit from 1699. Concerts. Open Mon. to Fri. 10–3, Sat. 10–1; closed Sun. except divine service 11 and 7.30. Admission free.

Gamle Aker Kirke (Old Aker Church). Akersbakken 26. Built around 1100, this is the oldest stone church in Scandinavia still in use as parish church. Tues. and Thurs. 12–2, Sun. service 11. Admission free.

Hovedøya Klosterruiner (Monastery Ruins). Constructed by Cistercian Monks, who arrived from Kirkstead in England in 1147. Ferry from Vippetangen to open-air site. Admission free.

Konserthuset (Concert Hall). Johan Svendsens plass. Inaugurated 1977, designed by Gøsta Åbergh. Facade covered with polished light Tolga granite. Concert hall and chamber music hall. Concerts of all kinds. Open for touring by appointment. See daily press and *Oslo This Week*.

Ladegården (Oslo Ladegård). Oslogate 13. Medieval Bishop's residence. The ecclesiastic center of ancient Oslo, together with the St. Hallvard Church. Later the Mayor's residence then pleasure residence. The present Baroque building dates from the 17th century, with vaults from the Middle Ages. Restored by the City of Oslo 1957–68. Open May through Sept., Wed. 6–7, Sun. 1–2. Admission free.

Oscarshall. Bygdøy. Pleasure palace built in 1847–52 by King Oscar I of Norway and Sweden. Open June through Sept., Sun. 11–4. Admission NOK 5 adults, NOK 1 children.

Rådhuset (Oslo City Hall). Foundation stone laid in 1931, inaugurated in 1950 for the celebration of Oslo's 900th anniversary. Lavishly decorated by Norway's leading painters and sculptors during the 1930s and 40s. Guided tours available. Open Apr. through Sept., Mon. to Sat. 10–3, Sun. 12–3; Jan. through Mar., Mon. to Sat. 11–2, Sun. 12–3. Admission free.

Slottet (Royal Palace). Drammensveien 1. Constructed 1825–48. Residence of King Olav V, King of Norway. Public admitted to the park only. Changing of the guard takes places at 1.30 P.M. When the King is in residence the band of the Royal Guard plays Mon. to Fri.

Stortinget (Parliament). Karl Johansgt. Built 1861–66. Richly decorated by contemporary Norwegian artists. Open July through Aug., Mon. to Sat. 11–3. Guided tours July through mid-Sept. at 11, 12 and 1. Admission free.

Tryvannstårnet (Tryvann Observation Tower). The largest observation tower in the north, with an optical horizon covering about 30,044 sq. km. (11,600 sq. miles). It is situated on the Tryvann hill on the outskirts of Oslo. Lift, binoculars, refreshments, souvenirs. Reached by Holmenkollen Railway from the National Theater to Frognerseteren, then a 25-minute walk. Open Mar. through Apr., Tues. to Sun. 10–6; May, daily 10–8; June and July, daily 9.30 A.M.–10 P.M.; Aug., daily 10–8; Sept., daily 10–6; Oct., Tues. to Sun. 10–4; Nov. through Feb., Sat. and Sun. 10–4. Admission NOK 11. adults, NOK 6 children.

Universitetet (Oslo University). Karl Johansgt. 47. The *Aula* (Hall) of the University with murals by Edvard Munch. Open July, Mon. to Fri. 12–2, otherwise on request by calling 02–330070 ext. 756.

SPORTS. Swimming. There are excellent bathing beaches on both sides of the fjord, all easily reached by bus from the City Hall. Out at Bygdøy, there is a popular beach at Huk, plus one reserved for nudists. On the east side you'll find: Ingierstrand, Katten, Hvervenbukta, Ljanskollen and Bestemorstrand, all reached by bus 75. On the west side, Hvalstrand, Asker, reached by bus nos. 261, 252, half-an-hour from the center. Also good are the two adjoining islands of Langøyene, owned by the city and with good sandy beaches; take the ferry from pier 4. Water temperatures in July and August average about 68° F (20° C). There are a number of very popular swimming pools dotted around the city, of which the most popular are by the Vigeland sculpture park and at Tøyen by the Munch Museum.

Tennis. Courts are available at Frogner Stadium near Vigeland Park.

Fishing. Good trout fishing can be had in many places around the city. Permits are necessary but may be bought at the many sports shops in Oslo and in the fishing chalets of Kobberhaughytta, Kikutstua and Løvliseter, where fishermen can also stay overnight.

Golf. The Bogstad golf course is 10 km. (6 miles) from the city center, enjoys unrivalled surroundings, and offers excellent golf from May to October.

Winter Sports. The season runs from Christmas to the end of March. There is fine skiing country in the hills around the city. Although the emphasis is naturally on cross country rather than downhill skiing, there are many fine slalom hills in Oslo and environs. All the trails and runs around the city can easily be reached from the center of town, and many are also floodlit. Ski schools and ski rental companies are plentiful. In addition, there are a number of skating and curling rinks and tobogganing trails. Details of all from the tourist office.

MUSIC, MOVIES AND THEATERS. Music. The musical life of the Norwegian capital is impressive, to say the least. The Oslo Philharmonic is the city's principal orchestra and has achieved much renown under its conductor Mariss Jansons for its recordings of Tchaikovsky's symphonies. It has frequent visits from soloists and conductors of international fame. Concerts are normally held in the *Konserthuset,* the Oslo Concert Hall, at Ruseløkkveien, a modern and lavish building completed in 1977. As well as the main auditorium there is also a smaller hall for chamber music and folk dance performances in summer on Mon. and Thurs. at 9 P.M.

In addition to the orchestra, the city has a thriving opera and ballet company, whose season generally lasts from September to June. Performances are most usually given at the *Den Norske Opera,* Storgaten 21. But there are also some performances at the *Henie-Onstad Art Center* at Høvikodden. For details of performances, see *Oslo This Week.*

Movies. There are numerous movie theaters around town. See the daily press or ask at the tourist office to see what's playing and when. A wide range of American and British movies are shown. Films are always screened in their original language with Norwegian subtitles. Smoking is not permitted in Norwegian cinemas.

Theaters. Oslo's principal theater is the *Nationalteatret* at Stortingsgaten 15 in the heart of the city. The main stage has now been renovated after a backstage fire. Note, however, that it is not open during the summer. Performances are in Norwegian, naturally enough, making their appeal somewhat limited as far as foreign visitors are concerned. But if you know, say, an Ibsen play well, it may be worth the experience. In the same building is the little *Amfiscenen,* used for both classical drama and more experimental work.

Among Oslo's other leading theaters are the *ABC Teatret,* St. Olavs plass 1; *Det Norske Teatret,* Kristian IV's gt. 8, Norway's most modern theater, opened in 1985, which presents works in *Nynorsk* or "new" Norwegian; the *Oslo Nye Teater,* Rosenkrantzgt. 10, which presents predominantly comedies and musicals, though again principally in Norwegian; the *Dukketeatret* in the City Museum, the Bymuseet, at Frognerveien 67, a puppet theater and an excellent place for families and children; the *Centralteateret,* Akersgaten 38, presents plays for children and young people. At Aker Brygge you will find smaller theater companies performing. For details of all performances, check *Oslo This Week.*

Finally, there are performances of folk dancing throughout the summer. The best and most colorful are held on Sundays at the *Folk Museum* at Bygdøy, and at the *Oslo Concert Hall* during July & Aug., but there are also displays, which you can join in if the spirit so moves you, at *Bygdelagssamskipnaden,* Nordahl Brunsgate 22, in the winter.

SHOPPING. In Norway, as in the other Scandinavian countries, you will find evidence of the peasant heritage in handicrafts—ceramics and textile weaving, wood carving and decorative painting. As prices are controlled, you may as well shop in Oslo where you will have the greatest choice. About 20% is charged (included in the price) in Value Added Tax (VAT), which will be refunded to any visitor who spends more than NOK 300 in any one shop. Ask for a special tax-free cheque and show your passport. All articles purchased must be presented together with the required tax-free cheque at the tax-free service counter at ports, airports, and border posts. The VAT will then be refunded minus 4½% service charge.

Glasmagasinet, at Stortorget 10, and *Steen & Strøm,* at Koagensgate 23, are Oslo's foremost department stores. The quayside *Aker Brygge* stores stay open late, until 8 P.M. (7 P.M. on Thursdays).

Arts and Crafts. *Basarhalene (Bazaar Arcade),* behind Oslo Cathedral, is a center for applied art, open all year. Artists present their own work. *Forum,* Rosenkrantzgate 7 (opposite the Bristol Hotel), has permanent exhibitions of contemporary Norwegian arts and crafts. Each item on display must first be accepted by a jury.

A similar establishment is *Norway Designs,* Stortingsgate 28 (entrance from Roald Amundsengate), the capital's largest center for the exhibition and sale of top quality Norwegian applied art, with special facilities for export.

For the most indigenous Norwegian handicraft try *Husfliden* (Norwegian Association for Home Arts and Crafts), Møllergate 4, near the cathedral and just behind the *Glasmagasin* department store. A non-profit organization for preserving and continuing the traditions of Norwegian handicrafts and rustic culture, it offers a wide range of home industry products including the well-known knitted sweaters, woven tapestries, dolls in national costumes, woodcarvings, ceramics etc.

Pewter, Ceramics and Crystal. A great Norwegian specialty is its pewterware: sugar bowls and creamers, all sizes of trays and bowls, candlesticks and pitchers. With a light-finish technique, Gunnar Havstad has created the best contemporary works, whereas the Groseth pewter bears the marks of the heavy sandstone presses that formed them after the old English manner.

Tinnboden, Tordenskioldsgate 7, has a good selection, as well as a splendid array of dolls in colorful regional dresses. *Glasmagasin* Department Store has a good selection of all three.

These ceramics are perhaps more primitive than those you have found in Denmark and Sweden—the plates and bowls often thicker and embellished with peasant figures and symbols of the life they know. Norway's best-known porcelain factory is Porsgrund. Also outstanding are the pottery works at Egersund and Stavanger, and the Hadeland Glass Works. Their products, however, should be available in Oslo pottery and ceramics stores and in larger department stores. Since their production, though of top quality, cannot incorporate all the vigorous ideas of young creative innovators, the works of individual craftsmen are equally numerous. Originality and taste are the rule in even the most common art glass, ceramics, and porcelain.

For the very best in crystal and glass etching be sure to go to *Christiania Glasmagasin,* Stortorget 10. In the glass department here you will find distinguished modern glassware, amusing cocktail glasses, and exquisite art glass in a range of delectable colors.

Knitwear. All department stores have good stocks of traditional Norwegian sweaters, but certain specialist shops also have particularly fine designs. Among them are:

Heimen, Rosenkrantzgt. 8, with handknitted sweaters and mittens. They can also make up authentic Norwegian costumes—each valley has its own—to order.

The *Oslo Sweater Shop* is in the arcade under the Hotel Scandinavia; *Maurtua,* Fridjof Nansensplass, opposite the City Hall, has a wide range of knitwear and textiles; *Trønderstna,* Vikaterrace, also has textiles and knitwear and a good selection of wool and patterns. If you can't find what you're looking for in these shops, try *Steen and Strøm,* the largest department store in Oslo.

Sports Shops. In Oslo the sports lover comes into his own. *Gresvig Sports Shop,* Storgata 20, also *Christiania Glasmagasin* at Stortorget 10, are probably the best in town and, in this sportsman's paradise, that means a lot. Norwegian packs, flies for your fishing rod—or the rod itself—skis, any kind of sports equipment for use during your trek through the countryside or for shipment home (which *Gresvig's* will happily and efficiently handle for you) are featured here.

Norway's famous ski jumper, *Sigmund Ruud,* has a shop at Kirkeveien 57.

RESTAURANTS. Oslo is singularly blessed with great numbers of excellent restaurants, particularly at the top end of the scale. Similarly, many of the more expensive hotels also have first-class restaurants, details of which are given in the Hotel listings above. But bear in mind that expensive restaurants here are very expensive, even by Scandinavian standards, while even a quick bite at one of the fast food spots, of which there are many, will also cost significantly more than in the U.S. Alcohol, especially wine, is also extremely pricey in all restaurants, with a humble bottle of table wine costing upwards of $35. Be careful!

For fast food, try the city center, which has any number of pizza and hamburger joints and small trendy cafés much favored by the young. Likewise, both the *Steen & Strøm* and *Glasmagasin* department stores have several restaurants featuring lunch buffets, ranging from the inexpensive to something a little more elaborate. A fair number of restaurants are closed on Sundays.

Expensive

Aker Brygge. Oslo's quayside pleasure park has restaurants in all price ranges and all nationalities.

Annen Etage. Hotel Continental, Stortingsgt 24/26 (419060). One of the very few Norwegian restaurants that has been internationally recognized. Excellent atmosphere and cuisine. Open daily except Sat.; piano music on Sun. from 3–7. AE, DC, MC, V.

Bagatelle. Bygdøy Alle 3 (446397). Sophisticated and elegant French spot to the west of the Royal Palace with excellent food. AE, DC, MC, V.

Blom. Karl Johansgate 41 (427300). Traditional artists' restaurant for nearly a century. Norwegian and international cuisine. Lunch buffet, "Fru Blom", lively café with outdoor terrace in more moderate price range; pâté, cheese, snacks and vintage wine by the glass. MC, V.

Caravelle. Fornebu Airport (122929). International restaurant overlooking the runways with excellent salad bar. Also has less expensive *Caravelle Cabin* (M), for pizzas, steaks and sandwiches, and *Caravelle Cafeteria* (M). AE, DC, MC, V.

De Fem Stuer. Holmenkollen Park Hotel, Kongevn. 26 (146090). Gourmet restaurant in traditional 19th-century timber building furnished in period style. Expensive, but good value; and interiors alone justify a visit. AE, DC, MC, V.

Frognerseteren. Holmenkollveien 200 (143736). By the Holmenkollen ski jump with spectacular views over the city. Old timber building in traditional Norse style with open hearth and Norwegian specialties. A must. MC, DC, V.

Grotten. Wergelandsveien 5 (209604). Located near the Royal Palace. Small, intimate restaurant with extensive à la carte menu. Closed on Sun. AE, MC.

OSLO

Holmenkollen. Holmenkollveien 119 (146226). Also up on the hill by the ski jump and with the same wonderful views. AE, DC, MC, V. Cafeteria (M) in same building.

La Brochette. Dr. Maudsgt 1/3 (416733). Select your own steak in this fine French spot; distinctive milieu and personal attention. AE, MC, V.

Ludvik. Torggt. 16 (42 88 80) (also at Aker Brygge). Specializes in fish. Situated in old city baths building. Good and unusual menu. AE, DC, MC, V.

Mølla. Sagvn 21 (375450). Charmingly-renovated spinning mill on the Aker river. Unique 19th-century atmosphere. Live music, cabaret and dancing in candlelit vaults; fish and game a specialty. AE, DC, MC, V.

La P'tite Cuisine. Solligaten 2 (444575). Grill restaurant with French atmosphere and cuisine in the west of the city. Fine wines. AE, DC, MC, V.

Tre Kokker. Drammensveien 30 (442650). Norwegian-style charcoal grill with excellent international cuisine near the Royal Palace; run by Norway's top gourmet. Dancing in bar. AE, DC, MC, V.

Moderate

Bella Napoli. Storgt. 26 (410052). Italian dishes and pizza. Friendly, informal atmosphere. Popular with young people. AE, MC, V.

Carl Johan Bistro. Karl Johansgt. 37 (417790). Good lunch buffet, special "dish of the day." Right in center of main street. AE, DC, MC, V.

Charly's. SAS Hotel Scandinavia (entrance from street only), St. Olavsgt. (113000). Salad bar, light meals, wine and beer; busy, noisy atmosphere. AE, DC, MC, V.

Engebret Café. Bankplassen 1 (360783). Newly renovated. Famous for its fish; cozy interior; piano music. Closed on Sun. AE, DC, MC, V.

Gamle Raadhus (old Town Hall), Nedre Slottsgt. 1 (420107). Oslo's oldest restaurant in building from 1640. Specializes in fish; noted for mussels and fresh shrimp. Closed Sun. AE, DC, MC, V.

Mamma Rosa. Øvre Slottsgt. 12 (420130). Informal Italian atmosphere, guitar music in evening; pasta and pizza as well as international menu. AE, MC, V.

La Mer. Pilestredet 31 (203445/203469). Fish and shellfish specialties. Closed Sun. AE, DC, V.

L'Océan. M/S Pibervigen, Rådhusbrygge 6, (419996/419997). Good fish restaurant on ship moored in front of the City Hall. In summer tours down the fjord during the day. Closed Sun.

Peking House. St. Olavsgt. 23 (114878). Good Chinese food. Pleasant interior, quick service. Near SAS hotel. One of three of the same name.

Stortorvets (Estasje) Gjestiveri. Grensen 1 (428863). Traditional restaurant in building dating from 1700. Outdoor courtyard service in summer. A genuine Christiania inn. AE, DC, MC, V.

Storyville, Chez Bendriss. Universitetsgt. 26 (429635). French and creole cuisine—barbecued spare ribs a specialty, and so is the Dixieland jazz. In same building, *Humla* (424420), with live music, cabaret, dancing in young atmosphere. Closed Sun. AE, DC, MC, V.

Theatercaféen. Stortingsgt. 24/26. Oslo's most visited restaurant; in the Hotel Continental. Good food, but best known for its lively, sophisticated atmosphere. AE, DC, MC, V.

Tostrupkjelleren. Karl Johansgt. 25 (421470). International restaurant, popular with those in the media; piano music. Closed on Sun. AE, DC, MC, V.

Inexpensive

Albin Upp (Gallery and Art Café). Briskebyv. 42 (557192). A real find for lovers of something different. Intimate wine and snack bar in renovated farmer's cottage right in the center of town. Contemporary Norwegian art on display includes graphics, jewelry, ceramics, watercolors. Open all year, but from June to Aug. on weekdays only 12–5. Tram no. 1 (Briskeby) from National Theater stops outside; get off at Uranienborg school stop. Good parking.

OSLO

Café Frølich. Drammensvn. 20 (443737). Oslo's only music café in old Viennese style. Several instruments including grand piano used by music students or any guest competent enough to play them—anything from classical to jazz and rock. Varied menu of small dishes, plus ice cream specials.

Café Sjakk Matt. Haakon VII's gt. 5 (423227). Popular with younger set. Snacks, salads, sandwiches, hot and cold meals.

Den Lille Fondue. President Harbitzgate 18 (441960). Oslo's only fondue restaurant; small and intimate; music. AE, DC, MC, V.

Herregårdsbroen. Frognerparken (552089). Features an open-air restaurant with à la carte menu. Open in summer.

Kaffistova, Grillstova, Torgstova. Recommended chain of coffee shops and cafeterias with generous helpings; check the *Oslo Guide* for locations.

Pinocchio Rica. Bogstadvn 53 (607786). Just by Colosseum cinema. Cheap and good. Closed Sun. AE, DC, MC, V.

Vega Vertshus Friskpartrestaurant. Munkedamsvn. 36 (428557). Vegetarian, salads, hot and cold meals; near National Theater station. AE, DC, MC, V.

NIGHTLIFE. A combination of high prices and puritanism have long conspired to render Norwegian nightlife a somewhat low key, not to say dormant affair. However, despite still strict licensing laws—no spirits can be served after midnight and not at all on Sundays and national holidays, and a bottle of scotch in a nightclub will certainly cost in excess of $50—the oil boom and its attendant influx of big-spending oil men, coupled with Norway's high standard of living, have resulted in a gradual hotting up of the nighttime tempo over the last few years. Over 90 restaurants, cafés and nightclubs are open after 1 A.M. Among the most popular spots are: *Sardines, Stravinsky* (very expensive), *Barock,* and *Cruise* (Aker Brygge).

A number of the larger and more expensive hotels have cabarets and dancing—either discos or to bands. Similarly, some, though by no means all, restaurants have entertainment of one sort or another. See our *Hotel* and *Restaurant* listings for details. In addition there are also a growing number of regular night spots, though their ranks are still thin. Most, not least as a result of their scarcity, tend to get very crowded, especially at weekends. The city also boasts a thriving jazz scene, not perhaps to be compared to Copenhagen's but lively enough nonetheless.

Among the recommended spots are:

Amalienborg Jazzhouse, Arbeidergate 2 (423024). Unpretentious with some frequently excellent jazz.

Ben Joseph (La Petite Cuisine). Solligate 2 (444575). Grill restaurant and nightclub in one.

Grand Café (Grand Hotel). Karl Johansgt. 31 (429390). Sunday Brunch, lunch with jazz concert.

Guldfisken. Rådhusgate 2 (411489). Good spot for trad. jazz.

Hot House. Pilestredet 15B (203989). Definitely for swingers; lots of jazz.

Jazz Alive. Observatoriegate 2B (440745). Live bands every night; one of the top jazz spots.

Stortorvets Gjaestiveri. Grensen 1 (428863). Beside the cathedral. Lunchtime jazz sessions on Saturdays in 18th-century building kept in period style. International menu, sandwich buffet, service in courtyard in summer. Attractive place even without the jazz.

THE OSLO FJORD DISTRICT

Vikings, Whalers and Twisting Valleys

Østfold is that section of Norway lying between the Oslo region, its major towns of Moss, Fredrikstad, Sarpsborg, and Halden are all points on the main rail line to the capital. At the same time Østfold also belongs economically to the forest and lumber district of eastern Norway and to the great valley of Østerdal, whose river Glomma flows through Sarpsborg to empty into the fjord just beyond Fredrikstad. It is a small section of the country, rich in history and modern industry. On the west side of the Oslo Fjord is located another small district, the opposite number of Østfold, quite logically called Vestfold.

Exploring the Oslo Fjord District

By leaving Oslo's Central Station some morning on a southbound express you will reach Moss in about an hour (if the wind's right, you'll know it by the smell!). Formerly known for its tremendous distillery, the town has now both paper and pulp and other types of industries. It is also the eastern terminus of the cross-fjord Horten-Moss ferry which links Østfold and Vestfold. Unless you intend to cross on this ferry, stay aboard the train another half-hour, then descend at Fredrikstad. Here is a thriving industrial town which converts animal and vegetable oil into many useful products, cans first-class anchovies, exports lumber, etc., yet is at the same time filled with historical monuments. Across the Glomma river in the New Town there is a super-cafeteria, part of Scandinavia's biggest food center—"Stabburet."

The fortified Old Town, with its earthen and stone ramparts, built in the 17th century as a protection against the Swedes, is fully worth wandering about. Particularly fascinating is the great stone fortress of Kongsten standing alone beyond the ramparts as an outpost to meet the first waves of attackers.

In Old Town, is the arts and crafts center—"PLUS." Many of its workshops are open for demonstrations and sales. You will find PLUS represented in many of the leading stores and centers for good Norwegian design.

East of Fredrikstad, route 110 runs in the direction of Halden. This road—also known as the Antiquity Road—is only 16 km. (ten miles) long but takes visitors back 3,000 years. Along it can be seen some of Norway's finest prehistoric finds, notably rock carvings and grave mounds, not all very clearly marked—you may want to get detailed directions from the local tourist office. The road also passes "Tomta," Roald Amundsen's birthplace at Borge.

Home of the internationally-known Borregaard Paper Mills, Sarpsborg has had a long and checkered history since its founding in 1016 by St. Olav. Like Fredrikstad, it was burned down many times during the conflicts with Sweden, but with the expansion of its paper industry in recent decades Sarpsborg is now a thriving and stable industrial town. Sarpsborg's only real attraction for visitors is the waterfall which the Glomma River forms in the middle of the town. This 20-meter (64-foot) waterfall is always impressive and simply marvellous at flood periods. Visitors interested in history might browse around the grounds of the Borgarsyssel Museum, where the ruins of St. Nikolas Church are found, or if it happens to be a Sunday, visit the charming Hafslund Manor.

Stay overnight at Halden and devote the next morning to visiting the Fredriksten Fortress, constructed on a steep hill in the town. The views over the border country and the tales told by the guide about sieges and sorties during the 17th and 18th centuries will amply reward one for the effort expended. The theater here is the only surviving Baroque theater in the country.

Vestfold, Home of the Vikings

Even smaller than its eastern twin, Vestfold has many links with the Oslo region as well as a thriving industrial life of its own which included until 1968 that unique occupation, Antarctic whaling. Historically Vestfold, like southern Norway, has had more contacts with Denmark than with Sweden, but what will stir the imagination most of all are the traces of Viking kings and seafarers to be found there. This district has no clearcut boundary such as the Swedish border provides for Østfold, but merges into the mountain district of Telemark.

The first half hour of the journey takes one as far as Drammen on the same main line that leads to Kristiansand and Stavanger.

The scenery is interesting but not spectacular; and it demonstrates, moreover, how quickly one gets from Oslo to the land of farms, forests and bare rock. And if you are wondering why more Norwegian railroads haven't been laid down in duplicate, the answer is easily seen on this 48-km. (30-mile) stretch to Drammen which has just been made doubletrack at staggering costs. Here you can see some of the difficulties that Norwegian railroad engineers encounter all over the country: steep up and down grades, cuts through solid rocks and tunnels. In fact the Norwegian State Railways on the Oslo–Drammen run has blasted Norway's longest tunnel (11 km./seven miles) through the mountains to open the double track. The Sisyphean job was completed in 1973. After the tunnel is passed there is a view over the valley and across Drammensfjord to the lumber, paper and shipping town of Drammen, sixth-largest city in Norway. Located at the mouth of the large timber-floating river, Drammen has the same strategic location as Fredrikstad on the other side of the Oslo Fjord, albeit without any walled town or fortress. The "Corkscrew Road" tunneled through the mountain to the top of the Bragernes Hill is a unique attraction.

The Vestfold express branches off here and inside an hour we pass through long, narrow Holmestrand, squeezed in between fjord and hillside, and Skoppum, from where the bus runs to the former naval base (also car-ferry) town of Horten. It is well worth making a detour to the coastal village of Åsgårdstrand, where Edvard Munch painted many of his well known works. His small, whiteframe house is open to the public from May to September. This unspoilt village is now a popular holiday resort. A short ride beyond brings Tønsberg which the inhabitants proudly claim as Norway's oldest town, founded in the year 870. The hill rising steeply beside the railway station demands a visit even though all that is left of the extensive fortress, castle and abbey which once crowned it are some ruined foundations. The outlook tower on top is of modern construction, erected in 1870 to commemorate the 1,000th anniversary of Tønsberg's founding, and it offers a panorama comparable in sweep to that from Frognerseteren in Oslo.

Because of the passages both to the Oslo Fjord eastwards and to the open sea southwards you can see at once why Tønsberg was a strategic place, not only for the old Viking raiders but also for shipping. From the sailing ships of the 18th and 19th centuries there has been a steady peaceful development to today's fleet of cargo liners and oil tankers which has won Tønsberg fourth place among shipping ports in Norway.

Looking back north along the railway from the Millenium Tower, one can almost locate Borre, site of many ancient Viking burial mounds; while much nearer Tønsberg is another famous site: Oseberg, where one of the Viking ships now at Bygdøy was found. You should really have a guide or Norwegian friend along to point out other historic spots, such as Ramnes, where rival pretenders to the throne fought decisive battles in the 12th century, and the old manor house at Jarlsberg, the seat of Norway's last family of nobility and still occupied by the family today. Hereditary titles were abolished by parliament early in the 19th century, but Count Wedel Jarlsberg was permitted to keep his distinction until he died in 1893.

Sandefjord and the World's Largest Mammal

Next stop is the picturesque town of Sandefjord, which was once the main base for the Norwegian whaling fleet. Sven Foyn, a native of Tønsberg, invented the explosive harpoon, but it was the skippers from Sandefjord who developed the business of Antarctic whaling to its recent level. The sight of the huge floating factories—up to 25,000 tonnes—and of their dozens of attending whale-catchers, tiny 200-tonners, used to be a fascinating and instructive sight. The great era of Antarctic whaling, nevertheless, has come to an end. With Japanese and Russian whalers joining the Norwegians after the last war, the whales are becoming fewer and fewer, and Sandefjord has withdrawn from the great hunt. However, in compensation, Sandefjord has acquired Norway's fifth-largest merchant fleet. By all means visit the Whaling Museum given to the town by the local "whale king", Consul Lars Christensen.

An interesting side-trip by taxi from Sandefjord is to Gokstad Mound where another of the Viking ships at Bygdøy was found in 1880. Only a grass-covered mound can be seen there now, but it will give some idea of the magnitude and pomp of medieval Viking burials.

Larvik is another of Vestfold's busy ports but it combines this with important lumbering activities, lying as it does at the mouth of another great timber-floating river; the Lågen from Numedal Valley.

Continue a few miles south from Larvik along road 301 to the coastal town of Stavern, famous for its many well-preserved 18th-century wooden houses. The Citadel here, once used by naval hero Tordenskjold, is now an artists' colony. Stavern has good bathing spots, particularly at the nearby fishing village of Nevlunghavn and a salmon fishing river.

PRACTICAL INFORMATION FOR THE OSLO FJORD DISTRICT

TOURIST INFORMATION. Tourist Information Offices are located in the following places: **Fredrikstad** (09–320330). **Halden,** Kongens Brygge (09–182487). **Larvik,** Stogaten 20 (034–82 623). **Horten,** Torggt. 2 (033–43 390). **Moss,** Christiesgt 3 (09–255451). **Sandefjord,** in the Town Hall (034–68 100). **Sarpsborg,** St. Mariegt 96 (09–153629). **Tønsberg,** Storgt 55 (033–14 819/10211).

TELEPHONE CODES. We have given telephone codes for all the towns and villages in the hotel and restaurant lists that follow. These codes need only be used when calling from outside the town or village concerned.

HOTELS AND RESTAURANTS. The region has a number of new hotels and modest family establishments. But in this district, as in other places, it is perfectly feasible to stay in modern town hotels and enjoy swimming on the neighboring beaches. The town hotels are mostly unpretentious, but the *Grand* at Larvik, the *Klubben* at Tønsberg, and the *Park* at Sandefjord are among the best in Norway. Some of the seaside resort hotels offer reduced terms before and after the peak season.

Drammen (Buskerud). *Rica Park* (L), Gamle Kirkeplass 3 (03–838280). 190 beds, all rooms with facilities, restaurant. MC, V. *Müllerhotel Drammen* (E), Strømsø Torg 7 (03–831590). 350 beds. All rooms with facilities.
Restaurant. *Skansen Restaurant.* At the top of the Spiral, a tunnel hewn out of the rock, running in six convolutions to a superb viewpoint at Skansen.
Youth Hostel. *Drammen Youth Hostel* (I), Korsvegen 62. 150 beds.

Fredrikstad (Østfold). *City* (E), Nygaardsgt 44–46 (09–317750). 250 beds. 50 rooms with bath, restaurant. AE, DC, MC, V. *Britannia* (I), Gunnar Nilsensgt 4 (09–311131). 23 beds, no rooms with bath or shower. Restaurant with à la carte menu. *Victoria* (M), Turngt 3 (09–311165). 82 beds, most rooms with facilities. AE, DC, MC, V. *Fredrikstad Motel og Camping* (I), Torsnesveien 16 (09–320315). 52 beds. Swimming.

THE OSLO FJORD DISTRICT 77

Restaurants. *Hawk Club A/S,* Storgt 20 (09-311035). *Løwendals Galei,* Storgt 4 (09-316944). *Peppe's Pizza,* Torvgt 57 (09-322202). *Tamburen,* Faergeportgt 78 (09-320313). *Tordenskiol Danserest,* Storgt 4 (09-316944).

Halden (Østfold). *Park* (E), Marcus Thranesgt 30 (09-184044). 90 beds, restaurant. MC, V. *Grand* (M), Jernbanetorget 1 (09-187200). 60 beds, all rooms with facilities. Fully-licensed restaurant. MC, V.
Restaurants. *Friluften,* Storgt 18 (09-181340). *Dickens,* Storgt 9 (09-183503). *Fredriksten Kro,* Fredricksten Festning (09-185425).
Youth Hostel. *Stangeløkka Youth Hostel* (I), 031-83 046. 40 beds.

Hankø (Østfold). Famous yachting center, summer only. *Hankø Fjordhotel* (L), 1620 Gresvik (09-332105). 140 beds, most rooms with facilities. Restaurant.

Holmestrand (Vestfold). *Holmestrand* (M), Langgt. 1 (033-53 100). 96 beds, 48 rooms with all facilities. Family rooms, many with panoramic views over fjord. Right on the waterfront. Restaurant, bar, and own pier for visiting boats.

Horten (Vestfold). *Grand* (M), Jernbanegt 1 (033-41 722). 48 beds, most rooms with facilities, all with TV, fridge, telephone; restaurant, bar, hire of sailboats and instruction.

Larvik (Vestfold). *Grand* (M), Storgaten 38-40 (034-83 800). 200 beds, most rooms with facilities. Overlooking fjord. Restaurants. AE, MC, V. *Holms Motel* (I), Amundrød E-18 (034-11 482). 126 beds. Cafeteria. AE, DC, MC. *Seierstad Gjestagård* (I), (034-11 092). 26 beds, no rooms with bath or shower. Self-catering,. Boats for hire.
Restaurants. *Hansemann,* Kongensgt 33 (034-86 148). *Blomsterhaven* (Grand Hotel), Storgt 38 (034-87 800). *Carina,* Jegersborggt. 4 (034-81360). AE, MC, V. *Otto Mat and Vinhus,* Torget 6 (034-81 811). *Hvalen Kro,* Ø. Halsen (034-26 099).

Moss (Østfold). *Refsnes Gods* (L), Godset 5 (09-270411). On Jeløy island. 90 beds, 30 rooms with bath. Charming. AE, MC. *Moss Hotel* (M), Dronningensgt. 21 (09-255080). 84 beds. Outstanding restaurant. MC, V.
Restaurant. *Ebas A/S,* Dronningens 1 (09-253898).
Youth Hostel. *Vansjøheimen Youth Hostel* (I), (032-55 334). 64 beds.

Sandefjord (Vestfold). *Park* (E). Strandpromenaden 9 (034-65 550). 270 beds, all rooms with facilities: Overlooking harbor, one of Norway's best hotels. Restaurant, bar, swimming, saunas. AE, DC, MC, V. *Atlantic* (M), Jernbanealléen 31 (034-63 104). 70 beds, some rooms with bath. AE, DC, V. *Granerød* (M), (034-77077). 250 beds, all rooms with all facilities. 12 rooms specially designed for handicapped guests. Conference center. *Kong Carl* (M), Torggt. 9 (034-63 117). 49 beds, all rooms with facilities.

Sarpsborg (Østfold). Industrial town with spectacular waterfall. *Grand* (M), Oskarsgt. 67 (09-154400). 53 beds, most rooms with bath or shower. Fully-licensed restaurant. AE, DC, MC, V. *Saga* (M), Sannessundvn 1 (09-154044). 120 beds, all rooms with facilities. AE, DC, MC, V. *St. Olav* (E), St. Olav's Plass, Glengsgt 21 (09-152055). 132 beds, 25 rooms with bath. AE, DC, MC, V.
Restaurant. *Dickens A/S,* St. Mariegt 109 (09-152892).
Youth Hostel. *Tuneheimen Youth Hostel* (I), (031-45 001). 70 beds.

Stavern (Vestfold). *Hotel Wassilioff* (E), Havngt. 1-3 (034-98 311). 88 beds, most rooms with facilities. At harbor's edge; outdoor terrace, pub, disco, new gourmet restaurant.
Restaurants. *Selma and Tatjanas Kjeller,* Hotel Wassilioff.

Tjøme (Vestfold). *Rica Havna* (E), (033-90 802), on coast in park. Chalets, hire of boats, wind surfers, cycles, tennis and squash courts, swimming pool, solarium. *Tjøme* (M), (033-90 232). 35 beds. Restaurant, café.
Restaurant. *Verdens Ende* (033-90 517). Overlooking rocks and sea.

Tønsberg (Vestfold). *Klubben* (E), Nedre Langgt 49 (033-15 111). 175 beds, all rooms with facilities, restaurant. AE, DC, MC. *Grand* (E), Øvre Langgt 65 (033-12 203). 160 beds, all rooms with facilities. *Maritim* (M), Storgt. 17 (033-17 100). 50 beds, all rooms with facilities.
Restaurants. *Bamboo Gardens,* Ø Langgt 49 (033-12 325). Good Chinese cuisine in intimate atmosphere. *Baronen & Baronessen,* Rådhusgt 2 (033-15 837). *Bonanza,* Ø. Langgt 65 inng. Møllegt (033-12 606). *Fregatten,* Storgt 17 (033-14 776). *Håndverkeren,* Kammegt 6 (033-12 388). *Kong Sverre,* Tollbugt. 14 (033-12 903). Pizza, grills. *Le-Ni Swing In Steak House,* Storgt 32 (033-11 892). *Pizzanini,* Munkegt 10 (033-11 915). *Vaegteren,* Storgt. 29 (033-13 909). *Vertshuset Greven,* Grev Wedelsgt. 3 (033-13 113).
Youth Hostel. *Tønsberg Youth Hostel* (I), (033-12 848). 47 beds.

Camping

There are good campsites near most towns by the Oslo Fjord, particularly along the main road in Østfold from Sweden to Oslo. *Kajerstranden* (Stavern) and *Oddane Sand* (Nevlunghavn) are 3-star camping sites. *Havna Skjaegardspark,* Tjøme. *Fjaerholmen Caravan/Camping,* close by Tønsberg Sailing Club on Nøtteroy Island.

HOW TO GET AROUND. There are good train services from Oslo down both sides of the Oslofjord—on the west side to Drammen, Tønsberg, Sandefjord and Larvik, and on the east side to Moss, Fredrikstad, Sarpsborg and Halden. It is possible to do a one-day round trip to either of these areas, allowing an hour or two in any one of the towns. There is a 40-minute car and passenger ferry crossing between Moss and Horten. Torp airport, between Tønsberg and Sandefjord, has regular connections with Stavanger, Bergen and Copenhagen. There are passenger ferries between Sandefjord and Strømstad (Sweden), Tønsberg and Strømstad, and Larvik and Fredrickshavn.

TOURS. For information on suggested touring routes, guided tours, boat trips and car ferries, visit the local Tourist Information Offices, listed at the beginning of this *Practical Information* section.

PLACES TO VISIT. The Oslo Fjord District has many churches and cathedrals of historical interest. The area also has its share of galleries and museums for the tourist to enjoy. Some of these places are listed below.

Drammen. Drammen Museum. Outdoor museum, with Marienlyst Manor from the 1770s. At Bragernesåsen.
Rock carvings. On Skogerveien road, these carvings are 6,000 years old.

Fredrikstad. Fredrikstad Domkirke. The cathedral is richly decorated by Norwegian artists. One of the largest and best organs in Norway.
Fredrikstad Museum. At the Gamle Slaveri. Open daily 10-4.
Gamelbyen (The Old Town). Scandinavia's oldest preserved fortress town, dating back to 1663.
Glemmen Church. Built in stone around 1100, with a Roman font. Crucifix and apostle sculpture from Lubeck, around 1450.
Kongsten Fort. Dates back to 1685. Now the property of the Town of Fredrikstad.
Oldtidsveien (Highway of the Ancients). The most concentrated collection of archaeological monuments in the country is to be found along Highway No. 110, between Fredrikstad and Skjeberg.

THE OSLO FJORD DISTRICT

Halden. **Fredristen Festning.** Mountain Fortress from the end of 1600s, empire style buildings. War and cultural history museum in the old prisons.

Larvik. **Larvik Bymuseum.** A manor house from 1673; the town museum. **Larvik Maritime Museum.** In the old customs house (1714).

Sarpsborg. **Borgarsyssel Museum.** County museum for Østfold with cultural history collections and old buildings.

Stavern. **Fredriksvern.** Naval station dating from 1750, now training school for air force. Open July through Sept. 9–8 daily. Many well-preserved 18th-century buildings.
Citadel. Artists colony in summer. 18th-century building; open to public.
Stavern Church. Baroque/Roccoco building dating from 1751.

Tønsberg. The oldest town in the north—once capital of Norway. **Haugar.** In the center of town, with old burial mounds. Site of local assembly in olden times.
Memorial Park. With sculptures by Gustav Vigeland and glass mosaics by Per Vigeland.
Oseberg Mound (where Oseberg ship, now in Viking Ship Museum in Oslo, was found). Borre National Park has several Viking burial mounds.
Slottsfjelle. Once the largest castle in Norway. Contains one of the largest collections of medieval ruins in Northern Europe.
St. Olav's Church. The largest circular church in the North. There has been a monastery in Tönsberg since the 1190s.
Tönsberg Cathedral. Erected in 1858 on the site of the old Lavran Church.
Vestfold County Museum. Includes outdoor museum, whaling and shipping sections. Viking ship from 800. Archeological section. Café serving waffles and traditional sour cream porridge *(rømmegrøt)*.

SPORTS. **Swimming** everywhere outside the Drøbak Narrows is pleasant in crystal-clear and surprisingly warm water (averaging 68°F. throughout the season). The bathing beaches at Ula and Lille Skagen at Hvasser are particularly good.

Sailing and boating are in evidence everywhere; the waters of the outer Oslo Fjord, with the mixture of open stretches and sheltered channels, are ideal for this activity. A sailing school with first-class instructors is run by the Hankø Hotel.

Faerder Lighthouse outside Hvasser marks entrance to the inner Oslofjord and is the scene of one of the first annual regattas marking the start of the sailing season: down the fjord from Oslo, round Faerder and back up the fjord again to Oslo. Boat trips round the lighthouse also possible from Hvasser. **Fishing** from a boat—or with a spinning-rod from the rocks—is a popular sport, best early (May) and late (September) in the season.

HELSINKI

Broad Avenues and Bright Prospects

Helsinki (Helsingfors to the Swedish-speaking minority) is very much a city of the sea, sprawling over peninsulas, curving round bays and spilling out across islands that are linked by bridges, causeways or even by boat to the central hub. This hub fills a chunky peninsula where, somehow, without overcrowding, are to be found the single-chamber Parliament, or Eduskuntatalo, the leading technical and educational institutes, art galleries, theaters, museums, business houses, the great Olympic Stadium (scene of the 1952 Olympic Games and 1983 World Athletics Championships), much outstandingly good architecture, the head offices of every big industrial enterprise—in fact all that constitutes the legislative, cultural, scientific, commercial and economic life of the country. And still there is space left for airy parks and broad streets.

Helsinki owes its origin to the chance whims of two monarchs, and its development has largely been the result of a series of accidents. Some 400 years ago King Gustav Vasa of Sweden ordered the citizens of four Finnish towns—Porvoo (Borgå), Tammisaari (Ekenäs), Rauma and Ulvila (Ulfsby)—to leave their homes and proceed to a place on the rapids of the river Vantaa. There they were to build a new town to attract the trade of the Estonian city of Tallinn, thus challenging the power of the Hanseatic League. Like many another city of this period, Helsinki's growth was interrupted by wars, plagues and fires. Not until 1809, when Finland became an autonomous Grand Duchy of Russia, was Helsinki really able to start developing; then three years later, it became the capital of Finland, primarily because the Czar found Turku (Åbo) was too far away from Russia and too close for comfort to Sweden to remain the capital of his newly-acquired territory.

The first of the accidents which stimulated the new capital's growth was the Great Fire in Turku. So much of the latter city was gutted that the University was moved bodily to Helsinki, which at once became the cultural as well as the political center of the country. In 1808, thanks to chance again, another Great Fire played a part in the young city's future. This time it was Helsinki that burned, allowing the German-born architect, Carl Ludvig Engel, an opportunity to plan the rebuilding of the city practically house by house and stone by stone. It is to Engel and to his partner, Ehrenström, that Finland must be grateful for her beautiful capital.

Around the Senate Square which Engel designed stand the Tuomiokirkko or Cathedral, the University and the State Council Building—a group built in one of the purest styles European architecture can boast. Perhaps it was Engel's inspiration, but from his day Finland has always had good architects. Two of them, Eliel Saarinen and Alvar Aalto, became world famous. You can hardly walk down any street in Helsinki without seeing splendid examples of the work of modern architects whose fame is already spreading beyond the frontiers of Finland, such as Heikki and Kaija Sirén, Rewell, Ervi, Petäjä, Pietilä, Penttilä.

Under the protective shadows of the island fortress of Suomenlinna (Sveaborg), Helsinki developed rapidly during the 19th century. The lovely park-strewn suburb of Töölö, and the island residential districts of Lauttasaari, and Kulosaari came into being quite recently. Still newer suburbs grew up in the post-World War II period, and the city continues to expand, as indeed it must, for like most capitals, it has not enough accommodations for all who wish to live there.

Exploring Helsinki

From the visitor's point of view, Helsinki has the virtue of compactness. Once you have oriented yourself and found out where you are on the city map, it will be difficult to get lost. The piers where ships from abroad dock, the railway station and, to a lesser extent, the air terminal, are all in the center of the city. So, however you come, you can start wandering around on foot at once.

It's an idea to begin by finding a good viewpoint from which to make your first survey of the city—such as the top of the Olympic Stadium Tower, the hill of Tähtitorninmäki, or comfortably installed in a top floor bar or restaurant as in the Torni, Hesperia, Inter-Continental, Palace or Vaakuna hotels. Probably the first buildings you will notice are the Cathedral and the railway station, both in the center of the town, together with the House of Parliament and the Stadium Tower. The great broad street running from the center of town through the city and out to the main Turku road is Mannerheimintie, or Mannerheimvägen (*tie* in Finnish, and *vägen* in Swedish, mean street or road.) Along this broad avenue, named after Finland's great hero Marshal Mannerheim, you'll be able to pick out the Post Office, the House of Parliament, the National Museum (Suomen Kansallismuseo), the fine new Concert and Congress Center of Finlandia Hall, and the Olympic Stadium.

Another simple introduction to the city is to take the No. 3T or 3B tram which describes a figure of eight through the city, bringing you back to

HELSINKI

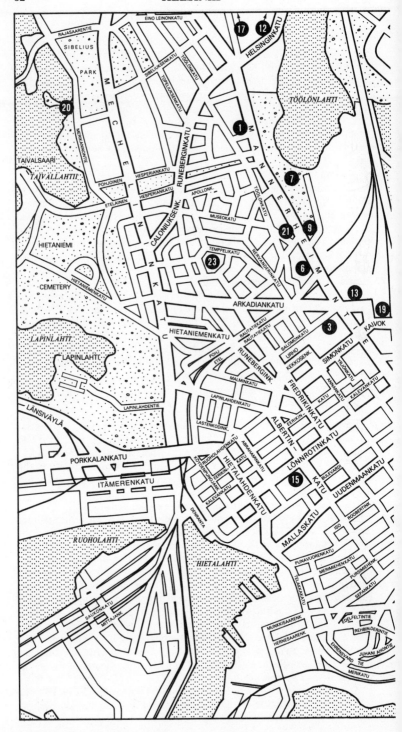

HELSINKI

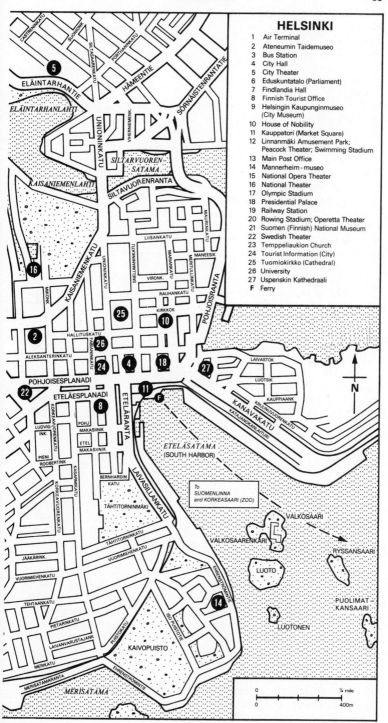

where you started. No. 3T has a commentary in several languages in summer (see "How to get around" in the *Practical Information*). After that, as good a way as any of planning your sightseeing is to start in the middle and work outwards. In point of fact, by far the greatest number of interesting sights are contained in the central part of the city, branching out from the Market Square (or Kauppatori).

The Helsinki Tourist Office has an excellent free booklet "See Helsinki on Foot," detailing six walking tours with maps. Their premises are near the Market Square down by the South Harbor, a few hundred meters from some of the passenger quays. The colorful open-air market flourishes each morning, ending around 1 P.M. and reopening in summer from 3.30–8, when the emphasis is more on arts and crafts. Grouped around the striking statue of Havis Amanda, by Ville Vallgren, are the flower sellers, and the fruit stalls with their mountains of strawberries, raspberries, blueberries, red currants and red whortleberries. You may even be fortunate enough to find the special cloudberry, *suomuurain,* which grows mostly north of the Arctic Circle and is ripened by the Midnight Sun. Fish are sold at the very edge of the harbor, straight from the boats in which they were caught earlier in the morning and so fresh they are still alive and flipping. Meat and dairy produce is sold in the covered market, just beyond the fish stalls.

Havis Amanda, incidentally, the beautiful lady loved by all Helsinkiites, is a center of *vapunaatto* (May Day Eve) revelry. She is crowned again and again on this festive night with the white caps of students who wade through the protective moat surrounding her and climb up to embrace her. Another statue of interest is the stone monument commemorating the time in 1833 when Nicolas I and his consort Feodorovna visited Finland. Known as the Empress Stone, it stands just opposite the quay used by the small boats which head out to the islands of the harbor archipelago. On the west side of the harbor is the Olympia Terminal where passenger and car ferries from Sweden, Poland, and Estonia dock—some of them huge vessels that loom as high as the buildings. Continue south and you come to the pleasant park and district of Kaivopuisto, where most of the embassies are to be found. On the shore, here and elsewhere, you will see small wooden structures from which some Helsinki housewives follow an old tradition of scrubbing their carpets in the sea (or lake, as the case may be).

Leading out of the Market Square are Pohjoisesplanadi and Eteläesplanadi (North and South Esplanades), with gardens running up the middle. Compositely known as Esplanadi, it is a favorite promenade and also features some of the display rooms and shops of Finland's top firms in porcelain, glass, fashion and crafts. Many of them are open on Sundays in July and August.

Along the edge of the Market Square facing the sea stands the President's Palace, with a sentry in field grey patrolling the entrance. Near it you can see the City Hall and various administrative buildings, and behind it towers Helsinki's most famous landmark, the Cathedral. Separating the North and South Harbors, the rocky headland of Katajanokka is dominated by the Orthodox Uspensky Cathedral with its gleaming "onion" domes. This rather neglected area of 19th-century warehouses and naval barracks has been given a new injection of life and is now a developing complex of shops, arts and crafts studios, and restaurants. Passenger ships from Sweden and Germany dock at the Katajanokka terminals on the South Harbor side of the headland.

HELSINKI

Senate and Railway Squares: Contrasting Hubs

Only a block away from the South Harbor market is Senate Square, one of the loveliest in northern Europe, with Engel's Cathedral and its domes soaring above it. In the middle of the square is Walter Runeberg's statue of Alexander II of Russia, the enlightened despot who was so well disposed to Finland.

On January 28, 1951, the great Marshal Baron Carl Gustaf Mannerheim, died in Switzerland. He was flown back to his native land and lay in state in the Cathedral for three days before his state funeral. The citizens of Finland were allowed to pay their last respects to him while he lay there in the dim vastness of this lovely church. Young war widows, children, officers and soldiers, who had fought in Finland's wars against Russia under Mannerheim's leadership, filed past in their thousands, and the only sound was one of weeping. Never in Finland's history has there been such an expression of national feeling.

Opposite the Cathedral the lively new Senaatti shopping center adds a new dimension to this gracious but rather quiet district. Most of the streets leading off the Senate Square contain government and administrative offices. Snellmaninkatu is named after J.V. Snellman, whose statue stands in front of the Bank of Finland. Known as the awakener of the Finnish national spirit, he was instrumental in persuading the Russian overlords to accept the idea of a separate Finnish currency and officially recognize the Finnish language. Nearby is the House of the Estates, site of Finland's Parliament during the Russian era, and now occupied by several scientific societies.

But let us leave the Senate Square and the "Whitehall district" of Finland and take a stroll up Aleksanterinkatu, the main shopping center of Helsinki. At its top end, where it runs into Mannerheimintie, is Stockmann's, Finland's largest department store. At this corner is the famous statue of the Three Smiths by Felix Nylund, a common rendezvous for people who have to meet somewhere in town.

Where Mannerheimintie meets Esplanadi stands the Swedish Theater where plays are given in the Swedish language. To reach its Finnish-language rival, the older National Theater, you must turn around and go back down Aleksanterinkatu to the first street on your left, which leads into the huge square in front of the railway station, which is also the hub of the city's impressive new metro network. Here the National Theater is overshadowed by the massive station itself, designed by Eliel Saarinen. Although he became an American citizen during the war, Saarinen's last wish was to be buried in his native country. His ashes were flown to Finland in 1950 and interred in the grounds of the beautiful home he built for himself along the shore of lovely Lake Hvitträsk.

Right opposite the Railway Station is the City Center, a complex of shops, restaurants, cafés, with underground passageway of shops leading to the railway station. Also on the opposite side of the Railway Square and facing the National Theater is the newly renovated Art Museum of the Ateneum (Ateneum in Taidemuseo), which houses specimens of the works of Finland's greatest painters. The paintings of Gallen-Kallela, Hugo Simberg, Albert Edelfelt, Eero Järnefelt, and Magnus Enckell are known far beyond the borders of Finland and are well worth a visit. You'll also find some sculptures by the world-famous Wäinö Aaltonen.

Just behind the railway station stands the Main Post Office. Opposite is Sokos House which contains a large hotel and restaurant, plus numerous business offices and shops. Nearby is one of Helsinki's latest shopping precincts, Kaivopiha, an attractive oasis linked to the railway station, with an entrance from Mannerheimintie.

The Post Office marks one boundary of the "downtown" part of the capital. Across Mannerheimintie from here is the bus station and, in the adjoining block, the glossy new Forum shopping center. A stone's throw north along Mannerheimintie is the House of Parliament, the impressive structure in red granite which seems so striking because of the ample space around it. It looks solid and, if you go inside you will agree that it is solid, built to withstand storms of debate within and criticism from without. It is lavishly and beautifully decorated inside, even to the special caucus room reserved exclusively for the three-score or more of lady representatives. Finland's 200 members of Parliament are elected by proportional representation.

National Museum and Olympic Stadium

A short distance west of Mannerheimintie in Temppeliaukio is the Temppeliaukio church, one of Europe's most unusual modern churches, built into the living rock. Designed by the brothers Timo and Tuomo Suomalainen, it is also used as a concert hall. Returning to Mannerheimintie, just a few hundred meters from the House of Parliament is an odd-looking edifice with a tower which gives it a church-like appearance. This is the National Museum, which houses a large collection of ethnographical exhibits illustrating Finland's history. This area, round the shores of Töölönlahti Bay, is the site of the big new city plan designed by Alvar Aalto. Part of this is Finlandia Hall, the Concert and Congress Center, designed by him, which opened in 1971, close to the shore of the bay and not far from the National Museum. The Intercontinental Hotel is nearby, while the ultramodern City Theater, designed by Timo Pentilä, is across the bay.

About half a mile beyond Finlandia Hall, on the corner of Helsinginkatu, is the site of the glossy new Opera House due to open in 1992. Further along Mannerheimintie, not half an hour's walk from the railway station and but ten minutes by tram, rises the imposing tower of the Olympic Stadium. One of the finest views of Helsinki can be obtained from the top of this tower. Further north still and to the east of Mannerheimintie, less than two miles from the city center, is Helsinki's fine new International Fair Center, which opened in 1975. Exhibition halls, a restaurant, cafeteria and well-planned open spaces make it a showplace of its kind.

The street leading off at right angles from Mannerheimintie, Helsinginkatu, leads to the beautiful Botanical Gardens and the Water Tower, from which there is a fine view. Nearby is Helsinki's Tivoli, or permanent amusement park, called Linnanmäki, offering top-class entertainment of universal family appeal. Continuing along this street we come to the "East End" of Helsinki where there is little to see except proof of the fact that Helsinki has indeed no slums.

If you return to Mannerheimintie and cross the street, you will find yourself in the hospital center of the capital. Actually, it is still Töölö, the biggest residential district, but in this little section are concentrated most of the city's biggest and newest hospitals.

Although it may seem a startling suggestion, you next ought to go and see the Hietaniemi Cemetery. When you get there, you will realize why it is a favorite rendezvous for a promenade, for it is a beautiful place. Marshal Mannerheim is buried in the military section. It is a custom to place candles on each grave on Christmas Eve, a moving sight.

Another place well worth visiting is Arabia. This is one of the largest pottery factories in Europe and can be visited by appointment. Although the Arabia plant is some distance out of town, a tram service runs practically to the gate.

Helsinki's Islands

A number of Helsinki's most interesting sights are on islands, a major one being the fortress of Suomenlinna. In fact, this covers a series of interlinked islands, and the entire Finnish army assisted in its construction, which began in 1748. Under the protection of this fortification, Helsinki first began to develop and flourish. Once called the Gibraltar of the North, it was indeed impregnable, never having been taken by assault. Twice, however, it was surrendered without a fight, first to the Russians in the war of 1808–1809, and then during Finland's war of independence when the German Baltic Division, assisted by the Finnish Civic Guard, captured the city of Helsinki. During the Crimean War a combined British and French fleet bombarded the fortress and the fires caused by the cannonade convinced the army that the fortress could not withstand modern artillery fire.

Yet Suomenlinna is more than an ancient military monument with several museums; its parks and gardens are lovely, especially in the spring. One of the forts near the historic King's Gate has an outstanding restaurant. Bearing the historic name of Walhalla, it has been changed as little as possible. This group of islands has now been developed into an all-purpose center for cultural and leisure activities. It includes the recently completed Nordic Arts Center, partly housed in a restored barracks dating from 1868, and focussing on exhibitions and the promotion and exchange of ideas on Scandinavian art.

Seurasaari, an island linked by bridge to the mainland, is another good spot to visit. It houses a delightful open-air museum which brings together houses, ranging from simple huts with turf roofs to lovely wooden villas furnished with original furniture, transported from various parts of the country.

Yet another island, Korkeasaari, houses Helsinki's zoo, reached by ferry from the South Harbor or by foot bridge from Mustikkamaa. The latter is the home of Helsinki's Summer Theater and is also an island, but accessible by road bridge. Close to Korkeasaari, the islet of Hylkysaari is the setting for the recently opened National Maritime Museum. Still more islands in this sea-girt city feature such amenities as bathing beaches, restaurants, yacht clubs.

Environs

A trip round some of Helsinki's suburbs will give you a fine idea of that special Finnish talent for creating imaginative residential districts in harmony with nature. These provide the theme for some sightseeing tours, but if you want to explore independently, head for Tapiola Garden City, situated in the forests and close to the sea, to the west of town.

PRACTICAL INFORMATION FOR HELSINKI

GETTING TO TOWN FROM THE AIRPORT. Frequent bus services link Seutula Airport with the air terminal (Hotel Intercontinental, Töölönkatu 21) and Railway Square in the city center. Journey time is 30 minutes. Check-in takes place at the airport.

TOURIST INFORMATION. Free publications such as *Helsinki This Week* and *Helsinki Today* are good sources of information on what's on and where. The City Tourist Office is at Pohjoisesplanadi 19 (169 3757).

Helsinki Card. This entitles you to free entry to about 40 museums and other sights, a guided sightseeing tour and unlimited travel on the city's public transport, and quite a few discounts. The cost is 65 Fmk (one day), 85 Fmk (two days), 105 Fmk (three days); about half-price for children. You can buy it from the City Tourist Office, hotels and some travel agencies.

USEFUL ADDRESSES. Embassies. *Canada,* Pohjoisesplanadi 25B (171 141). *U.K.,* Uudenmaankatu 16–20 (647 922); during 1990 moving to Itäinen Puistotie 19 (90–661 311). *U.S.A.,* I. Puistotie 14A (171 931).

Car Hire. *Avis,* Fredrikinkatu 37 (441 155). *Budget Rent a Car,* Malminkatu 36 (694 5300). *Hertz,* Polarpoint, Hernesaarenranta 11 (622 1100). *Inter-Rent,* Hitsaajankatu 7 (775 6133).

American Express. Katajanokan pohjoisranta 9–13 (661 631).

Main Post Office. Mannerheimintie 11 (1955 117).

Emergency hospital for foreigners. Helsinki University Central Hospital (4711). Information on health care available round the clock on (735 001).

Emergency (police, fire, ambulance) tel. 000.

TELEPHONE CODES. The telephone code for Helsinki is 90. To call any number in this chapter, unless otherwise specified, this prefix must be used. Within the city no prefix is required.

HOTELS. Reservations are highly recommended as the city is busy with conferences and exhibitions when it is not full of tourists. There is a Hotel Booking Service in the railway station for hotel and private accommodations, open mid-May through mid-Sept., Mon. to Fri. 9–9, Sat. 9–7, Sun. 10–6; mid-Sept. through mid-May, Mon. to Fri. 9–6, closed Sat., Sun. Unless otherwise stated, all the hotels listed below are open all the year and have licensed restaurants.

Deluxe

Hesperia. Mannerheimintie 50 (43 101). 385 rooms, pool, night club. A short stroll from center. AE, DC, MC, V.

Inter-Continental. Mannerheimintie 46 (441 331). 555 rooms, pool, nightclub. Perhaps Helsinki's plushest. A short stroll from center. AE, DC, MC, V.

Kalastajatorppa. Kalastajatorpantie 1 (488 011). 235 rooms, pool, tennis, boating, fishing. Glorious seashore situation and linked by underground passage-way with famous *Round Room* restaurant and *Red Room* nightclub. AE, DC, MC, V.

Palace. Eteläranta 10 (171 114). 59 rooms. Stunning view over South Harbor. AE, DC, MC, V.

Ramada Presidentti. E. Rautatiekatu 4 (6911). 500 rooms, several restaurants, pool, nightclub, all-night café. Central. AE, DC, MC, V.

Rivoli Jardin. Kasarmikatu 40 (177 880). 53 rooms; winter garden, no restaurant. New, central, with particularly well-equipped rooms. AE, DC, MC, V.

HELSINKI

Strand Inter-Continental. J. Stenberginranta 4 (39 351). Helsinki's latest with all facilities; 200 rooms, waterside location, pool. AE, DC, MC, V.

Expensive

Airport Hotel Rantasipi. Near Seutula Airport (826 822). 300 rooms, pool, nightclub. Excellent for transit stopovers with shuttle service to airport. AE, DC, MC, V.

Dipoli. Otaranta (435 811). 213 rooms, most with sea view, nightclub, disco, sports facilities. In garden suburb of Otaniemi, 9 km. from center. AE, DC, MC, V.

Helsinki. Hallituskatu 12 (171 401). 130 rooms, disco. Very central. AE, DC, MC, V.

Klaus Kurki. Bulevardi 2 (602 322). 130 rooms, central. AE, DC, MC, V.

Korpilampi. (Forest Lake) Lahnus (855 8431). 162 rooms, pool, nightclub, sports facilities, popular for congresses. Lovely forest setting in Espoo, 20 km. northwest of city. Some (M) accommodations. AE, DC, MC, V.

Merihotelli Cumulus. J. Stenberginranta 6 (708 111). 87 rooms, pool. AE, DC, MC, V.

Olympia. L. Brahenkatu 2 (750 801). 100 rooms. AE, DC, MC, V.

Seurahuone. Kaivokatu 12 (170 441). 114 rooms, nightclub, disco, elegant Café Socis. Very central, opposite rail station. AE, DC, MC, V.

Tapiola Garden. Tapiontori (461 711). 82 rooms, pool, nightclub. In the garden suburb of Tapiola. AE, DC, MC, V.

Torni. Yrjönkatu 26 (131 131). 158 rooms, several restaurants with different specialties, in high rise block. Central. AE, DC, MC, V.

Vaakuna. Asema-aukio 2 (171 811). 290 rooms, nightclub, disco. Central location on main railway station square. AE, DC, MC, V.

Moderate

Anna, Annankatu 1 (648 011). 58 rooms, cafeteria only. Nicely renovated small hotel in the center. AE, MC, V.

Aurora. Helsinginkatu 50 (717 400). 75 rooms, pool. AE, DC, MC, V.

Espoo (523 533). 13 km. (8 miles) from city. 94 rooms, rooftop pool. AE, DC, MC, V.

Haaga. Nuijamiestentie 10 (578 311). Not so central, part of the Hotel and Restaurant College, 110 rooms, pool. AE, DC, MC, V.

Helka. P. Rautatienkatu 23 (440 581). 150 rooms, some Expensive. AE, DC, MC, V.

Hospiz. Vuorikatu 17B (170 481). 141 rooms, unlicensed restaurant. AE, DC, MC, V.

Martta. Uudenmaankatu 24 (646 211). 44 rooms, unlicensed restaurant. AE, MC, V.

Ursula. Paasivuorenkatu 1 (750 311). Not so central, 43 rooms, cafeteria. AE, DC, MC, V.

Inexpensive

Academica. Hietaniemenkatu 14 (402 0206). Summer only, 216 rooms, pool, disco, tennis. AE, MC, V.

Dipoli Summer Hotel. Jämeräntaival (460 211). 240 rooms; sports facilities. Summer only. AE, DC, MC, V.

Finn. Kalevankatu 3B (640 904). 28 rooms; no restaurant. MC, V.

Satakuntatalo. Lapinrinne 1 (694 0311). Summer only, 64 rooms. AE, MC, V.

Cheapest accommodations are in boarding houses such as **Kongressikoti,** Snellmaninkatu 15 (174 839). **Clairet,** It. Teatterikuja 3 (669 707). MC, V. **Erottajanpuisto,** Uudenmaankatu 9 (642 169). **Lönnrot,** Lönnrotinkatu 16 (693 2590). **Omapohja,** It. Teatterikuja 3 (666 211). **Pensionat Regina,** Puistokatu 9 (656 937).

Apartment Rentals

Check with Art Travel (753 7018) or Yksitysmajoitus (445 048).

Camping

Rastila. 13 km. (8 miles) east of city center. Open May 15 to Sept. 15.

Youth Hostels

Olympic Stadium Youth and Family Hostel, Pohjoinen Stadionintie 3B (496 071). Open all year.

City Youth and Family Hostel. Porthaninkatu 2 (709 92590). Open May 15 through Aug.

HOW TO GET AROUND. By tram/bus. A ride costs 6.50 Fmk (small reduction for ten-ride tickets), allowing transfers within a one-hour period. A tourist ticket valid for 24 hours for unlimited travel is available from the Helsinki Tourist Office or public transport ticket offices (but not on board the vehicles), but better value is the Helsinki Card (see pg. 160), which gives many benefits including unlimited travel on all public transport within the city. The 3T tram, with commentary in several languages in summer, follows a figure-eight circuit right around the city center.

By metro. The first section of Helsinki's splendid new subway begins one stop beyond the main rail station and goes northeast to Itäkeskus, where it links with bus services to the outer suburbs. Same fare and transfer system as tram/bus above.

By taxi. These bear the sign "taksi." Minimum charge is 10,50 Fmk, with a surcharge added after 6 P.M. and at weekends. The fare increases according to the length of journey, amount of luggage and number of passengers. No tips are necessary or expected.

By boat. Regular ferries link the South Harbor with island communities, in addition to sightseeing boats throughout summer.

On foot. The Helsinki City Tourist Office have worked out some excellent itineraries, with maps. Ask for their free booklet "See Helsinki on Foot."

TOURS. There is a good selection of half- and full-day sightseeing tours of the city, some extending to the suburbs. Sightseeing trips by boat leave from the Market Square (South Harbor) visiting Helsinki's archipelago. Some include a lunch stop ashore.

Further afield is Hvitträsk with its lovely lake and the former studio-home of three leading Finnish architects. Another short excursion is to Ainola, near Järvenpää, the lovely home of Sibelius, now open to the public. The composer is buried in the grounds. Among other trips that can be made in one day, three are especially recommended: Porvoo (Borgå), Hanko and Hämeenlinna combined with Aulanko. You can travel to Porvoo by boat in three hours, returning by bus; or go both ways by boat.

Full details of all these trips are available from the tourist office.

MUSEUMS. The opening times given below are for the summer; check for other seasons. Entrance fees are usually 5–15 Fmk; in a few cases admission is free. Don't forget the Helsinki Card which gives free admission to around 40 museums and other sights.

Ateneumin Taidemuseo (Art Museum of the Ateneum). Railway Square. Reopening in 1990 after extensive renovation. Mainly paintings, sculptures, drawings, etc., by Finnish artists; some foreign and old masters. Open Mon. to Sat. 9–5, Wed. 9–8, Sun. 11–5.

Arabian museo (Museum of Arabia). Hämeentie 135. Table ware and ceramic art by this famous Finnish porcelain factory. Open Mon. 10–8, Tues. to Fri. 10–5, Sta.–Sun. 9–3. By terminal of tram no. 6.

HELSINKI

Gallen-Kallelan museo (Gallen-Kallela Museum). Leppävaara, Tarvaspää, reached by no. 4 tram to Munkkiniemi, then pleasant 2 km. walk. The home and works of one of Finland's greatest painters in charming surroundings. Open Tues. to Thurs. 10–8, Fri. to Sun. 10–5.

Helsingin Kaupunginmuseo (Helsinki City Museum). Karamzininkatu 2, beside Finlandia Hall. Art, furniture, archives illustrating history of city. Open Sun. to Fri. 12–4, Thurs. 12–8.

Helsingen kaupungin Taidemuseo (Helsinki City Art Museum). Tamminiementie 6, near Seurasaari. Finnish and French art from 20th century. Open Wed. to Sun. 11–6.30.

Heureka (The Finnish Science Center). Tikkurila in Vantaa, 15 minutes by train from the city center. The surrealist complex of this high-tech wonderland opened in 1989, covering everything from natural phnomena to the latest computer technology, with the whole range of audio-visual displays and working models. You can even conduct your own experiments. In the Center's Verne Theater, you'll get a new dimension on outer space. Open Mon.–Fri., 10–8, Sat.–Sun., 10–6.

Mannerheim-museo (Mannerheim Museum). Kalliolinnantie 14, Kaivopuisto. Home of Marshal Mannerheim, containing his collected trophies. Open Fri. and Sat. 11–3, Sun. 11–4.

Ruiskumestarin talo (Burgher's House). Kristianinkatu 12. Oldest wooden house in Helsinki (1817). Open Sun. to Fri. 12–4, Thurs. 12–8; closed Sat.

Seurasaaren ulkomuseo (Seurasaari Open-air Museum). Seurasaari island. Farm and manor buildings from different parts of the country. Open daily 11.30–5.30, Wed. 11.30–7.

Sinebrychoff Art Museum. Bulevardi 40. Collection of foreign old masters, especially Dutch and Flemish. Open Mon. to Fri. 9–5, Sat., Sun. 11–5.

Sports Museum. Olympic Stadium. Permanent and changing exhibitions, including memorabilia of some of the world's greatest athletes and skiers. There are also "ghosts" from the 1940 Olympics (pre-empted by World War II), such as the winners' podium that was never used. Open Mon.–Fri. 11–5, Thurs. 11–7, Sat.–Sun. 12–4.

Suomen kansallismuseo (National Museum). Mannerheimintie 34. Three sections: prehistoric, historic, ethnographic. Open 11–4 daily, Tues. also 6–9.

Suomen merimuseo (National Maritime Museum). Hylkysaari island, ferry 10 min. from Market Square (South Harbor). Also reached by footbridge from Mustikkamaa via Korkeasaari. Specialized maritime history museum. Open daily 10–3.

Suomen rakennustaiteen museo (Museum of Finnish Architecture). Kasarmikatu 24. Archives of Finnish architecture, past and present. Open 10–4. Closed Mon.

Taideteollisuusmuseo (Museum of Applied Arts), Korkeavuorenkatu 23. Development of design. Open Tues. to Fri. 11–5, Sat. and Sun. 11–4.

Urho Kekkonen Museum. Tamminiemi, Seurasaarentie 15. The late Urho Kekkonen, Finland's longest-serving President, lived here for 30 years. Near Seurasaari. Open daily 11–4.

PARKS AND ZOOS. The *City Conservatories* are in Eläintarha Park, open Mon. to Sat. 12–3, Sun. 11–3. Two central parks are *Tähtitorninmäki* (Observatory Hill) on the west side of the South Harbor and, a little to the south, *Kaivopuisto*—both rather more natural than formal. A beautiful oasis west of the center is the shoreside cemetery of *Hietaniemi;* Marshal Mannerheim is buried here. A little north of this is *Sibelius Park* with its distinctive sculpture by Eila Hiltunen commemorating the great Finnish composer.

Helsinki zoo is on the island of Korkeasaari, reached by ferry from the South Harbor, or by foot bridge from Mustikkamaa island which is accessible by road. Open June and July 10–9; shorter hours in other months.

HISTORIC BUILDINGS AND SITES. Eduskuntatalo (Parliament). Mannerheimintie. An imposing granite building, designed by Siren and completed in 1931. For entrance hours, contact the City Tourist Office. Public admitted to gallery during full session.

Stadionin torni (Olympic Stadium Tower). Eteläinen Stadionintie 3. Offers superb views. Open Mon. to Fri. 9–8, Sat. and Sun. 10–5.

Suomenlinna. Frequent ferry service from South Harbor. Fortifications on series of islands, now developed into a multi-purpose center: Nordic Arts center, museums, summer restaurants, summer theater, guided tours. Museums open daily 11–5.

Temppeliaukion kirkko (Temppeliaukio church). Lutherinkatu 3. Beautifully carved out of living rock to the plans of Timo and Tuomo Suomalainen. Open Mon. to Sat. 10–8, Sun. 12–2, 5–8.

Tuomiokirkko (Cathedral). Senaatintori. Fine classical building by Engel dating from the 1830s. Open Mon. to Fri. 9–5, Sat. and Sun. 9–6.

Uspenskin Kathedraali (Uspenski Cathedral). Kanavankatu 1. Completed in 1868, the most important Orthodox church in Finland. Open Mon. to Fri. 10–3.

Vanhakaupunki (Old Town). Original site of city founded in 1550, reached by tram no. 6.

SPORTS. Golf. There is a good 18-hole course at Talin kartano (Tali Manor), some 7 km. (4 miles) from city center. The tourist office can supply details about green fees and playing conditions.

Saunas. Nearly all hotels have them, but also recommended (and inexpensive) are those at swimming halls listed in *Helsinki Tourist Information.*

Swimming. The rocky shores and small beaches in and around the city offer plenty of opportunities. Among them are: Uunisaari, an island opposite the residential and diplomatic district of Kaivopuisto; the sandy beach of Hietaranta; the island of Seurasaari (accessible on foot); Mustikkamaa; farther out on the island of Pihlajasaari; Suomenlinna. Also at the Swimming Stadium or at Kumpula open-air pool.

Tennis. There are indoor courts at: Tennispalatsi, Ruskeasuo, Yrjönkatu 21B, Kulosaari, Meilahti Sports Park, Töölö Sports House, Tali Tennis Center, Myllypuro Tennis Center. Outdoor courts are at: Kaisaniemi, Kalastajatorppa, Kulosaari, Meilahti Sports Park, Taivallahti.

Winter sports. In winter, you can ski in the heart of the city through the parks (as some Helsinkiites do on their way to work!), or anywhere in the surrounding countryside. More specifically, Nuuksionpää, northwest of the city by bus, offers good terrain or, further afield, the ridges of Hyvinkää can be reached by bus or train. There is also ice skating at numerous public rinks in Helsinki.

MUSIC, MOVIES AND THEATERS. Music. The *National Opera Theater* at Bulevardi 23–27 (moving to a brand new complex on Mannerheimintie in 1992) offers performances of international and Finnish operas and ballets. Concerts are often held in the magnificent Aalto-designed *Finlandia Hall* on Mannerheimintie. Musical performances are also held in a number of attractive settings in summer, such as organ recitals on Sunday evenings in the Cathedral, concerts in *Temppeliaukion Church* and the *House of Nobility,* and open-air concerts of various kinds in several parks.

Movies. All films are shown in their original language with Finnish subtitles.

Theaters. The Finns are enthusiastic theatergoers and, though the main theaters will present most visitors with a language problem, it's well worth attending one of the several open-air summer theaters for the atmosphere and setting. The main ones are: *Helsinki Summer Theater* on Mustikkamaa island; *Operetta Theater* at the Rowing Stadium; *Peacock Theater* (variety shows) at Linnanmäki amusement park; *Rhymäteatteri* on Suomenlinna; *Student Theater,* Seurasaari; *Summer Theater,* Central Park, in the grounds of Laakso riding field; *Töölönranta Summer Theater* at Töölölahti Bay.

SHOPPING. Ask for the leaflet with full details of tax-free shopping, giving savings of about 11% on purchases of over 200 Fmk. The shop gives you a check for the appropriate amount which you can cash at most departure points; but you must also produce the items you have bought. Prices may not be low, but quality is high as is the standard of design of most Finnish products. Items to look out for especial-

HELSINKI

ly are glass, handwoven textiles, fashion wear, furs, stainless steel, metal and semi-precious jewelry, wooden toys. Hand-made candles in brilliant or subtle shades are charming inexpensive buys, while at the other end of the scale, the Finns produce beautifully designed modern furniture!

If you haven't much time to shop around, your best bet is to go to one of the big stores. The most famous is *Stockmann's,* founded in 1862, filling a block between Aleksanterinkatu, Mannerheimintie and Keskuskatu; it has an efficient export service. Nearby is the newly renovated Aleksi 13 department store.

Two big marketing groups with a nationwide network are SOK with their *Sokos* stores and hypermarkets, and E Marketing with their *Centrum* and *EKA-Market* (cut price) department stores.

The main shopping streets are Pohjoisesplanadi and Aleksanterinkatu, and the smaller streets off these. Stroll along Pohjoisesplanadi (North Esplanade) and you'll find the showrooms and shops of many major firms such as *Arabia* (ceramics and porcelain), *Nuutajärvi* (glass), *Marimekko* and *Vuokko* (fashions and fabrics), *Aarikka* (costume jewelry, wooden buttons and other crafts), *Pentik (leather) and Studio Tarja Niskanen* (furs). Most shops on Esplanadikatu are open on Sunday afternoons in summer. *Iso Roobertinkatu* is Helsinki's first pedestrian-only street, popularly known as Roba.

For a selection of small shops, go to the Station Tunnel (linking the rail station with the City Center complex opposite), or *Hakaniemi Market Hall,* where 50 shops above the covered food market in Hämeentie offer interesting variety. Several new and attractive shopping precincts include *Kaivopiha,* off Mannerheimintie and linked to the railway station. Another is the *Senaatti Center* opposite the cathedral.

A "must" is a morning visit to Kauppatori (Market Square) where the lively open-air market flourishes, year-round, by the South Harbor, selling fruit, vegetables, fish and household goods. It reopens in the afternoon in summer where the emphasis is on arts and crafts. Another main market place at Hietalahti includes a flea market from Mon. to Sat. 6.30–2.

Among specialist shops, the following are particularly worth a visit: Jewelry—*Kalevala Koru,* Unioninkatu 25 (especially beautiful traditional Kalevala motifs); *Galerie Björn Weckström,* Unioninkatu 30, or *Lindroos,* Aleksanterinkatu 48 (truly handsome modern jewelry). Furs—*Turkistuottaja* have an auction at Martinkyläntie 40 (in the suburb of Vantaa); *Ali Fur,* Erottaja 1–3; *Fur Shop,* Yrjönkatu 12–14. You can get anything and everything for the sauna from *Sauna-Soppi,* Aleksanterinkatu 28, Senate Square.

Finally Scandinavia's biggest bookshop is *Akateeminen Kirjakauppa* (Academic Bookstore), Keskuskatu 1.

RESTAURANTS. Helsinki's eating houses cater for every taste and pocket, ranging from the gourmet to the budgeteer in a hurry. All establishments listed below are fully licensed unless otherwise stated. Remember that set meals served between certain hours will bring costs down sharply.

Expensive

Alexander Nevski. Pohjoisesplanadi 17 (639 610). Helsinki's latest to capture the style and gastronomy of Imperial Russia. AE, DC, MC, V.

Amadeus. Sofiankatu (626 676). Quiet atmosphere, friendly service, game specialties. AE, DC, MC, V.

Bellevue. Rahapajankatu 3 (179 560). Russian style. AE, DC, MC, V.

Café Adlon. Fabianinkatu 14 (664 611). Smart. DC, MC, V.

Céline. Kasarmikatu 23 (636 921). One of the best. AE, MC, V.

Engel, Tehtaankatu 34 (628 865). One of Helsinki's latest, with ambitious *à la carte* menu. AE, DC, MC, V.

George. Kalevankatu 17 (647 662). Sophisticated gourmet restaurant voted "Restaurant 1987" by a Finnish Gourmet Club. AE, DC, MC, V.

Havis Amanda. Unioninkatu 23 (666 882). By the South Harbor; two sections of which one specializes in fish. AE, DC, MC, V.

HELSINKI

Kaivohuone. (177 881). In attractive location in Kaivopuisto Park looking out to the harbor; floorshow. AE, DC, MC, V.

Katajanokka Casino. Laivastokatu 1 (653 401). In fine seashore location. AE, MC, V.

König. Mikonkatu 4 (171 271). Subdued, sophisticated setting, below ground. AE, DC, MC, V.

Kulosaari Casino. Hopeasalmenpolku 1 (688 202). Pleasantly placed on island of the same name, but accessible by road. Dancing. AE, DC, MC, V.

Kultainen Sipuli (Golden Onion). Kanavaranta (179 900). One of Helsiniki's latest and most attractive in restored brick warehouse in the Katajanokka district. AE, DC, V.

Mestaritalli. Toivo Kuulan puisto (440 274). Formerly stables, now an elegant restaurant in a seashore park. Dancing. AE, DC, MC, V.

Piekka Finnish Cuisine. Sibeliuksenkatu 2 (493 591). Finnish specialties prepared in the traditional way in one of Helsinki's newest eating houses. AE, DC, MC, V.

Round House. Kalastajatorpantie 2 (488 011). A famous showpiece, beautifully situated near the seashore, above the Red Room nightclub. Floorshow. Part of the Kalastajatorppa hotel. AE, DC, MC, V.

Savoy. Eteläesplanadi 14 (176 571). A favorite lunch place for Finland's tycoons. Designed by Alvar Aalto. AE, DC, MC, V.

Svenska Klubben. Maurinkatu 6 (628 706). Intimate manorial atmosphere in listed historic house by North Harbor. AE, DC, MC, V.

Walhalla. (668 552). On fortress island of Suomenlinna, reached by short ferry journey from South Harbor. You dine in the authentic 18th-century atmosphere of a fortress never taken by storm, in a setting of ancient ramparts and flowering lilac bushes—one of the memorable sights of Helsinki. Summer only. AE, DC, MC, V.

Moderate

Agora Tea Room. Unioninkatu 30 (607 092). Especially for tea enthusiasts. DC, MC, V.

Amigo. Tehtaankatu 12 (625 311). Good for Spanish food.

Cafe Socis. In Seurahuone hotel, elegant rendezvous, lunch (M), coffee and cakes (E). AE, DC, MC, V.

El' Greco. Eteläesplanadi 22 (607 565). Greek food. AE, MC, V.

Elite. Eteläinen Hesperiankatu (495 542). Recently refurbished but maintaining its appeal to both locals and artists. MC, V.

Happy Days. Pohjoisesplanadi 2 (624 023). Adjoining Swedish Theater, with several restaurants of various price levels and types. MC, V.

Kappeli. (179 242). In the Esplanade near the South Harbor, recently renovated with several sections including open-air summer restaurant. AE, DC, MC, V.

Karelia. Käpylänkuja 1 (799 077). Karelian specialties. AE, DC, MC, V.

Kosmos. Kalevankatu 3 (607 717). Varied home-cooked fare in one of Helsinki's oldest restaurants in the heart of downtown; it's been in the same family since opening in the 1920s—and has kept the original ambience. AE, MC, V.

Omenapuu. Keskuskatu 6 (630 205). Cozy family restaurant in busy shopping center. Can be *Inexpensive.* AE, DC, MC, V.

Ostrobotnia. Museokatu 10 (408 602). Finnish food, good value.

Perho. Mechelininkatu 7 (493 481). Run by the Helsinki Hotel and Restaurant College and recently renovated. Excellent value. AE, DC, MC, V.

Rivoli. Albertinkatu 38 (643 455). French cuisine. AE, DC, MC, V.

Tamminiementien Café. Tamminiementie, near Seurasaari Open Air Museum. Homemade goodies (including Polish specialties) served in the restored faded elegance of the 1740s manor house of Meilahti. Lots of atmosphere, but definitely not for the calorie-conscious. MC, V.

Tervasaaren Aitta. Tervasaari (605 412). Excellent cold table. Summer only. AE, DC, MC, V.

HELSINKI

Troikka. Caloniuksenkatu 3 (445 229). One of a chain of three small eating places, specializing in Russian food. AE, DC, MC, V.

Vanha Maestro. Fredrikinkatu 51–53 (644 303). You can dance in the daytime here (Wed. and Sun. are Ladies Invitation Days). AE, MC, V.

Wellamo. Vyökatu 9 (663 139). Small, intimate, rustic atmosphere, good food if you like garlic. AE, MC, V.

Inexpensive

Carrols. Self-service hamburger restaurants in Mannerheimintie 19, in the City Passage, and Keskuskatu 3; disposable plates and cups; good value. Unlicensed.

Chez Marius. Mikonkatu 1 (669 697). French cuisine, beer and wine only.

Eliel. In the railway station (177 900). Genuine *art nouveau* style. Self-service. MC, V.

Kasvisravintola. Korkeavuorenkatu 3 (179 212). Self-service vegetarian restaurant. Unlicensed. DC.

Kellarikrouvi. P. Makasiininkatu 6 (655 198). Cozy wine cellar atmosphere. AE, DC, MC, V.

Kynsilaukka (Garlic). Fredrikinkatu 22 (651 939). Makes good use of garlic in rustic decor. DC, MC, V.

Vanhan Kellari. Mannerheimintie 3 (654 646). In cellar of Old Students' House. MC, V.

Wienerwald, Kaivokatu (663 589) and Lauttasaari (677 400). Part of the Austrian chain. AE, MC, V.

Many modern and attractive cafés (*kahvila* or *baari*), dotted about town, offer refreshments and sometimes hot meals, as well as coffee, cakes, etc. Look out for **Frazer.** AE, MC, V. Several cafés have lovely shoreside locations, such as the **Ursula,** Kaivopuisto.

A selection of English-style pubs includes: **Angleterre** (M), Fredrikinkatu 47 (647 371), AE; **Annan Pub** (M), Annankatu 3 (633 316). MC, V. **Richard's Pub** (M), Rikhardinkatu 4 (667 232); and **St. Urho's Pub** (M), Museokatu 10 (446 940).

NIGHTLIFE. Young people wanting to meet their Finnish counterparts can try one of the following discos: **Alibi,** Hietaniemenkatu 14; **Club Anna and Eric,** Eerikinkatu 3; **Harald's,** Kasarmikatu 40; **Ky-Exit,** Pohj. Rautatiekatu 21; **Tavastia,** Urho Kekkosenkatu 4–6.

For family fun, there's Linnanmäki amusement park (summer only), Helsinki's Tivoli with Peacock Theater, side shows, open-air dancing, Monorail and jungle train.

See under *Hotels* for establishments with nightclubs and under *Restaurants* for those featuring floor shows and dancing.

PRELUDE TO ICELAND

Land of Ice and Fire

When the Vikings landed in Iceland, they thought they had discovered the entrance to the Netherworld. Centuries later, the cone-shaped Snaefellsjökull glacier was made famous by Jules Verne in his *Journey to the Center of the Earth*. In Iceland you are on the edge of the world—and it feels that way too. This is a land of eerie icescapes and petrified lava fields, steaming thermal springs and spectacular glaciers. It is estimated that over the last 500 years a third of the volcanic lava to have reached the surface of the earth emerged in Iceland. Such is the pressure beneath the surface that the Giant Geysir, which gave its name to geysers all over the world, spouted boiling water and steam over 150 feet in the air. By contrast, the largest glacier here, Vatna-jökull, occupies an area equal to all the other glaciers in Europe put together.

Iceland has always been different—and in many different ways. The country is barren, with hardly a tree to be seen, but, with stark multicolored mountains, magnificent waterfalls, lakes and green valleys, is nonetheless strikingly beautiful. There are no frogs, snakes or reptiles. When the Vikings arrived, foxes were the only indigenous mammals. Since then, man has imported a wide range of animal inhabitants, including inadvertently-introduced mice and rats. Reindeer were first brought from Norway in the 18th century, and small herds can be found in the eastern counties.

Modern Comforts the Natural Way

Despite all this, Iceland is a modern Scandinavian country—though it is 500 miles from the nearest European landfall (Scotland) and nearly 1,000 miles from Copenhagen, which used to be its administrative capital. Nowadays the population is around 245,000—the same as the city of Derby in Britain, or just over half the size of Omaha, Nebraska. Half the Icelanders live in the capital Reykjavik, while over 80% of the rest of the island's 40,000 square miles remains uninhabited.

As its name suggests, Iceland is a chilly country. Though the Gulf Stream may keep its winters slightly warmer than those of New York, in summer a temperature of 70°F has them all swooning. But the summers here have one great advantage—it practically never becomes dark. And even in spring and fall there are long, long twilit evenings. But despite the tempting blue sea washing the weird black volcanic sand of the beaches, the sea is always too cold for swimming.

By contrast, Iceland has a flourishing horticultural industry, producing vegetables to meet the domestic demand, flowers for export, fruit—even bananas! This is all achieved by harnessing the abundant geothermal energy, which is put to a wide variety of use. For instance, most of the houses in Reykjavik are heated by naturally-produced near-boiling water. This is carried by two ten-mile-long, heavily insulated pipelines from the nearby hot spring. The heat lost while the water is running from the underground streams to the kitchen tap is less than 2°F, enabling the Icelanders to keep their houses at around 70°–75°F both winter and summer. However, you may sometimes notice a rather odd sulfur smell in the bathrooms.

If you happen to visit in winter, you'll find that it's dark for all but a few hours, partially explaining why the Icelanders are such good chess players. The real wizards come from the island of Grimsey, 30 miles off the northern shore on the Arctic Circle, where in mid-winter they only have a few hours of twilight every day. These long nights also explain why, per capita, more books are written, printed, bought and read in Iceland than anywhere else in the world.

However, before you set out for Iceland, there's one vital point you should know. Iceland is an expensive country. In 1987 record fish catches brought the country's balance of payments out of the red for the first time since 1978, and inflation is now at a manageable 11–12%. The falling value of the krona means your dollars and pounds go that much further. The main cause of inflation is that despite its small population, the island is anything but self-sufficient. Only just over 1% of the land is under permanent cultivation (hardly surprising when you realise that Reykjavik is on the same latitude as Archangel in Russia, and the Yukon in Canada). This lack of land development means that a high proportion of foodstuff has to be imported—and at a considerable expense owing to the distances involved. Indeed, Iceland's whole economy is based upon its sole major industry—fishing.

Despite these drawbacks, Iceland is host to a wide range of visitors, including many biologists, geologists, bird-watchers and photographers: all attracted by the unique colorfulness of the landscape—with its black lava, red sulfur, blue hotsprings, grey and white rivers with spectacular waterfalls creating high arching rainbows, and green, green valleys (unlike Greenland, which, paradoxically, is covered in ice). However, as you trek the wilderness you must be prepared for temperamental weather. Here you can have all four seasons in one day. Even so, when you step inside off the tundra, you enter Scandinavian-style living quarters: this is a land where primeval landscapes and modern comforts exist side by side.

Iceland may not be to everyone's taste—but there's no denying that it's different.

History and Development

The first people to arrive in Iceland were Irish monks. However, their time here was neither long or happy and they were either enslaved, or driven out, by the first recorded settlers, the Norsemen, who arrived in the year 874. The Norsemen were led by Ingólfur Arnarson, who was fleeing from the tyranny of Harold Fairhair in Norway. When Ingólfur first saw Iceland rising out of the sea before his longboat, he threw overboard a pair of high seat pillars carved with images of the heathen gods. He swore that he would make his home wherever the wooden pillars landed. Some time later they were found washed up in a mysterious smoke-shrouded bay. The smoke was caused by the steam from the nearby hot springs. The Icelandic word for smoke is "reykur," and for bay is "vík"—and that is how the capital of Iceland, Reykjavik, got its name.

To begin with the new colony prospered, attracting many Norsemen who had already settled in parts of Ireland, Scotland and the Faroe Islands. These new settlers brought with them their wives and slaves, which accounts for the preponderance of Celtic blood in the Icelandic population. Even to this day many of the natives have the appearance and temperament of Irish people.

In 930 the settlers established their first parliament—the Althing. Thus they created the first republic north of the Alps. The Althing still operates today, and is now the world's oldest surviving national legislature.

With prosperity, the forests melted before the axe, the sod was turned with primitive ploughs, imported sheep grazed the uplands, fish thronged the rivers, lakes and bays, and the skalds sang eulogies to the pagan gods. But with prosperity came rivalry and power-struggles. The Icelandic chieftain Eric the Red was forced to flee from his enemies (and in so doing discovered Greenland, founding an Icelandic settlement there). When Eric's son Leif fled, he discovered a land called Vinland—now widely believed to have been the northern shores of America. It was this era which gave birth to the famous Icelandic sagas. These sagas describe the life of the early powerful Viking settlers, their heroic deeds at home and overseas, their vicious blood-feuds, and their great love stories.

Meanwhile, the country continued to be rent by quarrels, feuds and power-struggles. By the beginning of the 13th century there was general civil war. Fratricidal strife continued for more than 50 years, periodically stirred up by the Norwegian kings who hoped to claim Iceland as their own. Their hopes were realized in 1264, when the Norwegian king stepped in as "arbiter" and sovereign. However, in 1380, both Iceland and Norway came under the Danish crown. The islanders then had to cope with the encroachment of Danish officials as well as natural calamities caused by volcanic eruptions. Their problems were further increased in the mid-16th century when the Reformation was imposed by the Danish king, and the last Catholic bishop, Jon Arason, was beheaded without trial. The king confiscated the property of the monasteries and churches, consolidating still more his grip on the country. At the same time, Spanish, Moorish and English pirates also raided the country. Then came famine, smallpox, leprosy, the Black Death, and worst of all, the imposition by the Danish king of a trade monopoly.

Iceland's unhappy story continued until the early 19th century when Icelandic nationalism began slowly to emerge in opposition to the oppressive Danish trade monopolies. But the movement thereafter gained popular momentum rapidly. Partial Home Rule came in 1904, and full sovereignty under the Danish King in 1918. When Denmark was invaded by Germany in 1940, Britain occupied undefended Iceland to keep it from falling into the hands of the Axis. A year later American forces replaced the British (and built Keflavík Airport); and on June 17th 1944, Iceland severed its remaining ties with Copenhagen to become a republic once more. The Icelanders then elected their first president. And in 1980, the Icelanders elected Vigdís Finnbogadóttir as president—the first woman to be elected a president in Europe.

Sagas, Song and Seafaring—Iceland Today

Alone among the world's myriad tongues, modern Icelandic has changed so little since early pagan times that reading the ancient sagas presents no more of a problem to the present-day Icelander than do Shakespeare's works to the average educated Englishman or American. Swedish, Danish and Norwegian all developed from the same stem, of course, but Icelandic bears about the same relationship to them as Anglo-Saxon does to English, and it's an exceptional Scandinavian who can make his way through Icelandic literature without the aid of dictionary and grammar. Even at this late date, Icelandic retains two peculiar letters of the alphabet which long ago disappeared from the other northern languages. One letter looks like a *b* combined with a *p,* and is pronounced like the *th* in *thin;* the other, pronounced like *th* in *leather* resembles a lazy *d* with a horizontal line drawn through the stem. Both look formidable on first acquaintance but yield to a little persistent lisping and buzzing.

In addition to its literary achievements, Icelandic has had a novel effect on matrimony and the position of women. In Iceland the custom persists of giving children the *first* instead of the *last* name of their father. Thus Magnus, the son of Svein, becomes Magnus Sveinsson, while Gudrún, the daughter of Einar, is known as Gudrún Einarsdóttir. What's more, Gudrún keeps her maiden name even after she marries, though her children will bear her husband's name.

Another custom is preserved amongst the older women. Many still wear the graceful national costume, which consists of a long, full black skirt and a black bodice, embroidered in gold and laced with gold cord over a colored blouse. An apron, worn as an ornamental panel, is usually of the same material as the blouse. Their hair is done up in two long braids which are looped up behind, and on their heads they wear small black velvet caps, with long black tassels, which are bound by two- or three-inch rings of gold or silver. Many of the younger women treasure the beautiful embroidered costumes worn by their mothers or grandmothers, though they do not wear them except on gala occasions.

Besides chess and books, singing has long been a favourite pastime to while away the long winter evenings. Even today the influence of medieval church music is revealed by the use of harmonies long ago superseded elsewhere. Choral groups are numerous and active—again there are more per capita than in any other country—and Iceland produces international opera singers. Singing developed naturally from ballad and saga recitals, and the tradition persists.

But fishing is really what Iceland is all about. The fishing industry and its by-products dominate the national economy. The main commodity available for export is fish, and about 75% of Iceland's trade is based in fish products. Per fisherman, the annual catch amounts to a staggering 290 tons, another world record.

Several years ago, over-fishing began to have a serious effect on Iceland's traditional fishing grounds. In consequence, Iceland extended her territorial limit to 200 miles, in a desperate effort to preserve stocks. More than this, it was also designed to protect the jobs of the more than one-in-seven of Iceland's workforce who are employed in the fishing industry. This action by Iceland led to a dispute with Britain—the so-called "Cod War"—which is now, fortunately, a thing of the past. A compromise was reached, and the rich harvest of the Arctic seas remains protected.

EXPLORING ICELAND

Volcanos, Hot Springs and Glaciers

Iceland is the second-largest island in Europe (only Great Britain is larger). It has approximately the same land area as England, or Kentucky, and for many years its strategic position in the north Atlantic made it an important staging post on trans-Atlantic flights. Nowadays, practically all flights go direct between Europe and America—though advantageous rates apply for those willing to make a short stop-over at Keflavik, Iceland's international airport, which is just 29 miles from Reykjavik.

Iceland's Capital

At the turn of the century, Reykjavik was a sleepy fishing village of just 6,000 people. Though it's now 20 times this size, its expansion has been carefully planned. The new apartment blocks are earthquake-proof, and the city is completely smokeless as all its heating is provided by the nearby hot springs. The city's resourcefulness was tested to the full in the fall of 1986 when, with all of one week's notice, President Reagan and Mikhail Gorbachev, plus attendant aides, advisors and sundry other camp followers—not to mention several thousand journalists—descended on it for an unexpected round of Disarmament talks. The talks may have failed, but they put Reykjavik firmly on the international map.

Set in its fjord, overlooked by snow-capped mountains, Reykjavik presents a colorful sight—with its concrete houses painted in light colors, and their striking red, blue and green roofs. Among the more important buildings are the Parliament or Althing, the Lutheran cathedral, the National

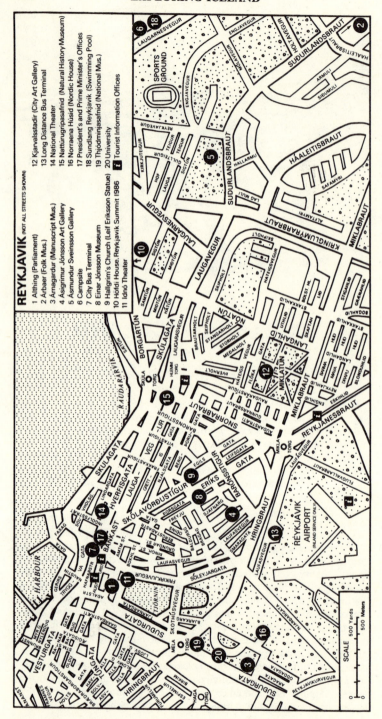

Theater, the University and the National Museum on Sudurgata beyond Mela Torg. Hallgrim's Church, with its famous statue of Leif Eiriksson, dominates a rocky plateau and a cluster of small wooden houses dating from the end of the last century.

Reykjavik's streets are ideal for window-shopping, but you'll find everything very expensive though some bargains can be found in street markets. Even so, an Icelandic sweater is a must. You'll find them all over town, but the best selection is in the Icelandic Handicrafts Center at Hafnarstraeti 3, down by the harbor near the City Bus Terminal. Good sweaters start at around 2,000 krona.

Besides being the island's center of government, Reykjavik is also its cultural center. Largely owing to those long dark winter evenings, the arts thrive here. Despite its comparatively small population, the city has its own symphony orchestra, two professional theaters, several museums and art galleries, and numerous cinemas and excellent bookstores. The more popular arts also exist here. Though Reykjavik is hardly known for its night life, there are some good discos. But a word of warning here: drinks in such places cost the earth.

Excursions from Reykjavik

Reykjavik makes a good base for exploring other parts of the country. About 56 km. (35 miles) east of the capital stretches the broad lava plain of Thingvellir, site of the first parliament and now a national park. A placid lake, Thingvallavatn, the biggest in Iceland, lends a deceptively idyllic air, for it was on this plain that chieftains and citizens from every village and farm met each summer to make the law. Here the decision was taken around the year A.D. 1000 to lay aside pagan ways and adopt the tenets of Christianity. The speaker's rock and the hollowed-out seats reserved for the most important men can still be seen, together with the ancient fairgrounds where wrestling matches took place, weddings were contracted and old scores settled. Nowadays Thingvellir is a favorite place for holiday-makers, and the modern campers' tents in the summer do, in a sense, carry on the tradition of the great meeting place, but in a much more gentle form. Do not miss a stroll along the Almannagja chasm, and the magnificent view from its upper rim.

A little further out from Reykjavik, the Great Geysir, which gave its name to hot springs around the world, bubbles away oblivious of the expectant crowds which gather there daily in hopes of some excitement. Geysir is getting old these days and cannot be relied upon to perform, but a junior geyser, Strokkur, seldom fails, throwing up boiling water to considerable heights at five-minute intervals. In the same area there are small boreholes from which steam arises, as well as beautiful pools of blue water.

Twenty km. (12 miles) away there is more thunder, this time in the form of the deafening Gullfoss waterfall. The river Hvitá plunges down a series of steps before throwing itself 30 meters (95 ft.) into a narrow canyon. The noise—and the spray—are on a heroic scale, and towards afternoon the sun illuminates the moist air, making it in fact, as well as name, the Golden Falls. Twenty nine km. (18 miles) from Geysir is Skálholt, a hallowed spot in Icelandic history. There has been a Christian church on this spot for nine centuries, and the present exquisitely simple building with its modern altar piece is the eleventh in its line. Jón Arason, last Catholic bishop in Iceland, and martyr to the Reformation, was beheaded without trial at Skálholt in 1550. A plaque marks the spot. A variety of one-day tours from Rekjavik are available for approximately $50.

To ascend 1,615 meter (5,000 ft.) volcanic Mount Hekla requires two full days, although by road it's only 120 km. (75 miles) from the capital. Getting up and down the mountain is a ten hour undertaking in itself, but the view into the crater, as well as out from the crater's edge, fully justifies the strenuous climb to the top. Hekla has erupted several times in recent years, and the new lava fields stretch for some miles around the crater. For those who dislike trudging, a four-hour plane trip combines a good look at Hekla with a glimpse of the glacier Vatnajökull, and a flight north to the Arctic Circle.

West Iceland

It's a long, sometimes monotonous drive to the Snaefellsnes peninsula. But you call always break it on the way by calling in at the whaling station at the head of Hvalfjördur. If you arrive at the same time as a whale, be prepared for a pungent and bloody experience. It is possible to shorten the journey by taking the ferry from Reykjavik to Akranes. Further north, turn inland to visit Reykholt, where you can see the small hot pool which belonged to Snorri Sturluson, Iceland's famous poet, who recorded the sagas. Touring westwards you reach Snaefellsnes peninsula with its glacier, Snaefellsjökull. This is the glacier where Jules Verne set the starting point for the *Journey to the Center of the Earth.* It is a wild beautiful place, where the main attractions are the hosts of seabirds nesting along the basalt cliffs, and the seals who pop up to gaze curiously at intruders.

On the other side of the peninsula there are weirdly shaped rock castles which are reached by crossing a grey lavafield. Continue along the northern side of the peninsula and you come to Stykkishólmur. The town is popular with many sea-sports fishermen who come for the halibut in Breidafjördur. It is a pleasant little place with a modern hospital run by Belgian nuns. Behind the town is a hill known as Helgafell. According to local superstition, anyone who climbs Helgafell for the first time will be granted three wishes—provided he doesn't look back or talk on the way up.

There are several islands in the large bay of Breidafjördur. A few are inhabited, and all have large colonies of birds and seals. A local ferry passing close to some of these islands takes you across the bay to Brjánslaekur Farm, on the remote Vestfirdir, the isolated region of the Western Fjords.

East Iceland

Not until 1974, when the final bridge was completed across the treacherous glacier waters pouring from the tongues of Vatnajökull glacier, was this area accessible by car from Reykjavik. It is still a long journey, but you can watch the miniature icebergs sliding towards the sea while the great skuas swoop overhead and across the black sands.

Following the southern road, you come to Skógar, a tiny settlement beside the impressive Skógafoss. Here you can lunch at the Edda hotel by prior arrangement, then visit the small museum consisting of turf houses brought from elsewhere in the district and re-erected. The locals used to fish this treacherous coast in small boats, and the last of these boats rests in the little museum together with many other interesting mementos from a tough and primitive way of life which persisted until comparatively recent times.

EXPLORING ICELAND

Press on eastward and you come to the Skaftafell reserve. This contains the famous Svartifoss waterfall, dropping thinly over a cliff whose sides resemble the pipes of a great organ. It's possible to walk on the glacier tongues here, but this should not be attempted without expert guidance and correct equipment. Höfn on the east coast is developing as a popular center from which to explore the extraordinary landscapes created by the outlying glaciers of Vatnajökull and the wild coastline. From here excursions are arranged to these, as well as to Skaftafell National Park.

On the very eastern tip of Iceland, you come to Borgarfjördur Eystri (a village and fjord with the same name). This is renowned as one of the most beautiful spots in the country. It takes its name from Álfaborg, a hillock just outside the village, reputed to be the legendary home of elves. Iceland's famous painter, Kjarval, lived here for a time. The village has a small hotel and restaurant.

South Iceland, Westmann Islands and Surtsey

The remote Westmann Islands are off the southwest coast of Iceland, and amongst them only Heimaey is inhabited. In 1973, after lying dormant for nearly 5,000 years the Helgafell (Holy Mountain) on Heimaey erupted, and the entire population of 5,000 was immediately evacuated by local fishing boats to the mainland. This was a disaster for the islanders. Their main industry was fishing, and they were dependent on the safe harbor at Heimaey as well as upon the fish processing plants there. However, with the grit and determination of people long used to living with the forces of nature, the inhabitants started to dig themselves out long before the eruption had ceased, removing tons of black lava dust from their buried houses and streets. Now the streets are cleared, the houses rebuilt and repainted, and fishing and processing working normally, though some of the plants were seriously damaged. However, the island now has 600 meters (1,900 ft.) of lava on the approaches to the harbor, and many of the houses which were closest to the eruption were buried for ever. The lava, still hot, is used for thermal heat by the islanders. Cold waterpipes are run through it, giving boiling water straight from the tap.

The islands are rich in sea birds, especially puffins, which are used in large quantities for food. The puffins were not too greatly affected by the eruption, but a considerable number of sea birds were lost and this has affected the task of egg-pickers, who estimate that it will take several more years before the colonies fully establish themselves again. Egg-picking is hazardous work. Dangling from ropes, the men swing from ledge to ledge down sheer volcanic cliffs to collect eggs from the nests, often attacked fiercely by the birds. Primitive winches haul the men back up with their fragile loads. Throughout the years there have been 18 fatal accidents, and legend has it that when the 19th man falls to his death the volcano Katla on the mainland opposite will erupt. (Its next eruption is in fact long overdue.)

A highlight of the Icelandic calendar is the festival held on the first weekend in August on Heimaey. It is well worth taking time to visit the Westmann Islands, despite the fact that the round-trip flight might be canceled by bad weather and you'll face a 10-hour sea journey instead. But if you really cannot spare more than a few hours, you can always take a shorter sightseeing tour from Reykjavik. A few miles west of the Westmann Islands is the new volcanic island of Surtsey, which was thrown up out of the sea by a submarine volcanic eruption in 1963. Already it is several hundred feet high. Scientists work there recording the progress of nature, but lesser folk are not allowed ashore. Sightseeing trips usually include a sail around the island and also to the multi-colored sea cave Kafhellir, on the island of Haena nearby.

Akureyri and the North

The north of Iceland was created by the interplay of fire and ice. The largest lava fields on earth are to be found here, for instance Odádahraun, some with plants and mosses, others barren and bare. The country is not all forbidding, and the valleys sheltered by the mountains are lush with vegetation and rich in color. There are also many rivers with good salmon and trout fishing, magnificent waterfalls and strange formations of basalt rock columns.

Iceland's second-largest town, Akureyri, is an hour from Reykjavik by plane. Ranged up and down a series of irregular hills on the western side of Eyjafjördur, the town is dominated by a simple ultra-modern Lutheran church whose twin spires accent the barren and treeless landscape. Some of the surrounding mountains reach a height of 1,400 meters (4,500 ft.) and offer fine climbs and ski runs.

Beside the Edda summer hotel there is an interesting statue. In bygone times, if a man transgressed the laws of the community, he was often banished, along with his family, to the lava fields. This was virtually a death sentence, for nothing could sustain life in those regions. This poignant statue, called the *Outlaw,* is by Einar Jonsson and depicts a man carrying his wife and child and accompanied by his dog, walking into outlawry.

From Akureyri you can get a boat to Grimsey, a particularly interesting spot for sea bird enthusiasts. This island is over 32 km. (20 miles) from the mainland and actually straddles the Arctic Circle. From Akureyri you can also take a long jolting bus ride over the weird volcanic plateaux to the magnificent waterfall of Godafoss, where the local chieftain threw his pagan household gods into its foaming depths when he was converted to Christianity in A.D. 1000. In the adjoining district is Glerárdalur, a valley where petrified wood is found. The bus continues to Lake Mývatn, a birdwatchers' paradise, where vast numbers of waterfowl make their homes. One can get a guide to some of the more remote nesting areas.

Mývatn also has an especially tasty breed of trout, which feeds on the midges that give the lake its name. Here there are all kinds of exotic phenomena, including Dimmuborgir (the black castles) where the fantastic landscape is said to resemble the lunar surface more closely than anywhere else on earth; Stóragjá and Grjótagjá, two pools of natural hot water in underground caves, where one can enjoy wonderful bathing; and Námaskard, where the purple sulfur boils like a witches' cauldron in the strange red and yellow valleys.

When the volcano Askja erupted here two centuries ago, the lava ran directly towards the lake and the small settlement which lay beside it. But in the path of the lava stood the settlement's tiny church; while the congregation prayed inside, the molten mass came to a halt within inches of its walls. There is a new church now, but the remains of the old one can still be seen, surrounded on three sides by solidified lava. Farther afield are Dettifoss, Europe's largest waterfall, and the fascinating lush national park of Ásbyrgi with the curious echoing rocks of Hljódaklettar. From here you can continue to Húsavik, an attractive port on the north coast, and thence back to Akureyri.

Central Iceland

The interior of Iceland is virtually uninhabited apart from the occasional isolated meteorological or scientific station. Though the Icelanders may get rather tired of having it likened to the Moon, the landscape really is strangely reminiscent of some science fiction vision—with its great stony deserts, extravagantly contorted lava fields, and towering glaciers from which crystal clear streams and green rivers drain across the land. The colors are superb, and there is a feeling of timelessness that few other places in the world can match.

This is *not* an area where you go exploring on your own. But there are excellent overland tours escorted by experienced guides. You don't have to be young and hearty or tremendously energetic to enjoy these, but you do need to be an outdoor enthusiast and prepared to camp. Transport is in specially constructed buses, and tents and all necessary equipment are provided; you are usually expected to be in charge of your tent during the trip, but meals are provided for you. Since this kind of tour tends to attract those who are interested in birds or flowers or geology, it's usually a fine meeting ground for like-minded souls of all ages and many nationalities. Over-night stops may be made near a small community or in the heart of a rugged uninhabited wilderness, perhaps on the edge of a lava field or at the foot of some craggy white glacier. There are opportunities to bathe in clear, naturally hot spring-water under the open sky, peer into volcanic craters, walk among wild lansdcapes, and experience a stillness that has barely been disturbed by human presence since time began.

These, then, are the distinctive features of Iceland, a land which beguiles all who have once stood on its grey shores, and felt the rock tremble beneath them with the subterranean forces of an unseen world.

PRACTICAL INFORMATION FOR REYKJAVIK

GETTING TO TOWN FROM THE AIRPORT. For arrivals at Keflavík International Airport, a bus service is stationed outside the terminal entrance which will provide transportation into Reykjavik. Fare at time of writing is $7, but sometimes your ticket includes the fare. Taxis are also available, though as driving time to Reykjavik is approximately 45 minutes, cost will be quite high.

From the town terminal there are bus connections and taxis on hand, night and day, to other parts of the city.

TOURIST INFORMATION. There are five main centers for tourist information in Reykjavik: The Information Center, Ingólfsstraeti 5 (623045); the nearby *Gimli,* Laekjargata 3 (28025); *Útsýn,* Austurstraeti 17 (26611); and the Iceland Tourist Bureaus at Reykjanesbraut (27488) and in Hotel Loftleidir at Reykjavik Airport (22322); also at Skógarhlid 6, (25855). There is also a branch office at Keflavík Airport Terminal. All these bureaus will be able to supply information on the city as well as for the rest of Iceland. Information can also be had concerning local and not-so-local accommodations, as well as special discount fares on city and country-wide bus services.

EXPLORING ICELAND

USEFUL ADDRESSES. Travel Agents. *Gudmundur Jónasson Tours,* Borgartúni 34 (83222). *Samvinn-Travel,* Austurstraeti 12 (27077). *Úlfar Jacobsen Tourist Bureau,* Austurstraeti 9 (13499). *BSI Travel,* Hringbraut (22300).

Embassies. *U.S. Embassy,* 21 Laufásvegur (29100). *Canadian Consulate,* Laufásvegur 77, (13721). *British Embassy,* 49 Laufásvegur (15883).

Car Hire. *ALP Car Rental,* Hladbrekka 2 Kopavogi (42837). *Geysir,* Borgartún 24 (11015). *Icelandair Car Rental* (22322).

Police. Headquarters at Hverfisgata 113, and at Hlemmtorg, tel. 11166.

Medical Services. Emergency telephone no. is 81200. From 8 A.M.–9 P.M., *Landspitalinn,* tel. 21230 and 29000. *Drugstore* (Apótek), tel. 18888.

TELEPHONE CODES. The telephone code for Reykjavik is 91 when calling from outside the capital. When calling Iceland from overseas the 9 is dropped and 1 becomes the code for Reykjavik. Within the city, however, no prefix is required. For all establishments outside Reykjavik, we have listed the necessary prefix immediately before the telephone number.

HOTELS. Apart from the top hotels in Reykjavik, Iceland's hotels are modest and simple. Breakfast is not included in the hotel price. However, all prices include 24% state tax and service charge. Somewhat less expensive accommodations are available in private homes; check with the Tourist Bureau for a list of homes participating. Students and other adventurous travelers who want to tour the countryside can usually obtain a night's lodging from $15, provided they supply their own sleeping bags. The summer hotels known as "Edda" hotels (university and school hostels used for tourists during the summer vacation) are moderately priced, but demand for rooms is high so book in advance if possible.

Expensive

Holiday Inn. Sigtún 38 (689000). 100 rooms. New, with restaurant and coffee shop. Fairly central. AE, DC, MC, V.

Hotel Esja. Sudurlandsbraut 2 (82200). 134 rooms. Conveniently located and with an exceptionally good view. AE, DC, MC, V.

Hotel Holt. Bergstadastraeti 37 (25700). 50 rooms. Central location. Decor features original works by leading Icelandic painters. AE, DC, MC, V.

Hotel Lind. Raudarárstíg 18 (623350). 44 rooms. A new hotel near to the city's main bus terminal. AE, DC, MC, V.

Hotel Loftleidir. Reykjavik Airport (22322). 227 rooms with bath or shower. All amenities, including theater, sauna, and solarium. AE, DC, MC, V.

Hotel Saga. Hagatorg (29900). 219 rooms, all above 4th floor. Recommended rooftop restaurant. All amenities. AE, DC, MC, V.

Moderate

Hotel Borg. Pósthússtraeti 11 (11440). 46 rooms. A traditional hotel; very central, beside the Cathedral. AE, DC, MC, V.

Hotel City. Ránargata 4a (18650). 31 rooms. Central.

Gardur. Hringbraut (15656). 44 rooms. Open summer only.

Ødinsvé. Odinstorg (25224). 20 rooms. 2 restaurants.

Stadur. Skipholt 27 (26210). 23 rooms. Open June 1 to Sept. 30.

Inexpensive

Guesthouse. Brautarholt 22 (20986). 24 rooms. Open summer only.

Guesthouse. Flókagata 5 (19828). 11 rooms. Central.

Guesthouse. Snorrabraut 52 (16522). 18 rooms. Comfortable.

Hotel Jörd. Skólavördustíg 13a (621739). 8 rooms. Central.

Royal Inn. Laugavegur 11 (24513). 11 rooms, in heart of town.

Salvation Army Guesthouse. Kirkjustraeti 2 (13203). 24 rooms.

Viking Guesthouse. Ránargata 12 (19367). 11 rooms.

Youth Hostel, Laufásvegur 41. Short walk from the center.

EXPLORING ICELAND

Camping

Reykjavik has only one campsite, and a pleasant one at that, conveniently located on Sundlaugarvegur, next to the largest swimming pool and near the sports stadium. Note that fires are not allowed, and all garbage must be collected and disposed of properly. All details from the Iceland Tourist Bureau.

Tjaldaleigan Rent-a-Tent, at Hringbraut v/Umferdarmidstodina 101 (13072), rents out all sorts of camping equipment, from cars with tent-trailers to camping kits including tent, sleeping bag, mattress, gas stove, and even a set of pots and pans. Prices run about $40 per person per week for the kit.

Youth Hostels

There are several hostels in Reykjavik; full details are available from the Youth Hostels Association (Farfugladeild Reykjavikur), Laufásveg 41 (24950). These hostels are well-equipped and very popular during the holiday season, so it's best to book beforehand. The Y.H.A. will also be able to give addresses of other inexpensive sleeping accommodations for those who have their own sleeping bags; cost usually as little as $15.

HOW TO GET AROUND. By bus. The major form of city transport is by buses which bear the letters S.V.R.—Straetisvaganar Reykjavikur (Reykjavik Buses). The two main stopping points are at Hlemmtorg in the eastern part of town, and the terminal at Laekjartog in the city center. These buses run fairly frequently, while most services start at 7 A.M. and finish at midnight. At weekends, the last buses finish at 1 A.M.

There are usually no ticket conductors on Icelandic buses. Tickets are bought directly from the driver (either individually or in sheets, which is cheaper), and then placed in a receptacle close to the driver's seat. Smoking is not allowed. If you want to get off, just press one of the buttons placed intermittently throughout the bus.

By taxi. Taxis are expensive, though you aren't expected to tip the driver anything over the metered amount. There are taxi stands in many parts of the city, and they also pick up en route. The sign *Laus* means that the cab is available for hire.

TOURS. An excellent way of getting acquainted with Reykjavik is to take one of the city's guided bus tours. Usually lasting around 2½ hours, these tours introduce the capital's past and present, and include a visit to the Museum and Art Gallery. Departures daily at 10 A.M. and 2 P.M. May through Sept.; cost approximately $21–$32.

A varied itinerary of day excursions is also available to and around the surrounding countryside. These day-tours include pony trekking on the Icelandic hills; the starkly dramatic lava arena of Thingvellir, where the ancient Viking parliament met for centuries; the famous Great Geysir, a seething area of erupting hot springs, mud pools, and geysirs, of which Strokkur, the world's most active geysir, is likely to spurt several times up to a height of 100 ft.; Reykholt, home of the famous Saga historian, Snorri Sturluson; and even an aerial tour for an eagle's-eye view of the rugged lavafields, volcanoes, and glaciers of southern Iceland.

All cost and departure details from the Icelandic Tourist Board; day excursion information can also be had from *Reykjavik Excursions* at Hotel Loftleidir at the airport (22322), or from *Gimli,* Laekjargata 3 (28025).

MUSEUMS. Being a small nation, Iceland cannot offer museums on the scale of the Louvre, the Prado, or the Metropolitan Museum of Art. She has, however, produced some very fine artists, many of whom have bequeathed their houses to the nation upon their death and whose works are displayed therein. These museums are normally open from 1.30–4 P.M., closed Mon. Admission is generally free, but occasionally there is a nominal charge.

Árbaer (Folk Museum). On the city outskirts. An interesting collection of old buildings, depicting rural life in the past.

Árnagardur (Árni Magnússon Manuscript Museum). Interesting collection of ancient manuscripts.

Ásgrímur Jónsson Art Gallery. Bergstadastraeti 74. An excellent collection of watercolors and oils by this well-beloved Icelandic painter.

Ásmundur Sveinsson Gallery. Kirkjumyrarbletti 10, Sigtún. An unusual dome-like house built by the artist himself, where you can see his creations throughout both house and garden. Open Sun.

Einar Jónsson Museum. Beside Eiríksgata, in the older part of the city. Most of the sculptures are displayed in the garden.

Gallerí Borg. Austurvöllur. Close to Hotel Borg. A modern gallery which sometimes has an art auction.

Hladvarpinn. The Women's Center; theater and exhibition hall. Vesturgata 3. Hours vary.

Kjarvalsstadir (City Art Gallery). Miklatún. Dedicated to the memory of the great Icelandic painter Johannes S. Kjarval, many of whose works are displayed here, along with those of other Icelandic and foreign artists.

Museum of Natural History, Hverfisgata. Open Sun., Tues., Thurs. and Sat.

National Art Museum. Sudurgata. A comprehensive collection of Icelandic art. Open Sun.

Norraena Húsid (Nordic House). Close to the University. A cultural center rather than just a museum, with exhibitions, lectures, and concerts.

Thjódminjasafnid (National Museum). On Hringbraut, close to the University. Viking artifacts, plus national costumes and silver work. Also displays of weaving and woodcarving, an ancient craft which has revived in recent years, and some unusual whalebone carvings.

PARKS AND GARDENS. Great efforts are being made to beautify Iceland's cities and towns by planting trees, flowers, and shrubs in parks and gardens, though the persistent wind prevents them blooming until June or even July. Tjarnargardar (Lakeside Gardens) are spread around Lake Tjörnin within Reykjavik's city center. The small but pretty garden behind the Parliament building is called Althingishússgardur. Overlooking the harbour and close to the National Theater is Arnarhóll, a grassy hill crowned by a statue of Ingólfur Arnarson, the first settler. Near the sports stadium and main swimming pool blooms Laugardalur, a lovely botanical garden.

SPORTS. Swimming. Every Icelandic primary school registers swimming as a compulsory subject, and it has become the national sport, somewhat like football to the Americans and cricket to the British. Most travelers will enjoy the marvelous swimming pools, and Reykjavik has many which are open year-round. It is particularly invigorating in winter months to dive from a snow-laden poolside into the warm waters of an open-air pool. All bathers are required to take a shower both before and after swimming.

Following are some Reykjavik pools and their addresses: *Sundlaugar Reykjavikur,* Laugardal (34039); *Sundlaug Vesturbaejar,* Hofsvallagata (15004); *Sundlaug Kópavogs,* Borgarholtsbraut (41299); *Sundlaug Breidagerdisskóla,* Breidagerdi (85860); *Sunóll Reykjavikur,* Barónsstig (14059); and *Sundhöll Hafnarfjardar,* Herjólfsgata 10 (50088).

Golf. The city has a number of golf clubs, though most boast only nine holes, except for the main club, *Golfklúbbur Reykjavikur,* (84735), which is about 8 km. (5 miles) east of the city center and has 18 holes. Another smaller golf club is at *Seltjarnarnes,* in the western part of the city. Clubs are open daily from May to Nov., and play continues as long as the daylight lasts (it's scarcely necessary to stop at all during June!).

EXPLORING ICELAND

Gliding. Gliding enthusiasts should contact *Flugmálafélag Íslands* (the Icelandic Gliding Club), on (24354).

Fishing. Many foreign anglers return year after year for the excellent fishing opportunities that Iceland offers, Prince Charles among them. Trout and salmon are especially good, and sea angling is also possible. Check with the Tourist Office for more details. Remember that not only is a permit necessary, but the angler must usually limit his catch to a quota.

Hiking. For information on day and weekend outings, contact *Ferdafélag Íslands,* Oldugata 3 (19533).

Winter Sports. Skating is popular; Lake Tjörnin in particular, in the heart of the capital, is a bustling spot for skaters.

Skiing is practised on the slopes between Reykjavik and Selfoss. Regular bus service from Hlemmtorg and Lackjartorg during the winter. Summer skiing at Kerlingarfjöll.

The Sports Stadium in Laugardal (83377), next to the large swimming pool, has excellent facilities, both indoor and outdoor, including **badminton** and **tennis.**

Details of all sports and facilities from the Tourist Office.

MUSIC, MOVIES, AND THEATERS. Music. Reykjavik has an active symphony orchestra, with several well-known Icelandic and foreign guest conductors. An opera, operetta, or musical is staged at least once a year at the National Theater. The Icelandic Opera has been operating for some years with a great response by the public, and some Icelandic opera singers are internationally known. As in other Scandinavian countries, there are several male-voice choirs and some mixed ones. Brass bands are very popular.

Movies. There are several cinemas in Reykjavik and its suburbs. Most films shown are British or American with Icelandic subtitles. Now, however, some new Icelandic films are coming onto the circuit which usually portray life from the Saga Times. Icelandic nature and volcano films are shown daily in the *Osvaldur Knudsen Film Studio,* near the Hotel Holt. The *Volcano Show,* Hellusundi 6a (13230), consists of two hours of Icelandic volcano and nature films.

Theaters. Reykjavik's *National Theater,* opened in 1950, is a splendid building at Hverfisgata (11200), close to the city center. The Theater performs both classical and modern works, but be warned that these are in Icelandic and will therefore be somewhat impenetrable to most (though the spectacle itself is still enjoyable). Ballet is also performed here, and though not as advanced as drama productions, some good programs can be seen, usually during the winter months. Another smaller theater is the *L.R.* (Reykjavik Theater) in Vonarstraeti by the lake (16620), which is planning to move its productions in the near future to the new City Theater in the New Center of Kringlumyri. The National Theater, Reykjavik Theater, and the Icelandic Opera are all closed during Aug.

The Icelandic Marionette Show at Jón Gudmundsson, Kaplaskjólsveg 61 (16167) gives performances to both large and small groups. *Light Nights* is a multi-media show in English, depicting Icelandic culture through the ages; it appears regularly during the summer tourist season at Tjarnarbió, near the lake. Performances start at 9 P.M., Thurs. through Sun.

SHOPPING. Iceland does not exactly qualify as a shopper's paradise, but locally-made sweaters and scarves of undyed Icelandic wool are beautiful and extremely soft and warm. Also worth considering are the sheepskins, lava ceramics, and silver items. Beware of the duty-free shop at Keflavík Airport. Some items are more expensive than in shops in town. The following shops are also recommended: *Álafoss Store,* Vesturgata 2, *Framtidin,* Laugavegur 45, *Gallerí Langbrók,* Amtmannstigur 1, *The Handknitting Association of Iceland,* Skólavördustig 19, *Hilda,* Borgartún 22, *The Icelandic Handicrafts' Center,* Hafnarstraeti 3, *Kúnst,* Laugavegur 40, *Parisartízkan,* Laugavegi, and *Rammagerdin,* Hafnarstraeti 19.

In food stores you can buy specially packed samples of Icelandic food to take home yourself or to mail to your friends. The smoked salmon, herring, and shrimps are all excellent.

RESTAURANTS. Reykjavik and the surrounding suburbs have seen some welcome additions recently as far as restaurants go, and there is now an attractive selection of eating places catering for all pocketbooks. Note that all of the expensive hotels mentioned earlier in this chapter have reasonable restaurants. Reservations are necessary from Thurs. to Mon. during the summer.

Expensive

Alex. Laugavegur 126 (24631). A popular all-rounder. AE, DC, MC, V.

Arnarhóll. Hverfisgata 8–10 (18833). Very exclusive and formal. Central location. AE, DC, MC, V.

Hotel Holt. Bergstadastraeti 37 (25700). The best hotel-restaurant in town. Exclusive and business-like ambience.

Vid Sjavarsduna. Tryggvagat (15520). Good French cuisine; lamb and seafood specialties. Close to the harbor—you can watch the boats sailing in and out. AE, DC, MC, V.

Vid Tjörnina. Templarasund 3 (18666). Highly recommended. This unique restaurant is located just behind the Parliament building and the Cathedral; and has a typical late 19th-century Scandinavian decor. The chef is a pioneer of modern Icelandic seafood cuisine; try the marinated codgills. AE, DC, MC, V.

Thrir Frakkar. Baldursgata 14 (23929). French cuisine. AE, DC, MC, V.

Moderate

Hard Rock Café. Kringlan (689888).

Hornid Restaurant. Hafnarstraeti 15 (20366). Attractive atmosphere, and very central. Icelandic lamb among specialties. AE, MC, V.

Krákan. Laugavegur 22 (13628). Very popular. AE, MC, V.

Potturinn og pannan. Brautarholt 22 (11690). Excellent food in a pleasant setting. American salads. Unlicensed. AE, MC, V.

Náttúran. Laugavegur 20b (28410). Vegetarian. Reasonably priced.

Torfan. Amtmannsstígur 1 (13303). Icelandic specialties in charming 19th-century atmosphere. AE, MC, V.

Inexpensive

Café Hressó. Austurstraeti 20 (14353). Popular meeting place. AE, MC, V.

El Sombrero. Laugavegur 73 (23866). Spanish food and pizzas. AE, MC, V.

Múlakaffi. Hallarmúli (37737). Typical Icelandic meals.

Pítuhornid. Bergthórugata 21 (12400). Pita, soups, and salads. Value for money.

Saelkerinn. Austurstraeti 22 (11633). Central. Italian dishes. AE, MC, V.

NIGHTLIFE. As your grandmother probably used to say, a word to the wise is sufficient: Iceland doesn't have what you would call a red-hot after-hours scene, and some tourists might find it unbearably tame or quaint. But following is a list of the more popular Reykjavik discos, one of which may take your fancy: *Broadway,* Álfabakka 8, Breidholti (77500); *Europa Discotek,* Borgatun 32 (35355); *Hotel Isleand,* Armuli 9 (687111); *Glaesibaer,* Álfheimar 74 (86220); *Hollywood,* Ármúli 5 (83715); *Klúbburinn,* Borgartún 32 (35355); *Kreml,* Austurvelli (11322) and *Odal,* Austurvöllur (11322, 11630).

Bars

All the major hotels in Reykjavik listed earlier in this chapter have licensed bars. It's important to note that the term "bar" to the Icelander refers to snack bars selling fast foods and soft drinks, so don't get confused. Icelandic law prohibits the sale of strong beers, but low alcohol beers are readily available. Wine bars in restaurants are new.

PRACTICAL INFORMATION FOR THE REST OF ICELAND

TOURIST INFORMATION. Akureyri. Ferdaskrifstofan Akureyri, Rádhústorg 3 (96–25000). **Westmann Islands.** Ferdaskrifstofan Utsýn, Hólgata 6 (98–1515).

TELEPHONE CODES. We have given telephone codes for all the towns and villages in the hotel and restaurant lists that follow. These codes need only be used when calling from outside the town or village concerned.

HOTELS AND RESTAURANTS. It's important to note that although Iceland is a large island, the total population is only around 240,000, so it's not overflowing with huge, sprawling urban areas by any means. Given which, we haven't been able to provide many addresses for hotels and restaurants outside of those in Reykajavik and Akuyeri.

In the following sections, we have divided Iceland into four areas—North, South, East, and West—and list all hotels and restaurants under the appropriate town or village name. In most of the smaller places, there are no other restaurants except for those in the hotels, but these are usually quite adequate.

The hotels and restaurants listed below fall into three categories: Expensive (E), Moderate (M), and Inexpensive (I). We give approximate prices for these gradings in the *Facts at Your Fingertips* section.

NORTH ICELAND

Akureyri. *Hotel K.E.A.* (E), Hafnarstraeti 89 (96–22200). 28 rooms, all with bath or shower. First-class hotel with a friendly atmosphere; several bars, a restaurant and cafeteria. AE, MC, V. *Hotel Akureyri* (M), Hafnarstraeti 98 (96–22525). Comfortable hotel in the town center. V. *Hotel Vardborg* (M), Geislagata 7 (96–22600). 24 rooms. Very close to the center, with personal service and a good restaurant. AE, MC. *Skídahotel Hlídarfjall* (M), 96–22930. A ski-hotel in the hills about 2 miles above the town; open Jan. through May. Four chair-lifts, and floodlit ski-trails. *Dalakofinn* (I), Lyngholt 20 (96–23035). Very small (4 guest maximum), with bath, private entrance, and breakfast available on request. Good cooking facilities. *Edda* (I), (96–24055). 68 rooms without bath. Summer only. V. *Guesthouse Árgerdi* (I), Túngusída 2 (96–24849). Bed and breakfast for one to four persons. Swimming pool and sauna. Buses nos. 3, 4, and 5 all days from central square.
Restaurants. *Sjallinn* (M), Geislagata 12 (96–22770). Popular restaurant serving all sorts of seafood. Disco and band from Thurs. to Sun. V. *Smidjan* (M), adjacent to Bautinn (96–21818). Try the spiced lamb chop. MC, V. *Bautinn* (I), Hafnarstraeti 92 (96–21818). First-class restaurant near the town center. MC, V. *H. 100* (I), Hafnarstraeti 100 (96–25500). Combination restaurant and disco.
Camping. The camping site is at Thórunnarstraeti, just south of the swimming pool (96–23379). Toilet facilities, and hot and cold water available.
Youth Hostel. Stórholt 1 (96–23657).

Blönduós. *Edda* (M), (95–4126). 30 rooms, all with bath or shower. V.

Dalvík. *Hotel Vikurröst* (M), (96–61354). 20 rooms. Swimming pool and restaurant. Also allows sleeping bag stays. MC.

Hrútafjördur. *Edda Reykir* (M), (95–1003). 28 rooms. Swimming pool and steam bath. Summer only. V. *Stadarskáli* (M), (95–1150). Motel with good restaurant. MC.

Húnavellir. *Edda Svínavatn* (M), (95–4370). 23 rooms. Very comfortable hotel in a picturesque setting near Lake Svínavatn. Swimming pool and sauna. V.

Húsavik. *Hotel Húsavik* (E), Ketilsbraut (96–41220). 34 rooms with bath or shower. AE, V.

Kópasker. *Guesthouse* (I), (96–52121). 3 rooms.

Laugar. *Hotel Laugar S. Thingeyjarsýsla* (M), (96–43120). 70 rooms; summer only.

Mývath. *Reykjahlíd* (M), (96–441412). 12 rooms without bath; summer only. *Reynihlíd* (M), (96–44170). 44 rooms, swimming pool. U.S. astronauts were trained in the lunar-like atmosphere of the surrounding area. AE, MC, V.

Raufarhöfn. *Hotel Nordurljós* (M), (96–51223). 30 rooms; summer only.

Saudárkrókur. *Hotel Maelifell* (I), Adalgata 7 (95–5265). 7 rooms. MC.

Siglufjördur. *Hotel Höfn* (M), Laekjargata 10 (96–71514). 14 rooms, none with private bath. MC, V.

Skagafjördur. *Hotel Varmahlíd* (M), (95–6170). 17 rooms, none with private bath.

Stórutjarnir. Alongside Lake Ljósavatn. *Edda* (M), 96–43221. Comfortable, with 24 rooms. On route from Akureyri to Húsavik. Not far from the magnificent waterfall of Godafoss. Summer only.

SOUTH ICELAND

Flúdir. *Summerhotel Flúdir* (M), (99–6630). 27 rooms; summer only. *Motel Skjólborg* (I), (99–6624). 8 rooms.

Grindavik. *Guesthouse Bláa Lónid Svartsengi* (M), (92–8650). 10 rooms. Hot sea baths for sufferers from rheumatism and psoriasis. Good restaurant. Transport from airport.

Hella. *Guesthouse Mosfell* (I), (99–5828). 20 rooms without private bath.

Hveragerdi. *Hotel Ork* (E), (99–4700). 59 rooms with showers. Brand new, modern hotel. MC. *Hotel Hveragerdi* (M), Breidamörk 25 (99–4231). 12 rooms; summer only. MC. *Hotel Ljósbrá* (M), (4588). 10 rooms. MC.

Hvolsvöllur. *Hotel Hvolsvöllur* (M), (99–8187). 20 rooms, some with bath.

Keflavík. *Hotel Keflavík* (M), (92–4377). 27 rooms with showers. MC.

Kirkjubaejarklaustur. *Hotel Edda* (M), (99–7626). 32 rooms, some with bath or shower. Open all year. V.

Laugarvatn. *Hotel New Edda* (M), (99–6154). 27 rooms; summer only. *Edda Hotel* (I), (99–6118). 88 rooms, all with bath or shower. Swimming pool and steam baths; situated close by a lake. V.

Njardvík. *Hotel Kristina* (M), (92–4444). 10 rooms with showers. MC.

Selfoss. *Thóristún* (M), (99–1633). 17 rooms.

EXPLORING ICELAND

Skálholt. *Guesthouse Skálholt* (M), (99–6870). 10 rooms with bath; summer only.

Skógar. *Hotel Edda* (I), (99–8870). 34 rooms without bath; summer only. V.

Thingvellir. *Valhöll* (M), Lyngas 4 (99–4080). 37 rooms; summer only. AE, DC, MC.

Vík Mýrdal. *Hotel K.S.* (I), (99–7193). 10 rooms.

Westmann Islands. *Hotel Gestgjafinn* (M), (98–2577). 14 rooms, all with bath or shower. V. *Guesthouse Heimir* (I), (98–1515). 22 rooms, none with bath.

EAST ICELAND

Breidalsvík. *Hotel Bláfell* (M), (97–5770). 8 rooms, none with private bath. *Hotel Edda Stadarborg* (M), (96–5683). 9 rooms; summer only.

Djúpivogur. *Hotel Framtid* (I), (97–8887). 9 rooms.

Egilsstadir. *Hotel Valaskjálf* (M), (97–1500). 24 rooms, all with bath. V. *Hotel Egilstadir* (I), (97–1114). 15 rooms with bath; summer only.

Eidar. *Hotel Edda* (I), (97–3803). 60 rooms, none with bath. Summer only. V.

Eskifjördur. *Hotel Askja* (I), (97–6261). 7 rooms.

Hallormsstadir. *Hotel Edda* (I), (97–1683). 22 rooms, none with private bath. Summer only. V.

Hornafjördur. *Hotel Höfn* (E), (97–8240). 40 rooms, all with bath or shower. DC, V. *Hotel Edda Nesjaskóli* (I), (97–8470). 30 rooms, none with bath. Summer only. V.

Raufarhöfn. *Nordurljós* (I), (96–51233). 8 rooms.

Reydarfjördur. *Guesthouse K.B.H.* (I), (97–4200). 3 rooms without bath.

Seydisfjördur. *Snaefell* (M), (97–21460). 9 rooms. Restaurant.

Vopnafjördur. *Guesthouse Tangi* (M), (97–3224). 12 rooms without bath.

WEST ICELAND

Akranes. *Hotel Akranes Bárugata* (M), (97–2020). 11 rooms, none with bath.

Borgarfjördur. *Hotel Bifröst* (M), (93–5000). 31 rooms; summer only.

Borgarnes. *Hotel Borgarnes* (M), Egilsgötu (93–7119). 35 rooms, all with bath or shower. MC, V.

Búdardalur. *Hotel Bjarg* (I), (93–4161). 7 rooms.

Isafjördur. *Hotel Isafjördur* (E), (94–4111). 31 rooms, all with bath or shower. V. *Hotel Hamrabaer* (M), (94–3777). 8 rooms. *Guesthouse Isafjördur* (I), (94–3043). 17 rooms.

Króksfjördur. *Hotel Edda Bjarkalundur* (M), (94–4762). 12 rooms; summer only.

Ólafsvik. *Hotel Nes* (M), (93–6300). 38 rooms, none with bath.

Reykholt. *Hotel Edda* (M), (93–5260). Summer only. V.

Saelinsdalur. *Hotel Laugar* (M), (93–4111). 27 rooms, none with bath. Summer only.

Snaefellsnes. *Hotel Búdir* (M), (93–8111). 20 rooms, none with bath. Summer only.

Stykkishólmur. *Hotel Stykkishólmur* (E), (93–8330). 26 rooms, all with bath or shower. MC, V.

Thingeyri. *Guesthouse Höfn* (I), (94–8151). 3 rooms.

Vatnsfjördur. *Hotel Edda Flókalundur* (M), (94–2011). 14 rooms, all with bath or shower. Summer only. V.

Detail from Picture-stone: Gotland, 8th Century.

SCANDINAVIAN HISTORY

Prosperity Out of Conflict

Scandinavia today presents a picture of harmonious unity: five countries, linked by a common culture, geography and history, politically and technologically sophisticated, at peace with themselves and the world. There are, to be sure, differences between them. Finland, for example, has a language that owes nothing to the other Scandinavian tongues. Norway, Sweden and Denmark are monarchies, Finland and Iceland are republics. Denmark is the only Scandinavian member of the EEC, the Common Market. Sweden and Finland have long been politically non-aligned, Norway, Denmark and Iceland are all active members of NATO. But what unites Scandinavia is ultimately of greater significance than what divides her, and it is difficult to think of any other grouping of countries in the modern world more happily or naturally united.

But it was not always so. Her present enviable prosperity and stability are a striking tribute to the new maturity of once rival and warring lands, with little more than a common tongue—Finland excepted—and their harsh climate and isolation on the northern fringes of Europe to unite them.

Bog People and Berserkers

More than anything else, it is the fact of her isolation that provides the key note of much early Scandinavian history. With the exception of Denmark and parts of southern Sweden, Scandinavia is a vast and frequently inhospitable land, underpopulated even today; a land of endless forests and mountain fastnesses, laced by rivers and lakes and buffeted by the long northern winter. This combination of remoteness and vast scale long conspired to ensure that she remained in the backwaters of early European history.

Not surprisingly, Scandinavia's earliest inhabitants seem naturally to have gravitated towards its most fertile and temperate regions. Though relics dating back six or seven thousand years—in particular primitive skis—have been found in the empty wastes of Finland and northern Sweden, it was in the south of Scandinavia, in present day Denmark and southern Sweden, that the first sizeable settlements existed. There is considerable evidence to suggest that by the Bronze Age (c. 1500 B.C.–500 B.C.) the early Scandinavians had become successful farmers and hunters, skilled also at pottery and weaving. A number of Scandinavian museums—the Nordic Museum in Stockholm pre-eminently—contain sizeable collections of jewelry, pottery and other artefacts from burial mounds which attest to the relative sophistication of these early inhabitants. Remarkably, two of the men themselves, pickled by the peat bogs in which they were buried, have also been found. The severed heads of these grisly remains—Graubolle man and Tollund man—are today on view, for those with strong stomachs, at the Århus and Silkeborg museums in Denmark.

Yet despite this evidence of a not inconsiderable population, Scandinavia remained isolated from the main centers of Europe. Even the Romans baulked at her trackless forests and vast unpopulated expanses, no doubt discouraged also by her brutal winters, and the northernmost limits of their empire stopped far to the south of the Scandinavian lands. Nonetheless, it seems clear that merchants from the south were happy to barter with the mysterious northern tribes. The pieces of amber that could be picked up on Denmark's beaches were particularly prized by the Romans, who traded ivory, silver and gold for them. Roman coins have even been found in remote and rugged Iceland—*Ultima Thule* indeed.

By about A.D. 700 much of coastal southern Scandinavia had been settled, though vast areas of the interior remained uninhabited. Interestingly, though perhaps not surprisingly, the most densely populated areas, at the heart of the most important agricultural lands and strategically placed for trade, were subsequently to grow into modern Scandinavia's capitals. But in addition, Trondheim, on the northwest coast of Norway, also developed as an important center.

As well as being successful hunters and farmers, the Scandinavians also traded extensively. The Swedes, for example, controlled the fur trade between north and south Scandinavia, while the Norwegians of the Atlantic coast had trade links with both southern Sweden and Denmark and the Frisian islands on the west coast of Germany. However, the inhospitable interior meant that most trade was dependent on sea travel, and it is evident that despite their primitive navigational know-how the early Scandinavians were skilled shipwrights and routinely undertook long and arduous sea voyages. At the same time, increasingly persistent warring between rival tribes also made the possession of sea-going vessels necessary.

Around A.D. 800 something very strange happened to these somewhat primitive hunters and farmers, relegated to the outer fringes of Europe. Without warning, and for reasons that still remain the subject of speculation, they exploded onto the European scene, sallying forth from Scandinavia in their long ships and wreaking havoc—pillaging, looting and terrorizing—over the length and breadth of Europe. The Vikings had arrived.

"From the fury of the Norsemen, Good Lord deliver us," was to become a deeply-felt and oft-uttered prayer in many parts of Europe.

Whatever the reasons for the sudden appearance of the Vikings—whether economic pressure created by population increases in their homelands, changes in the climate, or just a simple-minded taste for a wandering life of excitement and exploration (the ultimate test of Viking manhood was to enter battle bare-chested or "berserk")—one thing is clear. The Vikings were successful because the disintegration of the Roman empire had created a power vacuum in Europe, leaving the continent weak and disordered, a prey to any who chanced upon her. Thus the Vikings remorselessly swept through Europe, as though a cannon loaded with grapeshot had been suddenly fired.

Swedes thrust southeastwards across the Baltic, founding Russia some say (*rus* means Swede), and reaching the Black Sea by means of the Dnieper river, and Persia by the Volga river and Caspian sea. In Constantinople they enrolled as Varangian (or Viking) guards, elite bodyguards to the Byzantine emperor. The Norwegians sailed west and north, overtaking Orkney and Shetland, which remained Scandinavian until 1468 when they were mortgaged to the Scottish crown. Step by step, they then bridged the Atlantic, reaching the Faroes (850), Iceland (874), Greenland (984) and finally Vinland—North America—(1000). The Atlantic leap itself was achieved in just two generations. Eric the Red left Norway to farm in Iceland, and then moved on to found the Greenland colony. It was his son, Leif, who discovered America.

The Norwegians also swept down the west coast of Britain, to the Isle of Man, the Lake District and Ireland. The Danes meanwhile landed in eastern England, establishing York as their major center. In the south of England, the Danish king Canute eventually reigned (1016–1035) over a combined English, Danish and Norwegian domain. At the same time Northern France became Normandy, the land of the northmen, soon to emerge as an independent country and, under Duke William, to begin the conquest of Britain in 1066.

The Coming of Christianity

Though the impact of the Vikings was great, the Viking age itself was relatively short lived, lasting from about 800 to 1050. Perhaps its very vividness was such as to ensure that it exhausted itself quickly. At all events, by the middle of the 11th century, the Viking period was rapidly being superceded by a new and much more stable economic and political order that was to last right up to the Renaissance. And at the heart of this new medieval society was Christianity, slowly but inevitably dispersing the seemingly endless night of the Dark Ages.

The Vikings themselves yielded to the forces of the "pale Galilean." Some indeed appeared positively to welcome the new religion and proved themselves enthusiastic converts and, later, missionaries, happy to despatch those whose interest was more tepid to the Viking Valhalla. Nonetheless, the old beliefs and religions of the Vikings lingered on—their Gods Tyr, Wodon, Thor and Frey are still with us, disguised as Tuesday, Wednesday, Thursday and Friday. For a time, Christianity fused with the Viking religions to create curious hybrids, nowhere better illustrated than by the 12th-century stave churches of Norway, a number of which have survived to the present day at Fantoft, Borgund and Lom. These tall,

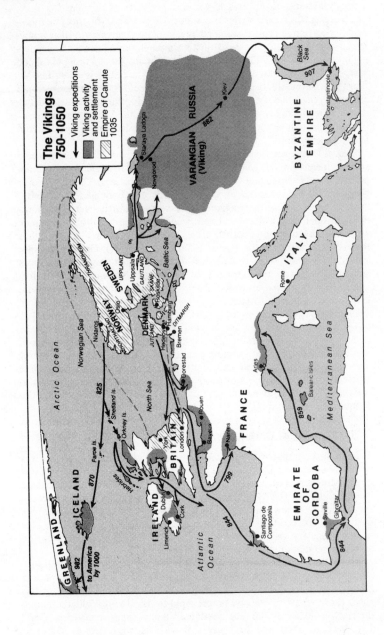

pagoda-like structures, whose tiered wooden roofs rise delicately skywards, are always surmounted by a cross, but on their eaves and along the door jambs dragons and other pagan symbols are carved. Even today there are clear traces of the old Scandinavian religions in the far north among the Lapps and in Finnmark.

But Christianity proved itself an irresistable force and by 1300 had established itself throughout Scandinavia. Sweden even produced a saint, Bridget, born in 1303. She subsequently moved to Rome where she wrote a series of widely influential mystic *Revelations* and founded an order of nuns, the Bridgettines.

The Middle Ages

For all that Christianity underpinned Scandinavian society in the Middle Ages, Scandinavian history in this period nonetheless presents a confused picture of succeeding dynasties, recalcitrant nobles and scheming bishops. And for much of the period, that is until the beginning of the 17th century, Scandinavia remained essentially remote from developments on the wider European stage, a minor player in an increasingly important game. Even Denmark, for example, long the most developed and prosperous of the Scandinavian countries, largely by virtue of its proximity to the European mainland, was reduced to bit part status, falling under the sway of the Hanseatic League, the predatory merchants of Hamburg and Lübeck in north Germany who negotiated for themselves lucrative trading monopolies among the hapless Scandinavians. The Hansa quays in Bergen, Norway, have survived as potent evidence of Hanseatic power.

At the same time that Scandinavia was groaning under the Hanseatic yoke in the 13th and 14th centuries, another catastrophe struck in the form of the Black Death. Norway alone lost a third of her population between 1349 and 1350. Essential reading for an idea of the impact of the Black Death on the infant Scandinavian states is Sigrid Undset's sprawling novel *Kristin Lavransdatter.*

Literature of another sort was actually being produced during this period, in Iceland, by the aristocratic and cultured Snorri Sturlson (1179–1241). He it was who committed to writing the achievements and adventures of the Viking age, and celebrated early Iceland's turmoil and warring, in the Sagas and Eddas, the greatest monuments of early Scandinavian literature and an invaluable treasure house of historic myths and tales. Ironically perhaps, he did so at a moment when not only had the Vikings all but faded from the scene but when Iceland itself, until the 13th century a considerable political force in Scandinavian affairs and a proudly independent land—it is Iceland's happy boast that she is the site of the oldest republic north of the Alps—was fast fading herself, a decline continued in 1264 when Iceland succumbed to Norwegian rule, as had Greenland three years earlier.

However, this period of Norwegian expansion in the 13th century was to prove brief and, the Hanseatic League notwithstanding, by the 14th century it was Denmark that had emerged as the dominant voice in Scandinavian affairs, consolidating her hold on the whole of the region in 1389 in the shape of the Kalmar Union by which Sweden, Finland and Norway were united under Danish rule. The Kalmar Union, which lasted until 1521, was essentially the work of the remarkable Queen Margrethe of Denmark. She was, however, Regent only and in 1397 handed the reigns of power to her incompetent nephew, Eric of Pomerania. The combination of his maladministration and the greed of his henchmen was more than sufficient to cause a seemingly endless series of revolts among his subject peoples, especially in Sweden. The Danish rulers that followed Eric were hardly less inept, but nonetheless the Union struggled precariously through the 15th century. By the end of the century, following the ascendency of the energetic and authoritarian Christian II of Denmark, it appeared set for greater things, however. Determined to stamp out dissent among the Swedes once and for all, in 1520 Christian initiated a massacre of the leading members of the so-called Freedom Party in Stockholm. But his efforts were to prove entirely counter-productive, and only sparked greater demands for Swedish independence. This the Swedes were dramatically and violently to achieve, principally under the imaginative and forceful leadership of Gustavus Vasa. Capitalizing on a popular uprising in the province of Dalecarlia, Gustavus fanned the flame of revolt and by 1523 had established himself as undisputed ruler of a newly-independent and aggressive Sweden. Thus the stage was set for Sweden's greatest moment of glory and expansion.

The Reformation and Sweden's Rise

The Sweden now ruled by the indomitable Gustavus Vasa was still an essentially impoverished and downtrodden land following almost two centuries of Danish domination. Similarly, though the Danes had been ousted from Sweden, their military intentions toward her were by no means exhausted and they remained in control of parts of southern Sweden, a permanent threat to Gustavus. Thus much of Gustavus's reign was characterized by an urgent need to consolidate Sweden's independence from Denmark and to build up trade as rapidly as possible in order to finance his increasingly ambitious military goals.

In this, Gustavus shrewdly and pragmatically took advantage of the slow spread of the Reformation into Scandinavia. Like his contemporary Henry VIII in England, Gustavus, guided largely by political rather than spiritual considerations, took advantage of the split with Rome to support and eventually to establish as the new national church the Reformed—that is, the Protestant—religion. Simultaneously, he systematically confiscated much of the considerable wealth of the old Catholic church in Sweden, using it to finance his armies.

As Sweden grew in strength, in the process ridding herself of the remaining monopolies enjoyed by the waning Hanseatic League, so Gustavus began to interest himself more and more in foreign affairs. And it was under Gustavus that for the first time since the Vikings a Scandinavian country began to enjoy influence and status on the wider European stage. An alliance with Francis I of France against the future emperor of the Holy Roman Empire, Charles V, represented only the first stirrings of Sweden's ambitions toward, and influence over, the affairs of the Holy Roman Empire on the European mainland.

The Reformation enjoyed equal success in the rest of Scandinavia, spreading throughout the joint kingdom of Denmark and Norway and into Swedish controlled Finland, and finally to Iceland. To some extent, the Reformed Church acted as a new focus of nationalism for the Danes, still smarting from their defeat at the hands of Gustavus Vasa. Sweden's position by the end of the 16th century was still somewhat precarious. Her only outlet to the North Sea, for example, was a narrow strip at the mouth of the Göta river between hostile Denmark and Norway, and her ambitions in the Baltic were permanently under threat from Russia and Poland as well as Denmark herself. Moreover, by the beginning of the 17th century Denmark had acquired a new ruler in Christian IV (1588–1648) whose dynamism and ambition were formidable. As well as being an indefatigable builder—Copenhagen's fairy-tale summer palace of Rosenborg and the Borsen (Stock Exchange) with its barley-sugar-twist spire both owe their existence to the energetic Christian; similarly, he rebuilt Oslo, moving it nearer to its present location and renaming it Christiania in the process—Christian made strident efforts to regain the dominance Denmark had enjoyed during the heyday of the Kalmar Union. Denmark still controlled all shipping passing through the narrow sound between Copenhagen and southern Sweden—the Sound of Sounds, as it came to be known, and the principal link between the Baltic and the North Sea. Similarly, her maritime prowess in the Baltic remained impressive.

Under Christian the Danes embarked on an extended series of military campaigns against the Swedes. However, while the Danes were fortunate to have so outstanding a ruler in Christian, the Swedes were even more blessed. And in Gustavus II Adolphus, the Lion of the North who roared his way to the throne in 1611, they found themselves a ruler of outstanding military abilities, more than the equal of even one as apparently awesome as Christian IV.

Under Gustavus, Sweden swept confidently into the 17th century and her age of greatness, during which she defeated the Danes, driving them out of southern Sweden, and turned the Baltic into what was to amount to her own private preserve. In addition, the brilliant military campaigns waged by Gustavus were to ensure Sweden a decisive role in the complex entanglements of the Thirty Years War (1618–1648), in which the Catholic forces of the Holy Roman Empire, ruled by the Habsburgs, grappled brutally and somewhat pointlessly with the Protestant forces of northern Europe, represented principally by Sweden. By 1632, in fact, the Swedes under Gustavus had swept through the whole of present day Germany and were poised to take Austria, the heart of the Holy Roman Empire, when Gustavus was killed at the battle of Lutzen in 1632. The Swedes were victorious at Lutzen, but the death of their charismatic general and king broke the momentum of their campaign, and the battle was to mark the high point of the European adventures.

Gustavus Adolphus was succeded by his young daughter, the enigmatic and ambivalent Christina. In the early part of her reign, however, when Christina was still a child, the country was governed by a Council headed by the able statesman Axel Oxenstierna. Though Sweden under Oxenstierna remained a major military influence in the Thirty Years War, which, as it neared its climax, was to turn Germany into one vast and chaotic battlefield, Oxenstierna himself turned his attentions increasingly towards developments in the Baltic, seeking to establish Sweden as the pre-eminent power there. In this, as in other matters of foreign policy, Christina played no very significant role once she had come of age. Though a woman of striking intelligence (but of less-than-lovely appearance), Christina devoted herself almost exclusively to establishing luxury, elegance and learning in her court. Her reckless extravagance and neglect of matters of state, despite the warnings of Oxenstierna, were eventually to prove her undoing and in 1654 she was forced to abdicate. Her disgrace in the eyes of her

countrymen, who by now she affected to despise for their ignorance and crudity, was compounded by her subsequent conversion to Catholicism in Paris. She thereafter settled in Rome, living in the same house that St. Bridget had used, where she died in 1689.

However, the combined efforts of Oxenstierna and Christina's successors Charles X Gustavus and Charles XI Gustavus were equal to the task of ensuring that Sweden's dominant role in Scandinavia and the Baltic was continued. Indeed it was under Charles X in the Danish-Swedish war of 1657–60 that Sweden eventually reclaimed the remaining Danish territories in southern Sweden, confining Denmark once and for all to the areas west of the Sound.

By the end of the 17th century Sweden was again ruled by a man of outstanding military ability, the romantic soldier-king Charles XII Gustavus. He needed to be, too, for in 1700 Sweden was attacked simultaneously by the combined armies of Poland, Denmark and Russia. Despite the overwhelming numerical superiority of his enemies, Charles achieved a remarkable victory over the Russians at Narva in 1700, which effectively destroyed the enemy alliance. He subsequently marched on Moscow but was defeated—as much by the Russian winter as by the Russian army—at Poltava in 1709. Charles sought refuge in Turkey from where, extraordinarily, he continued to rule over distant Sweden. By now, however, Sweden faced an even larger alliance, made up of Russia, Poland, Denmark, Britain and two of the north German states, Hanover and Prussia. Hopelessly outnumbered, Charles then attempted to disrupt the alliance between Russia and Britain, to which end he returned, incognito, to Scandinavia in 1718. In the middle of these clandestine negotiations, Charles was mysteriously murdered in Norway, ending all hope of disrupting the powerful forces ranged against him. The Swedes were forced to capitulate.

Much of Sweden's Baltic empire was ceded to the Russians, including large parts of Finland, and by 1721 the once indomitable Swedes found that their empire had all but vanished leaving the way clear for the Russians, who soon after emerged as the dominant power in the Baltic.

Rococo and Revolution

Though Sweden remained the dominant power in the 18th century among the Scandinavian nations, the period as a whole witnessed the gradual decline of Scandinavian influence. For example, while Denmark continued to enjoy considerable maritime prestige, she was also to fall increasingly under the influence of Prussia in northern Germany, a trend that continued into the 19th century. Similarly, Norway and Finland, the one still ruled by Denmark, the other partitioned between Sweden and Russia, remained obscure and generally insignificant lands. And Sweden herself was forced to watch the gradual erosion of what remained of her Baltic empire.

Nonetheless, it was in Sweden that the most interesting developments occurred, especially during the reign of Gustavus III, who came to the throne in 1771. He was responsible both for a radical reshaping of Swedish government—a vital early step in the development of democracy in Sweden—and for a great upsurge in the importance of Swedish arts. His marvelous palace at Drottningholm, just outside Stockholm, with its delightful Rococo theater, is eloquent proof of the artistic revolution that occurred under this most enlightened of Swedish kings. The period also saw Sweden step into the intellectual and scientific limelight. Carl von Linée—we know him as Linnaeus—was the leading botanist of his day, whose revolutionary *Systems of Nature* pioneered the same essential system of classification for plants as that used today. Gustavus—a great admirer of all things French—also founded the Swedish Academy, modeled on its famous French cousin.

But in 1792 Gustavus was assassinated, a victim of the violent political opposition his far-reaching reforms had stirred up among the Swedish aristocracy. Yet to some extent even his death amounted to little more than a sideshow, for by the end of the 18th century, internal events in Scandinavia were being more and more overshadowed by the turmoil engulfing Europe as a whole following the French Revolution. As Napoleon and his revolutionary armies marched across the Continent, the Scandinavians found themselves inexorably drawn into the greater European conflict, with consequences that were to influence decisively the further development of Scandinavian history.

Thus in 1801, for example, Nelson attacked Copenhagen to prevent Napoleon obtaining the Danish navy for his intended invasion of Britain. Six years later, Wellington bombarded the capital again and seized the fleet himself. Similarly, Sweden under Gustavus IV Adolphus, having declared herself for Britain largely on the strength of her trading links, was attacked by the Russians in 1807 following a recent alliance forged between Napoleon and Russia. The Swedish–Russian conflict was in fact to have a number of very important consequences. Not only did Sweden lose her remaining Finnish territories to the Russians, she also found herself with a new, and very unexpected ruler. This was one of Napoleon's marshalls, one Bernadotte, who, with the active collusion of Napoleon (who saw Bernadotte as a swift means of obtaining control over Sweden), was elected king of Sweden in 1809. However, the French emperor's hopes were quickly dashed when Bernadotte revealed himself as both profoundly opposed to Napoleon's scheming and shrewd in the extreme. At the Congress of Vienna in 1815, which settled the fate of post-Napoleonic Europe, Bernadotte was able to obtain considerable compensation for the loss of Sweden's Finnish lands, and even more spectacularly confirmed the transfer of Norway, which had been ruled by Denmark since the 14th century, from Denmark to Sweden. Denmark meanwhile was left only with the politically and economically insignificant North Atlantic islands of Iceland, Greenland and the Faroes.

Industrialization and Independence

More than the political map of Scandinavia was changed by the events of the first decades of the 19th century, however. By about 1820, it was evident that Scandinavia was economically crippled, unable to keep pace with the ever more rapid developments of the Industrial Revolution or to exploit the growing opportunities for trade created by the opening of new markets outside Europe by the leading European nations, among whom the Scandinavians emphatically no longer numbered.

The 19th century was in fact a generally dismal time for the Scandinavians. Lacking the capital to develop their own modern industries, their trade was gradually taken over by foreign concerns, causing a decline in home markets that made only all the more remote the likelihood of the industrialization that by 1850 had become long overdue. Simultaneously,

Scandinavian agriculture also declined, giving rise to wide-spread rural poverty which in turn led to massive emigration, particularly to America. This reached a peak between 1880 and the turn of the century.

But bankruptcy was in some senses the mother of Scandinavian invention, and from the middle years of the 19th century, a slow industrialization spread throughout the region. Such breakthroughs as Ørsted's in electro-magnetism helped the Nordic lands, lavishly endowed with water for electricity, to industrialize efficiently. Nobel's invention of dynamite changed the nature of war and mining. Similar inventive genius assisted in the growth of Danish dairying, Norwegian nitrates and Swedish ball-bearing factories. Developments in steamships helped found an expanding Norwegian merchant navy for fishing, world trade and, at home, provided the coastal services from Bergen to Kirkenes and back, forerunner of today's Coastal Express. Railways opened up vast interior tracts and serviced mines in Sweden and Finland, while canals bypassed the Baltic, linking Stockholm with Gothenburg through the great lakes. The Danes established Esbjerg in 1868 especially for trade with Britain, while the United Steamship Company was created two years earlier to link the nation's scattered areas, and is still with us as DFDS.

Scandinavians, with their small populations, were also among the first to realize the importance of an educated, fully participatory majority. Here the chief figure was the Dane Gruntvig (1783–1872), whose deep reading in the Sagas, widely-based religious views, boundless energy and patriotism led him to create the highly influential Folk High School movement. These schools, somewhat misnamed in English, offered "Education for Life"—culture, history and poetry, moral and practical subjects and economics for all.

While the latter half of the 19th century saw a slow rise in prosperity in Scandinavia and the political foundation of the modern Scandinavian states, it also saw the only serious foreign entanglement to befall Scandinavia since the end of the Napoleonic wars. This occurred on Denmark's southern border with Prussia in Germany, long a source of friction between Danes and Germans. By the 1860s, the Prussians, guided by their wily Chancellor Bismarck, had begun to cast covetous eyes on Denmark's border provinces, the acquisition of which they saw as the first step in the unification of Germany under Prussia. When war came in 1864 the military might of the Prussians was rapidly decisive and Denmark, having lost Norway only 50 years earlier, now found herself stripped of one sixth of her remaining lands. That the Danish monarchy survived such a crushing national humiliation spoke volumes for its stability and popularity. (Denmark's southern provinces were eventually restored to her in 1920).

The latter part of the 19th century was also marked by the growing spread of democratic and nationalistic ideals, culminating in 1905 with the dissolution of the joint kingdom of Sweden and Norway and the granting of full independence to Norway. Finland's independence from Russia in 1917, however, was achieved at much greater cost. All the Scandinavian nations had managed to remain neutral in World War I (though all, especially Norway, suffered considerable disruption of their trade). The Finns were thus well placed to take advantage of the Russian Revolution in 1917, which plunged an already war-torn Russia into terrible chaos, and declare themselves independent. Though the new Russian regime under Lenin soon recognized this independent Finland, a large body of opinion in Finland did not and civil war broke out; the "whites" favoring independence, the "reds" continued union with Russia, or the Soviet Union as it had now become. The whites were quickly victorious, however, and in 1920 the borders of modern Finland were established.

The Modern States

The Scandinavian nations continued on their peaceful course until the late '30s, all by now determinedly neutral and essentially removed from the growing tensions in Europe caused by the rapid rise of Nazism and the Soviet Union. But in 1939, despite their professed neutrality, the Finns were invaded by the Soviet Union, with whom they had signed a pact of non-agression in 1932. Remarkably, Finland resisted the vast but disorganized Soviet army for over 100 days before capitulating in March 1940. Under the terms of the subsequent peace treaty the Finns were obliged to cede large parts of their eastern lands to Russia.

This, however, was only the beginning of Scandinavia's troubles. As in World War I, all the Scandinavian nations attempted to remain neutral following the outbreak of World War II. The Swedes alone succeeded in doing so. Both Norway and Denmark were invaded by Nazi Germany in April 1940, while Iceland was occupied by Britain and, later, by the Americans who used it as a vital staging post for ferrying men and supplies across the Atlantic. Finland, meanwhile, then sided with the Nazis; not, as they are quick to point out, for any ideological reasons but because they saw the Nazi invasion of Russia in 1941 as an ideal opportunity to regain the territories lost in 1940. In this they were singularly unsuccessful, and ended the war by fighting the Russians *and* the Germans. Though non-combatants, the Danes and, even more particularly, the Norwegians, had suffered almost equally grave destruction by the end of the war. To some extent the very effectiveness of the Resistance movements both spawned was responsible, provoking the occupying Nazis into terrible acts of reprisal.

By 1945 Norway, Denmark and Finland were all seriously weakened, the Finns in addition having lost again to the Russians all the territory they had regained following their initial invasion with the Germans. Even neutral Sweden ended the war with severe economic problems caused by the disruption of her trade and the expense of the rapid armaments program she had been forced into in order to maintain her neutrality.

Thus it is really only in the immediate post-war period that Scandinavia has grown into the plenty and excellence that so distinguishes her today. Politically, the major developments of this period were the granting of full independence to Iceland in 1944, followed by the granting of full autonomy to Greenland in 1979. 1956 saw the formation of the Nordic Council, a loose grouping of all the Scandinavian states designed to further cooperation and development. Still a thriving organization today, it expresses eloquently the new and happy unity of this much-troubled region.

Yet even in today's affluent society—and Scandinavia seems to have weathered the recessions of the '70s and early '80s better than most—there are many reminders that the Scandinavia of the past, the vast and trackless land that even the Romans failed to penetrate, lingers on, a permanent reminder of an ancient people. In the far north Eskimos still hunt seal and polar bear where best they can be found, and Lapps still wander in search of fresh pastures for their reindeer. They may have walkie-talkies and central heating, but their lives are otherwise little changed from those of their ancestors two thousand years ago.

SCANDINAVIAN HISTORY

FOOD AND DRINK

How to Skal and Survive

Although the Viking custom of drinking toasts out of somebody else's skull went out of fashion quite some time ago, it's only fair to warn you, as a visitor to Scandinavia, that you're still in danger of losing your head. But the threat to the visitor is more subtle these days, as you'll discover when you first slide your feet under a Scandinavian table.

When Do We Eat?

The first thing which will puzzle you as you edge uncertainly towards the *spisesal* (dining room) is the question of mealtimes. Breakfast, of course, is a natural, and is consumed sometime between the early morning bath and a glance at the newspaper. But now the difficulty begins. The next meal of the day defies definition. Some Anglo-Saxons are tempted to call it dinner, counting the sandwiches and glass of milk that many businessmen eat at their desks around noon as lunch. There are even those who stick by this theory doggedly, refusing to notice that the clatter of silverware against china, which starts up around 4.30 P.M. and becomes deafening towards 6.00 P.M. has completely disappeared, in Norway at least, by the dinner hour. The Scandinavians, being practical people, avoid the dispute by calling it *middag*. We advise you to do the same, thereby working for peace in a troubled world.

Instead of sowing discord, the Scandinavians are interested merely in making maximum use of the long and bright summer evenings. Accordingly, families sit down to the main meal of the day as soon as father comes home from work, somewhere towards the tag end of the afternoon. The great advantage of this arrangement is that, once *middag* is over, everyone is free for the rest of the day. If you come hotfoot from South Dakota or South Kensington with a hatful of introductions to near relations or business acquaintances, you can turn this custom into a game. Don't refuse three or four dinner invitations you received for the same day. Just fix a different hour for each.

While you have your napkin unfolded and are wondering who's going to eat all that food, we should urge you to save some room for *aftens* or supper, the final meal of the day, not counting incidental snacks. This may be no more than cakes and coffee or it may consist of no less than a complete cold buffet, depending on the circumstances and whether or not your eyes have the socially-accepted glaze. No one is looked down upon for starting this as early as 7.00 P.M. although, at a formal party, it might well not appear until midnight.

With this overall timetable in mind, let's get down to particular dishes. The typically Scandinavian breakfast is more varied than the typical English or American one. The larger hotels, accustomed to catering to visitors from abroad, will be able to offer you bacon and eggs, though this honorable combination is not indigenous to the Scandinavian ménage. Instead, eggs, cheese, cold meats, herrings in a number of guises, jams, and fruit are all likely to make their appearance, in addition to less usual items such as cereals, porridge, hot meatballs, and salad. These you'll discover together with a great variety of bread, many kinds rarely found in other countries. One of them, *Knekkebrød*, is of the hard, unleavened type which you've undoubtedly seen elsewhere under the proprietary name of Ry King. Unless you specify otherwise, your egg will normally be served soft-boiled and still in its shell.

By the time you've tried everything, chances are you'll have a solid foundation which will carry you through to mid-afternoon. But if you find your fancy gradually turning towards thoughts of food around about noon, you have a number of choices. In most of the bigger cities there are sidewalk stands displaying signs reading *Pølser* or *Varm Korv*. At these you will be able to buy hot dogs, often wrapped in what looks like a pancake instead of a roll. They are smaller than what you're used to, and you will probably agree that they taste better.

If all you want is something cool, look for another kind of sidewalk stand, marked *Is* or *Glass*. The name has nothing to do with the verb "to be" or with windowpanes, but informs you that here you can have ice cream. The Finns, incidentally, call it *jäätelö*.

The Mysterious Open Sandwich

Failing both of these (and still assuming you're interested), make for the nearest restaurant. If you see the word *smørbrød*, you're in luck, for this is Scandinavia's most typical dish (the Swedish spelling is *smörgasbørd)*. The word means simply, "butter-bread," but there's nothing simple about it, as you'll discover when the waiter hands you a menu listing dozens of varieties.

Smørbrød is the rich uncle of its English or American nephew, the sandwich. Unlike the anonymous sort of thing served at garden parties or railway stations, it is a single-decker, and presents its offering naked and unashamed. Lobster, smoked salmon, prawns, shrimps, smoked herrings, all appropriately and artistically garnished, cold turkey, chicken, roast beef, pork, a host of sausages, cheeses, eggs, and salads, all tastefully and appetizingly arranged. Variously called *smörgås* by the Swedes and *voileipä* by the Finns, three of them taken with a cool lager are generally considered an excellent lunch, whether or not you abandon all caution and succumb to a piece of pastry for dessert. Hot food is available too, if you are still hungry.

Wherever you may be in Scandinavia, the sea is never far off, and this is a good thing to remember when you sit down to *middag*. Perhaps because the fish served in restaurants and hotels is invariably fresh, the Scandinavians are all great fish-eaters. Whatever the reason, their seafood dishes are justly renowned for their variety and excellence. Lobster, salmon, and trout are great favorites, but you will also have your choice of cured herrings, crayfish, crab, oysters, shrimps, prawns, hake, eel, and other seaborne morsels. Boiled cod may sound unromantic, yet you'll find it transformed when served *à la Scandinave* with melted butter and parsley. In the summer the Swedes and Finns indulge in traditional crayfish weeks when you can go on eating these succulent little creatures until your conscience begins to bother you. In Denmark you'll compare the Limfjord oysters to the best that Baltimore or Colchester has to offer.

Then there are a number of fish dishes which only the bolder spirits are advised to try. The first of these is *rakørret*, which is trout that, like Keats' wine, has "lain long years in the deep-delved earth." There is actually much more to the preparation of this highly odiferous *spécialité de la maison* than burying it in the backyard, but it is undoubtedly an acquired taste. Next comes *surströmming*, another form of man's inhumanity to fish, except that this time it's a herring who suffers. As the name sugests, the taste is distinctly sour; that is, if you get that far. The third of our "don'ts" for cautious gourmets is *lutefisk*, which is codfish steeped in a lye of potash. The finished product has the consistency of frog spawn and a taste which can only be experienced and not described. The Norwegians who eat this "delicacy" anesthetize themselves with such copious drams of *akvavit* one might suspect that the *lutefisk* is only an excuse.

While we are on the subject of dishes which should be approached circumspectly, we may as well complete the story with a mention of *geitost* or goat's cheese, which has the hue of scrubbing soap or milk chocolate and the texture of plastic wood. Give it a try anyhow; you'll be called on for your own opinion sooner or later. And if you are too disappointed, all the Scandinavian countries produce excellent imitations of such well-known favorites as Roquefort, Camembert, Gruyère, and even England's Stilton. Danish Blue is another local variety with which no cheese-lover could possibly quarrel.

Scandinavian cooks use margarine or butter for their cooking, and not oil as the Latins do. Game and roasts are usually served with a cream sauce which is delicious. In some cases, sour cream is used, and *ryper* (a variety of grouse or ptarmigan) prepared with this sauce and accompanied by cranberry jam is a rare treat.

By now you are doubtless wondering what has happened to the renowned Swedish *smörgåsbord*. It's doing fine, thank you. But let me first explain to the uninitiated that the *smörgåsbord* (called *voileipäpöytä* by the Finns) is a very special *hors d'oeuvre*, offering the diner a stupendous number of small dishes, each more calculated than the last to whet his appetite and make him forget all rash resolutions to respect his waistline. The beauty of this institution is that it contains no *pièce de résistance* to dominate the table. You roam at will like the honey bee, savoring here a morsel of smoked eel, there a little lobster, and roving through the delicacies of the animal kingdom, with regular rounds of *akvavit* and beer to give you fresh incentive. These days, the *smörgåsbord* is seldom the prelude to a four-course dinner in private homes, but some restaurants feature it as a specialty, maybe on a certain day in the week.

Desserts do not run to the English or American pattern. Neither the English pudding nor the American ice cream desserts are as prevalent as soufflés, large, tiered cream cakes, and berries in season. Strawberries reach the table somewhere around the end of June and manage to survive for a commendable number of weeks. Later on in the year, Finland, Norway and Sweden offer a delicious wild berry which is hardly known elsewhere, the cloudberry, called *suomuurain* or *lakka* in Finnish, *hjortron* in Sweden, and *multer* in Norway. In appearance rather like an overgrown unripe raspberry, it has a delicate aroma which is unique. Incidentally, the Finns make a delicious liqueur from the juice of this berry.

Speaking of liquid refreshments, we should note that the Scandinavians are coffee-drinkers rather than tea-drinkers, and they make their coffee good and strong, in the best Continental tradition. In Denmark and Norway, coffee is somewhat expensive, and families who drink a lot have to make up for it with some sort of substitute. This trend has, of course, resulted in an increase in tea-drinking, but on the whole the Scandinavians have not yet acquired the English touch. So be sure to emphasize that you want your tea strong. Don't expect to find that the cult of tea has made the Scandinavians tea-conscious. The buttered toast, crumpets and muffins of Belgravia have no afternoon counterpart in Bergen or Bornholm. Instead, look for a restaurant-type of place with the sign *"Konditori"* over the door. The waitress will bring cakes to your table along with tea, coffee, milk or a soft drink. You'll be hard put to choose among the several delicious varieties.

Skål

Scandinavia's local brand of firewater is known as *akvavit,* and a glass of this is known in Denmark, Sweden and Finland as *snaps,* whereas the Norwegians call it a *dram.* Served at the beginning of the main meal of the day—at the *hors d'oeuvre* stage, or occasionally with the first course— it is invariably taken with a beer chaser. *Akvavit* emphatically is not a drink for the tyro toper and you'll find it takes a little practice to attain proficiency in the local ritual of gulping it down without falling off your chair. The mysteries of the *skål* or toast, apart from regional variations, are too complicated to explain here, but you won't go far wrong if you stick to the following procedure.

First, at the start of any meal, wait for someone to give the signal. At a formal party, the host, after clearing his throat ominously or belaboring the nearest piece of china or crystal with a soup spoon, will seize his glass and launch into a *velkommen til bords* speech. All this means is "welcome to the table" and you may even find it a gracious gesture of hospitality. Anyhow, the crucial thing is to listen intently for the word *skål.* This is your cue. Seizing your own glass, you hold it firmly in a position of tantalizing proximity to your parched lips, though preferably far enough away from your nose to avoid asphyxiation. Then you nod your head north, south, east, and west as you echo *"skål."* Now, and not a moment sooner, your *akvavit* starts its downward journey. This is the supreme test. As all hell breaks loose somewhere in your gullet, you may be tempted to reach convulsively for the beaker of cool beer that beckons by your plate. Not so the trained snapser. He returns his glass to its original position just south of his chin, nods blandly to the four points of the compass while simulating an air of complete indifference to the fires consuming within, and then sends a mouthful of malt brew in pursuit of the *akvavit*.

When the urge to wet your whistle descends on you, don't try a surreptitious drink on your own, but pick up your glass boldly, fix a fellow diner with a purposeful stare, pronounce the word *"skål,"* and proceed as above. Anyone is fair game for this except your hostess; after all, someone has to keep track of the time. Apart from achieving a drink, you will undoubtedly have won the undying gratitude of your friend across the table, who was almost certainly contemplating a similar move. Remember that husbands are expected to *skål* their wives, who, if slighted, are entitled to collect a pair of stockings by way of damages.

Although there are so many striking points of similarity between the food and drink of each of the Scandinavian countries, it is surprising that in a few unimportant details, which only indirectly affect the table, there should be some startling discrepancies. For example, one may say without any risk of offending the Swedes and the Danes, that the Finns and Norwegians make infinitely better dessert and eating chocolate. On the other hand, the Danish Aalborg akvavit and the Swedish Norrland akvavit can be said to be the best of its kind—but the Norwegians have gone one step further by producing their *linje akevitt,* which is stored in huge sherry vats of American white oak, and then sent on Norwegian cargo liners to Australia and back. It is said that the rolling of the ship, combined with the change of climate when crossing the Equator—the "Linje"—adds an unusual flavor to the "scalplifter." Lager beer in Scandinavia is of top quality, whether you drink Danish Carlsberg or Tuborg or Norwegian Ringnes or Schou, all of which are exported around the world.

There is, unfortunately, one more essential piece of advice to impart while on the subject of liquor in Scandinavia—namely, that it is very expensive. The Danes get away quite lightly in this respect, but in all the other Scandinavian countries, alcohol, especially the imported variety, is very, very pricey. And just to add insult to injury, you'll also discover that, except for the carefree Danes, the Scandinavians, like the British, have strict and inflexible licensing hours, outside which it is not possible to buy so much as the humblest glass of beer. Don't say you haven't been warned.

A Final Word

You will find that the Scandinavians have elevated the culinary arts to a high place among the graces which add flavor to life. Wherever you dine you will discover that the serving is on a par with the cuisine. Helpings are generous, dishes and drinks which are supposed to be hot really are hot, and iced drinks never arrive in a semitepid state. This is only natural where hospitality is regarded as one of the supreme virtues.

After finishing a meal in Scandinavia, it is a time-honored custom for the hostess to stand near the door of the dining room. The guests, one by one, shake her hand on their way into the living room and pronounce the words, *"takk for maten."* Badly translated, this means "thank you for the food." A phrase well-worn by usage, perhaps, but nonetheless welcome from those who have dined well in congenial company.

INDEX

INDEX

COPENHAGEN
Practical Information

Airport transportation, 36
Auto rentals, 36

Bars, 48
Bicycles, 40
Buses, 39

Camping, 39
Climate, 25
Clubs & discos, 48

Embassies, 36
Excursions from Copenhagen, 35–36.
 See also listings in geographical index

Fishing, 44

Golf, 44

Historic buildings & sites, 42–43. *See also listings in geographical index*
History & background, 26–27
Horse-drawn cabs, 40
Horse racing, 44
Hotels, 37–39
 deluxe, 37
 expensive, 37–38
 general information, 37
 inexpensive, 38–39
 moderate, 38

Information sources, 36. *See also alphabetical listings*

Map, 28–29
Movies, 44
Museums, 30–36, 41–42; general information, 41.
 See also listings in geographical index
Music, 42, 44

Nightlife, 48

Parks & gardens, 42. *See also listings in geographical index*

Restaurants, 46–48
 expensive, 46–47
 general information, 46
 inexpensive, 47–48
 moderate, 47

Sailing, 44
Seasonal events, 25–26
Shopping, 44–46
Sports, 43–44. *See also alphabetical listings*
Swimming, 43–44

Taxis, 40
Telephone code, 36

INDEX

Tennis, 44
Theaters, 44
Tourist information office, 36
Tours, 40
Train system, 39
Transportation, 39–40. *See also alphabetical listings*

Travel agents, 36

Youth hostels, 39

Zoos, 42

Geographical

Absalonsgade, 31
Amalienborg Palace, 34, 42
Andersen, Hans Christian, statue of, 34
Aquarium (Danmarks Akvarium), 35, 42

Bakken (amusement park), 25
Botanical Gardens (Botanisk Have), 35, 42
Bredgade, 34

Charlottenlund, 35
Christian V, statue of, 33
Christiania, 32
Christiansborg Slot (Christiansborg Palace), 31, 43
Christianshavn, 32
Church of Our Lady (Vor Frue Kirke), 33
Citadel (Kastellet), 27, 34, 43
City Museum (Kobehavns Bymuseum), 31, 41

Danish Academy of Fine Arts, 33
David Collection, 41
Deer Park (Dyrehaven), 35, 42
Dragør, 36, 43

Elsinore (Helsingør), 35
English Church, 34
Esplanaden, 34

Fish market, 32
Frederiksberggade, 31
Frederiksholms Canal, 31
Frihedsmussett, 34
Fyrskib XVII (lightship), 33, 41

Gammeltorv Square, 31
Gefion Fountain, 34
Geological Museum, 41
Glyptotek Museum, 30, 41
Grundtvigs Kirke, 36, 43

Hans Christian Andersens Boulevard, 30

Hareskov (woods), 36
Hirschprung Collection (Den Hirschprungske Samling), 35, 41
Højbro, 32
Holmens Kirke, 32, 43
House of Danish Design (Den Permanente), 30
Hunting and Forestry Museum, 41

King's Gardens (Kongens Have), 35
Klampenborg, 35
Knippelsbro (bridge), 32
Kongelige Theater, 33
Kongens Nytorv, 33–34
Kyrstalgade, 33

Langelinie Promenade, 34
Liberty Museum (Frihedsmuseet), 34, 41
Little Mermaid (statue), 34
Lyngby, 35–36

Marble Church (Marmokirken), 34
Museum of Decorative Arts (Kunstindustrimuseet), 34, 41

National Gallery (Statens Museum for Kunst), 35, 41
National Museum (Naitonalmuseet), 31, 41
Nikolaj Kirke, 32
Nyhavn Canal, 33
Nytorv Square, 31

Open Air Museum (Frilandsmuseet), 35–36, 43
Ordrupgård Collections, 41
Our Saviour's Church (Vor Frelsers Kirke), 32

Pantomine Theater, 42

Radhüs Pladsen. *See* Town Hall Square
Regensen (college), 33
Rosenborg Castle (Slot), 34, 35, 43
Round Tower (Runde Tårn), 32–33, 43

INDEX 141

Royal Arms (Arsenal) Museum (Tøjhuset), 31, 42
Royal Library (Det Kongelige Bibliotek), 31, 43

Scala Center, 30
Slotsholmen, 26, 31–32
Stock Exchange Building (Børsen), 31–32, 43
Strøget (area), 31, 33

Thorvaldsen Museum, 32, 41

Tivoli Gardens, 30, 42
 restaurants, 42
Tivoli Guards, 30, 42
Town (City) Hall & Square (Rådhuset), 27, 30, 31, 43

University, 33

Vesterbrogade, 30–31

Zoological Museum, 42

HELSINKI
Practical Information

Airport transportation, 88
Apartment Rentals, 90
Auto rentals, 88

Buses, 90

Camping, 90

Embassies, 88
Emergencies, 88
Emergency hospital for foreigners, 88

Ferries, 90

Golf, 92

Historic Buildings and Sites, 91–92
History & background, 80–81
Hotels, 88–89
 deluxe, 88–89
 expensive, 89
 general information, 88
 inexpensive, 89
 moderate, 89

Information sources, 88. *See also alphabetical listings*

Map, 82–83
Metro, 90
Movies, 92
Museums, 84–86, 90–91. *See also listings in geographical index*
Music, 92

National Opera Theater, 92
Nightlife, 95

Parks, 91. *See also listings in geographical index*
Post Office (Main), 88

Restaurants, 93–95
 expensive, 93–94
 general information, 93
 inexpensive, 95
 moderate, 94–95

Saunas, 92
Shopping, 92–93
Skiing, 92
Sports, 92. *See also alphabetical listings*
Swimming, 92

Taxis, 90
Telephone codes, 88
Tennis, 92
Theaters, 92
Tourist information, 88
Tours, 90
Trams, 90
Transportation in Helsinki, 90. *See also alphabetical listings*

Youth hostels, 90

Geographical

Alexander II (statue of), 85
Aleksanterinkatu, 85
Amanda, Havis (statue of), 84

Arabia (Potter Plant), 87, 90
Art Museum of the Ateneum (Ateneum in Taidemuseo), 85, 90

INDEX

Botanical Gardens, 86
Burgher's House (Ruiskumestarin talo), 91

Cathedral (Toumiokirkko), 81, 84, 92
City Center (complex), 85

East End, 86
Eläintarha Park (City Conservatories), 91
Empress Stone, 84
Environs of Helsinki, 87
Esplanadi, 84, 85, 93

Finlandia Hall, 81, 86, 92
Finnish Science Center (Heureka), 91
Forum Shopping Center, 86

Gallen-Kallelan Museum, 91

Helsinki City Art Museum (Helsingin kaupungin Taidemuseo), 91
Helsinki City Museum (Helsingin Kaupunginmuseo), 91
Helsinki Summer Theater, 87, 92
Hietaniemi Cemetery, 86–87, 91
House of Parliament (Eduskuntatalo), 81, 86, 91
House of the Estates, 85
Hylkyssaari (islet), 87

International Fair Center, 86
Islands of Helsinki, 87. *See also* alphabetical listings

Kaivopiha (shopping precinct), 86
Kaivopuisto (park & district), 84, 91
Katajanokka (island), 84
Korekeassaari (island), 87, 91

Lake Hvitträsk, 85
Linnanmäki (amusement park), 86

Mannerheimintie, 81, 85, 86
Mannerheim Museum, 91
Market Square (Kauppatori), 84, 93
Museum of Arabia (Arabian museo), 87, 90
Museum of Finnish Architecture (Suomen rakennustaiteen museo), 91

Mustikkamaa (island), 91

National Maritime Museum (Suomen merimuseo), 87, 91
National Museum (Suomen kansallismuseo), 81, 86, 91
National Theater, 85
Nordic Arts Center, 87

Olympic Stadium Tower (Stadionin torni), 80, 81, 86, 92
Orthodox Uspenski Cathedral (Uspenskin Kathedraali), 84, 92

Post Office (main), 86
President's Palace, 84

Railway station (building), 85

Saarinen, Eliel, home of, 85
Senaatti shopping center, 85
Senate Square, 81, 85
Seurasaari (island), 87
Seurasaari Open Air Museum (Seurasaaren ulkomuseo), 87, 91
Sibelius Park, 91
Sinebrychoff Art Museum, 91
Snellmaninkatu, 85
Sokos House, 86
South Harbor, 84
Suomenlinna (island fortress), 81, 87, 92
Swedish Theater, 85

Tähtitorninmäki Park (Observatory Hill), 81, 91
Tapiola Garden City, 87
Temppeliaukion Kirkko, 86, 92
Three Smiths, statue of, 85
Töölö (district), 86–87
Töölönlahti Bay, 86

Uspenski Cathedral, 92

Walhalla (fort/restaurant), 87

Zoo, 87, 91

OSLO
Practical Information

Airport transportation, 60

Auto rentals, 60

INDEX

Bicycles, 63
Buses, 63

Camping, 63

Embassies, 60

Fishing, 68

Folk Dancing, 69

Golf, 68

Historic buildings & sites, 67–68. *See also listings in geographical index*
History & background, 50–51
Hotels, 60–62
  deluxe, 61
  expensive, 61–62
  general information, 60–61
  inexpensive, 62
  moderate, 62

Information sources, 60. *See also alphabetical listings*

Map, 52–53
Metro, 63
Movies, 68
Museums, 54–55, 56–60, 64–66. *See also listings in geographical index*
Music, 68

Nightlife, 72

Parks & gardens, 66–67. *See also listings in geographical index*

Restaurants, 70–72
  expensive, 70–71
  general information, 70
  inexpensive, 71–72
  moderate, 71

Shopping, 69–70
Skiing, 68
Sports, 68. *See also alphabetical listings*
Sports Shops, 70
Swimming, 68

Taxis, 63
Telephone codes, 60
Theaters, 68–69
Tourist office, 60
Tours, 63–64
Trams, 63
Transportation, 63. *See also alphabetical listings*
Travel agents, 60

Youth hostel, 62

Zoo, 66

Geographical

Aker Brygge (shopping center), 56
Akershus Fortress (Slot), 50, 55, 67
Armed Forces Museum (Forsvarsmuseet), 55, 64
Arts & Crafts Center, 54, 69

Bogstad Manor, 67
Botanical Gardens (Botanisk Hage), 59, 66
Bygdøy, 55, 56, 57

Cathedral (Domkirken), 54, 67
Christian IV, statue of, 54
City Hall (Rådhuset), 55–56, 67
City Museum (Oslo Bymuseum), 66
Concert Hall (Koncerthuset), 67, 68

Flower Market (Stortoget), 54
Framhuset (Polar exploration ship), 57, 64
Frogner (Vigeland) Park, 56, 66–67

Gamlebyen Ruiner (park), 67
Gjoa (ship), 57

Haakon VII, state of, 54
Harbor area, 55–56
Henie-Onstad Art Center, 56, 59–60, 64
Historical (Historisk) Museum, 54, 55, 64
Holmenkollen, 56, 58–59
  hotel & restaurants, 59

International Children's Art Museum (Barnekunst Museet), 64

Karl Johans Gate, 51, 54
Kon-Tiki Museum, 57–58, 64–65

Ladegården, 67

INDEX

Maritime Museum (Norsk Sjøfartsmuseum), 57, 65–66
Market area, 54
Monastery ruins (Hovedøya Klosterruiner), 67
Munch Museum, 56, 59, 65
Museum of Applied Art (Kunstindustrimuseet), 54, 55, 65

National Gallery (Nasjonalgalleriet), 54–55, 65
National Theater, 51, 68
National History Museum (Geologisk Museum), 59, 65
Norwegian Folk Museum (Norsk Folkemuseum), 58, 65
Norwegian Museum of Science & Industry (Norsk Teknisk Museum), 66

Old Aker Church (Gamle Aker Kirke), 67
Oscarshall, 67

Parliament (Stortinget) building, 54, 67

Resistance Museum (Norsk Hjemmefrontmuseum), 55, 65
Roosevelt, F.D., statue of, 56
Royal Palace (Slottet), 50–51, 54, 67

St. Olavs Gate, 55
Ski Museum (Skimuseet), 59, 66
Sørenga Ruiner (park), 67
Studenterlunden (park), 51

Theatre Museum (Teatermuseet), 66
Tordenskiold, Peter, statue of, 55
Tryvannshøgda Observation Tower, 58, 67–68

University of Oslo (Universitetet), 51, 68

Vigeland Museum, 56–57, 66
Viking Ship Museum, 58, 66

Zoo (Dyre Parken), 66

OSLO FJORD DISTRICT
Practical Information

Camping, 78
Churches and cathedrals, 78–79

Fishing, 79

Hotels & restaurants, 76–78

Information sources, 76

Museums, 78–79

Sailing & boating, 79

Sightseeing, 78–79
Sports, 79. *See also alphabetical listings*
Swimming, 79

Telephones, 76
Tours, 78
Transportation, 78

Youth hostels, 76–78

Geographical

Antiquity Road, 74
Åsqårdstrand, 75

Borgarsyssell Museum, 74, 79
Borge, 74
Borre, 75

Drammen, 74–75, 78
  hotels & restaurants, 76

Fredrikstad, 73–74, 78
  hotels & restaurants, 76–77
Fredriksten Fortress, 74, 79

Gokstad Mound, 76

Halden, 73, 74, 79
  hotels & restaurants, 77
Hankø
  hotels & restaurants, 77
Highway of the Ancients (Oldtidsveien), 78
Holmestrand
  hotels & restaurants, 77
Horten, 75
  hotels & restaurants, 77

INDEX

Jarlsberg, 75

Kongsten Fortress, 74, 78

Larvik, 76, 79
   hotels & restaurants, 77

Moss, 73
   hotels & restaurants, 77
Munch, Edvard, house of, 75

Oseberg, 75, 79
Östfold, 73

Ramnes, 75

Sandefjord, 75–76
   hotels & restaurants, 77
Sarpsborg, 74, 79
   hotels & restaurants, 77
Stavern, 76, 79
   hotels & restaurants, 77

Tjøme
   hotels & restaurants, 78
Tönsberg, 75, 79
   hotels & restaurants, 78

Vestfold, 74–75

REYKJAVIK
Practical Information

Airport transportation, 107
Auto rentals, 108

Bars, 112
Buses, 109

Camping, 109

Embassies, 108

Fishing, 111

Golf, 110

Hiking, 111
Hotels, 108
   expensive, 108
   general information, 108
   inexpensive, 108
   moderate, 108

Information sources, 107–108. *See also alphabetical listings*

Map, 102
Medical services, 108
Movies, 111
Museums, 109–110. *See also listings in geographical index*

Music, 111

Nightlife, 112

Parks & gardens, 110. *See also listings in geographical index*
Police, 108

Restaurants, 112

Shopping, 111
Skiing, 111
Sports, 110–111. *See also alphabetical listings*
Swimming, 110

Taxis, 109
Telephone codes, 108
Theaters, 111
Tourist information, 107
Tours, 109
Transportation in Reykjavik, 109. *See also alphabetical listings*
Travel agents, 108

Youth hostels, 109

Geographical

Arnarhóll (hill), 110
Arni Magnússon Manuscript Museum (Arnagardur), 110
Asgrímur Jónsson Art Gallery, 110

Asmunder Sveinsson Gallery, 110

City Art Gallery (Kjarvalsstadir), 110

INDEX

Einar Jónsson Museum, 110
Eriksson, Leif, statue of, 103

Folk Museum (Arbaer), 110

Hallgrim's Church, 103

Icelandic Handicrafts Center, 103

Lakeside Gardens (Tjarnagardar), 110
Laugardlur (Botanical Garden), 110
Lutheran Cathedral, 101

National Museum (Thjódminjasafnid), 103, 110
National Theater, 101, 103, 111
Natural History Museum (Nattúrugripasafnid), 110
Nordic House (Norraena Húsid), 110

Parliament Building (Althing), 101

Tjarnargardar (Lakeside Gardens), 110

University, 103

Rest of Iceland
Practical Information

Climate, 97

Fishing industry, 100

History & background, 96–100
Hotels and restaurants, 113–116. *See also alphabetical listings in geographical index*

Information sources, 113

Language, 99

Telephone codes, 113

Geographical

Akranes
  hotels, 115
Akureyri, 106
  camping, 113
  hotels & restaurants, 113
  youth hostels, 113
Alfaborg (hill), 105
Almannagja chasm, 103
Asbyrgi (national park), 106
Askja (volcano), 106

Blönduös
  hotels, 113
Borgarfjördur Eystri, 105
  hotels, 115
Borgarnes
  hotels, 115
Breidafjördur (bay), 104
Breidalsvík
  hotels, 115
Brjánslaekur Farm, 104
Búdardalur
  hotels, 115

Central Iceland, 107

Dalvik
  hotels & restaurants, 113
Dettifoss (waterfall), 106
Dimmuborgir (black castles), 106
Djúpivoguir
  hotels, 115

East Iceland, 104–105
  hotels, 115
Egilsstadir
  hotels, 115
Eidar
  hotels, 115
Eskifjördir
  hotels, 115
Eyjafjördur, 106

Flúdur
  hotels, 114

Giant (Great) Geysir, 96, 103
Glerardalur (valley), 106
Godafoss (waterfall), 106
Grimsey (island), 106
Grindavik
  hotels & restaurants, 114
Grjótafjá (pool), 106
Gullfoss (waterfall), 103

Haena (island), 106
Hallormasstadir
  hotels, 115
Heimaey Island, 105
Hekla, Mount, 104
Helgafell (Holy Mountain), 104, 105
Hella
  hotels, 114
Höfn, 105

INDEX

Hornafjördur
  hotels, 115
Hrútafjördur
  hotels & restaurants, 113
Húnavellir
  hotels, 114
Húsavik, 107
  hotels, 114
Hvalfjördur, 104
Hveragerdi
  hotels, 114
Hvitá (river), 103
Hvolsvöllur
  hotels, 114

Isafjördur
  hotels, 115

Kafhellir (sea cave), 106
Katla (volcano), 105
Keflavik
  hotels, 114
Kirkjubaejarklauster
  hotels, 114
Kópasker
  hotels, 114
Króksfjördur
  hotels, 115

Laugar
  hotels, 114
Laugarvatn
  hotels, 114

Mývatn (town & lake), 106
  hotels, 114

Námaskard (town & lake), 106
Njardvík
  hotels, 114
North Iceland, 106-107
  hotels & restaurants, 113-114

Ólafsvik
  hotels, 116

Raufarhöfn
  hotels, 114, 115
Reydarfjördur
  hotels, 115
Reykholt, 104
  hotels, 116

Saelinsdalur
  hotels, 116
Saudárkrokúr
  hotels, 114
Selfoss
  hotels, 114
Seydisfjördur
  hotel and restaurant, 115
Siglufjördur
  hotels, 114
Skaftafell (national park & reserve), 105
Skagafjördur
  hotels, 114
Skálholt, 103-104
  hotel, 115
Skógafoss, 104
Skógar, 104
  hotels, 115
Snaefellsjökull (glacier), 104
Snaefellsnes (town & peninsula), 104
  hotels, 116
South Iceland, 105-106
  hotels, 114-115
Stóragjá (pool), 106
Stórutjarnir
  hotels, 114
Strokkur (geyser), 103
Stykkishólmur, 104
  hotels, 116
Surtsey (volcanic island), 105-106
Svartifoss (waterfall), 105

Thingeyri
  hotels, 116
Thingvallavatn (lake), 103
Thingvallir (national park), 103
  hotels, 115

Vatnajökull (glaciers), 96, 105
Vatnsfjördur
  hotels, 116
Vestfirdir (region), 104
Vík Mýrdal
  hotels, 115
Vopnafjördur
  hotels, 115

West Iceland, 104
  hotels, 115-116
Westmann Islands, 105
  hotels, 115

Index
General Information for Scandinavia

Food and drink, 130-135
  akvavit, 133-134
  beers, 134
  breakfast, 131
  cakes, 133
  cheeses, 132

INDEX

Food and drink (*continued*)
  coffee & tea, 133
  desserts, 133
  fish, 132
  games & roasts, 132
  liquor, 133–134
  sandwiches (smørbrød), 131
  seafood, 132
  sidewalk stands, 131
  smorgåsbord, 132–133

History and background, 117–129
  coming of Christianity, 119–121
  early history, 118–119
  industrialization & independence, 126–128
  middle-ages, 121–122
  modern Scandinavia, 128–129
  the Reformation & Sweden's rise, 122–125
  revolution & rococco, 125–126
  the Vikings, 119–121

Maps
  rise of the modern states, 129
  Swedish empire, 124
  Viking Lands & conquests, 120

Stockholm
Practical Information

Airport transportation, 12
Auto rentals, 12

Bars, 24
Bicycling, 20
Boat transportation, 16
Buses, 16

Camping, 15
Canoeing, 20
Climate, 2

Embassies, 12
Excursions from Stockholm, 11–12

Fishing, 20

Golf, 19

Historic buildings & sites, 18–19. *See also listings in geographical index*
History & background, 1–4
Hotels, 13–15
  deluxe, 13–14
  expensive, 14
  general information, 13
  inexpensive, 15
  moderate, 14–15

Information sources, 12. *See also alphabetical listings*

Maps, 6–7
Movies, 20

Museums, 4–5, 9–12, 17–18
  general information, 17. *See also listings in geographical index*
Music, 11, 20

Nightlife, 23–24

Parks & gardens, 18. *See also listings in geographical index*

Restaurants, 21–23
  expensive, 21–22
  general information, 21
  inexpensive, 23
  moderate, 22–23

Shopping, 21
Skiing, 20
Sports, 19–20. *See also alphabetical listings*
Subways, 16
Swimming, 19

Taxis, 16
Telephone codes, 12
Tennis, 19
Theaters, 20–21
Tourist center, 12
Tours, 16
Transportation in Stockholm, 16. *See also alphabetical listings*
Travel agents, 12

Youth hostels, 15–16

Geographical

Aquarium, 9, 18

Bank of Sweden (former bldg. of), 5

INDEX

Biological Museum, 17
Blue Hall, 10

Chapel Royal, 5, 19
China Palace, 11, 18
City Hall, 10, 19
City Museum, 18
Concert Hall, 11, 20
Court Theater, 20–21

Djurården (island), 4, 9, 11, 18
Drottningholm Palace, 11, 18–19

Ethnographical Museum, 17

Fjällgatan (park), 18

Gamla Stan. *See* Old Town
German Church, 8
Golden Hall, 10
Grand Hotel, 4
Great Church (St. Nicholas), 2, 5, 8, 19
Gröna Lund Amusement Park, 18, 20
Gustavsberg (ceramic works), 12

Haga Palace & Pavilion, 12, 19
Hall of State, 5
Hallwyl Museum, 17
Helgeandsholmen, 4
Hötorget, 4, 11
House of the Nobility, 5, 19

Island of the Holy Spirit. *See* Helgeadsholem
Isle of the Knights. *See* Riddarholmen

Kaknäs Tower, 11, 19
Katarina elevator, 8
King Charles XII, statue of, 4, 18
Klarabergsgatan, 4
Kungsholmen, 4
Kungsträdgården. *See* Royal Gardens

Lake Mälaren, 1, 2, 8, 10, 11, 18
Långholmsparken, 18
Lidingö (island), 11

Maiden Tower, 10
Markets, 11
Mårten Trotzigs Gränd, 8, 19
Mediterranean Museum, 17
Milles, Carl, home of (Millesgården), 11, 17
Museum of Far Eastern Antiquities, 10
Museum of Modern Art & Photography, 10, 17

Museum of National Antiquities, 11, 17

National Maritime Museum, 17
National Museum & Art Gallery, 10, 17, 20
Nedre Norrmalm, 4
Nordiska (Nordic) Museum, 9, 17
Norrbro Bridge, 4–5
Norrmalm, 4

Old Town, 2, 4–5, 8, 19
Östermalm, 4, 11

Parliament building, 5
Parliament House, 3
Prästgatan, 8
Prince's Gallery, 10

Riddarholm Church, 8, 19
Riddarholmen, 4
Riddarhuset. *See* House of the Nobility
Riddarhustorget (square), 5
Royal Armory, 17, 19
Royal Army Museum (Armemuseum), 17
Royal Cabinet of Coin, 10–11, 17
Royal Dramatic Theater, 20
Royal Gardens, 4, 18
Royal Opera House, 4, 18, 20
Royal Palace, 4, 5, 19
Royal Treasury, 5, 19

Saltsjöbaden, 12
Science & Technology Museum, 18
Sergels Torg, 1
Skansen (amusement park), 4, 9–10, 18
Skansen (open air museum), 4, 18
Skeppsholmen, 10
Skinnarviksparken, 18
Södermalm, 4
Stock Exchange Building, 8
Storkykobrinken, 5
Stortoget (square), 8
Strandvägen, 9
Strindberg, August, house of, 18
Supreme Court Building, 5, 19
Swedish Academy, 8, 19

Thiel Art Gallery, 18
Town (City) Hall, 3, 4, 8, 10, 19
Toy Museum, 17

Waldemarsudde, 9–10, 18
  museum, 9, 18
Wasa Museum, 9, 18
Waterfront areas, 9

Zoos, 9, 18

Fodor's Travel Guides

U.S. Guides

Alaska
Arizona
Atlantic City & the
  New Jersey Shore
Boston
California
Cape Cod
Carolinas & the
  Georgia Coast
The Chesapeake Region
Chicago
Colorado
Disney World & the
  Orlando Area

Florida
Hawaii
Las Vegas
Los Angeles, Orange
  County, Palm Springs
Maui
Miami,
  Fort Lauderdale,
  Palm Beach
Michigan, Wisconsin,
  Minnesota
New England
New Mexico
New Orleans

New Orleans (Pocket
  Guide)
New York City
New York City (Pocket
  Guide)
New York State
Pacific North Coast
Philadelphia
The Rockies
San Diego
San Francisco
San Francisco (Pocket
  Guide)
The South

Texas
USA
Virgin Islands
Virginia
Waikiki
Washington, DC

Foreign Guides

Acapulco
Amsterdam
Australia, New Zealand,
  The South Pacific
Austria
Bahamas
Bahamas (Pocket
  Guide)
Baja & the Pacific
  Coast Resorts
Barbados
Beijing, Guangzhou &
  Shanghai
Belgium &
  Luxembourg
Bermuda
Brazil
Britain (Great Travel
  Values)
Budget Europe
Canada
Canada (Great Travel
  Values)
Canada's Atlantic
  Provinces
Cancun, Cozumel,
  Yucatan Peninsula

Caribbean
Caribbean (Great
  Travel Values)
Central America
Eastern Europe
Egypt
Europe
Europe's Great
  Cities
France
France (Great Travel
  Values)
Germany
Germany (Great Travel
  Values)
Great Britain
Greece
The Himalayan
  Countries
Holland
Hong Kong
Hungary
India,
  including Nepal
Ireland
Israel
Italy

Italy (Great Travel
  Values)
Jamaica
Japan
Japan (Great Travel
  Values)
Kenya, Tanzania,
  the Seychelles
Korea
Lisbon
Loire Valley
London
London (Great
  Travel Values)
London (Pocket Guide)
Madrid & Barcelona
Mexico
Mexico City
Montreal &
  Quebec City
Munich
New Zealand
North Africa
Paris
Paris (Pocket Guide)
People's Republic of
  China

Portugal
Rio de Janeiro
The Riviera (Fun on)
Rome
Saint Martin &
  Sint Maarten
Scandinavia
Scandinavian Cities
Scotland
Singapore
South America
South Pacific
Southeast Asia
Soviet Union
Spain
Spain (Great Travel
  Values)
Sweden
Switzerland
Sydney
Tokyo
Toronto
Turkey
Vienna
Yugoslavia

Special-Interest Guides

Health & Fitness
  Vacations
Royalty Watching

Selected Hotels of
  Europe

Selected Resorts and
  Hotels of the U.S.
Shopping in Europe

Skiing in North America
Sunday in New York